Pan Breakthrough Books

Using Statistics in Business 2

Peter Clark

A Pan Original
Pan Books, London and Sydney

First published 1982 by Pan Books Ltd,
Cavaye Place, London SW10 9PG

ISBN 0 330 26751 5

Printed and bound in Great Britain by
Richard Clay (The Chaucer Press) Ltd, Bungay, Suffolk

If you wish to study the subject-matter of this book in more depth, write to the National Extension College, 18 Brooklands Avenue, Cambridge CB2 2HN, for a free copy of the Breakthrough Business Courses leaflet. This gives details of the extra exercises and professional postal tuition which are available.

Pan Breakthrough Books

Pan Breakthrough Books open the door to successful self-education. This series provides essential knowledge using the most modern self-study techniques.

Expert authors have produced clear explanatory texts on business subjects to meet the particular needs of people at work and of those studying for relevant examinations.

A highly effective learning pattern, enabling readers to measure progress step-by-step, has been devised for Breakthrough Books by the National Extension College, Britain's leading specialists in home study.

Peter Clark is principal lecturer in business studies at Kilburn Polytechnic, London. He is a former lecturer in the teaching of statistics at Garnett College (a teacher training college) in London and is a past adviser to the ILEA on business education. He has worked in further education for a considerable time, teaching on a variety of courses at different levels, and has also spent several years working in business.

Pan Breakthrough Books

Other books in the series:

The Business of Communicating:
  Improving Communication Skills
Keep Account:
  A Guide to Profitable Bookkeeping
Making Numbers Work:
  An Introduction to Business Numeracy
Management: A Fresh Approach
Practical Business Law
Using Statistics in Business 1
What Do You Mean 'Communication'?
  An Introduction to Communication in Business

Acknowledgements

To my wife and small son, who were very tolerant about me being locked away in the study for hours on end writing.

To Eileen, who typed the initial manuscript very competently despite often being given very little time.

To Michael Skudder, for his comments on the book and to all the various other people who read through it and tried the exercises. To Richard Freeman of the National Extension College, whose advice on the presentation of the material in the book was invaluable. The final responsibility for the book is, however, mine, and the responsibility for anything in it which may be incorrect or misleading must be laid at my door.

Contents

Introduction

Both volumes of *Using Statistics in Business* have been written as an introduction to statistics for those people who are preparing themselves for a career in business; also for those people already in business who want to refresh their memory of statistics, or to begin studying – and using – statistics for the first time.

Using Statistics in Business is especially suitable for people studying for a Business Education Council (BEC) award at national level, since it covers much of the statistics element of the Numeracy and Accounting core module and of the option module Applied Statistics. However, it can also be used profitably by students of statistics at RSA Stage II and LCCI Intermediate levels; as well as by students of various professional bodies – in particular, the Institute of Marketing, the Institute of Personnel Management, the Institute of Chartered Accountants, the Institute of Cost and Management Accountants, the Institute of Chartered Secretaries and the Association of Certified Accountants.

Volume *1* introduces you to the 'discipline' of business statistics and describes how statistical data is collected, validated, sorted and simplified. It tells you how to get hold of accurate and reliable statistical data, economically, and how to reduce it to a manageable level. The last chapter (Chapter 13) shows how chance plays a part in determining exactly what data is collected and acts as an introduction to the methods of drawing conclusions from statistical data, which start the present volume. An appendix, 'Where to find statistical data', lists sources of various statistical data which may be used instead of collecting it yourself.

Volume *2*, the present volume, uses the ideas developed in Volume *1* to show how you can draw conclusions from statistical data and warns you about some of the errors that can occur when doing so. It covers the presentation of statistical data and outlines some of the pitfalls that may be encountered when using such data. The last chapter (Chapter 8) shows you how to make a case based on statistical evidence and draws upon the ideas and methods discussed in both volumes.

No algebra is used in either volume; all you will need is a knowledge of arithmetic.

How to use this book

Throughout this book you will find questions which you are encouraged to answer before reading on. There are three types of question:

Self-check. Usually short questions requiring quick answers. They either help to prepare you for the text which follows, or they provide a means for you to test for yourself whether you have understood a particular principle or technique. Answers almost invariably follow directly after the questions.

Review. These are similar to self-checks in their purpose, but are usually placed at the end of a chapter, or at the end of a section, and are intended to review your understanding of several principles or techniques.

Activity. Again, these are designed to test your understanding of the text, but they usually ask you to use some information which you will not find in the text. To answer these questions you have to use your own experience, discover some fresh facts for yourself, or try out an experiment away from the book.

It is obviously best for you to try to answer all questions before reading on, but, whether you think you've got the answer right or wrong, read the answer before moving on to the next topic. If you have somehow made a mistake, the answer will usually tell you where you went wrong. You can, of course, 'cheat' and read the whole book from beginning to end without attempting to answer the questions at all. But you probably don't need me to tell you that you will only be cheating yourself if you do.

Graphic examples, and answers to the self-check questions in the text, have been drawn by a professional artist. Your answers need not be so elaborate. The three-dimensional effect of the illustrations in the text is for visual impact only.

A note on the 'scenarios'

As with Volume *1*, this book contains a number of 'scenarios' based on a fictional company, Gourmet Foods Limited. The company was introduced to you in the first scenario of Volume *1* (on page 15 of that volume), and by now you should be quite familiar with the activities of the company and some of the problems it has faced.

As I said in the previous volume, each scenario acts as an introduction to a topic, or several topics, by providing a realistic situation which illustrates why and how statistical techniques should be used in business. Each scenario provides information which the chapters immediately following it make use of, so don't be tempted to skip them. They are designed to broaden your understanding of statistics and to show you how statistical techniques can be applied, not just in a food manufacturing business but in a wide range of business or public organizations.

The first chapter of this volume makes use of some of the information given in scenario 8 of Volume *1*, the scenario which told the story of a machine breakdown at the Gourmet Foods plant. You may find it useful to re-read that scenario before starting Chapter 1. The other scenarios in this volume appear on pages 50, 116, 159, 209 and 284.

Part 1
Drawing conclusions

1 Some naturally occurring patterns

Tossing a coin

A trial in which there are only two possible outcomes or classes of outcome, each with a fixed probability, is called a 'Bernoulli trial', after the mathematician who investigated their properties.

Self-check

What Bernoulli trial is commonly used for making a random choice between two possibilities, such as which team kicks off at a football match?

Tossing a coin is a Bernoulli trial which is often used for making a random choice between two possibilities. We saw in Chapter 13 of Volume *1* how the probability of 'heads' and of 'tails' is 1/2. We also saw how two simultaneous tosses of different coins, or, equivalently, two successive tosses of the same coin, resulted in the following relative frequency distribution. Given the earlier definition it is also a 'probability distribution'.

TABLE 1. TWO TOSSES OF AN UNBIASED COIN

*Event**	*Relative frequency (probability)*
Both heads [HH]	1/4
One head, one tail [HT *or* TH]	1/2
Both tails [TT]	1/4

This is an example of a 'binomial distribution'. It results from a sequence or set of *independent* Bernoulli trials – in this case, *two* of them. The outcome of one trial must *not* influence the outcome of another, as explained in Volume *1*, Chapter 13. It gives the relative frequencies (probabilities) of the various different possible combinations of outcomes of each trial, *regardless of order*; that is, we do not distinguish between a head on one toss and a tail on the other and vice versa.

If there were three tosses, there would be eight different possible outcomes: HHH, HHT, HTH, etc. (where H = head and T = tail). In a series of triple tosses, each of these outcomes should, with an unbiased coin, occur an equal number of times in the long run. Thus the relative frequency of each should be 1/8. The relative frequency distribution for these outcomes would appear as in table 2(a) and for the various combinations as in table 2(b). These results were obtained in review 1 at the end of Volume *1*, Chapter 13.

TABLE 2. THREE TOSSES OF AN UNBIASED COIN

(a)	*Outcome*	*Relative frequency (probability)*
	HHH	1/8
	HHT	1/8
	HTH	1/8
	HTT	1/8
	THH	1/8
	THT	1/8
	TTH	1/8
	TTT	1/8

(b)	*Event**	*Relative frequency (probability)*
	HHH	1/8
	HHT/HTH/THH	3/8
	HTT/THT/TTH	3/8
	TTT	1/8

(b) is, again, a binomial distribution. The number of Bernoulli trials here is three. The binomial distribution in **(b)** is symmetric. But this is only so because the probabilities of the two outcomes of tossing an unbiased coin are equal. If we had a biased coin the result would have been a skewed distribution, as you will see from the next section.

* We often call a set of outcomes an 'event'.

Self-check

Which of the following form binomial distributions and which do not?

1 The probabilities of getting the various different possible sums of the numbers on two dice rolled together.
2 The probabilities of two cards drawn one after the other from a pack both being aces, only one being an ace and neither being an ace.
3 The probabilities of getting 'two wins', 'only one win' or 'no wins' on two successive plays on a roulette wheel. (NB: A roulette wheel is spun to generate a random number. The player has to guess which number will come up. If he is right he wins.)

ANSWERS

1 If you said it was a binomial, look back to the definition. There has to be a set, or sequence, of Bernoulli trials. What is the Bernoulli trial here? Tossing a die is *not* a Bernoulli trial if we are interested in the six different possible outcomes. By definition, a Bernoulli trial may only have two. In passing, it is worth noting that if we were only interested in whether or not the result was a 6, there would only be two possible outcomes, a 6 or not a 6. We would then have a Bernoulli trial.

So the answer here is that it is not a binomial distribution.

2 Here there is a Bernoulli trial, namely drawing a card from a pack. There are only two outcomes, an ace or not an ace. However, the distribution is *not* binomial because the two Bernoulli trials involved are *not* independent. If you said it was a binomial, then think if the chances of the second card being an ace will be affected by the fact that the first card was or wasn't an ace. How many aces are there in the pack? If the first one of the cards *is* an ace, how many are left in the remainder of the pack, and how many are left if the first card *isn't* an ace. The answers are different in each case, aren't they! This will then alter the probability of getting an ace the second go.

3 Here too there is a Bernoulli trial, that is spinning the wheel, with the outcome a win or not a win. But here the successive

spins *are* independent; the result of the first spin can have no affect on the result of the next one, if the wheel is fair! It is a binomial distribution in this case then.

Machine breakdowns

There are two particular Bernoulli trials that are important in production. One is whether or not a machine breaks down in some given period. The other is whether some item produced is defective or not. Suppose now that experience has shown that some machine, say the one that puts the food in the jars at the Baby Gourmet plant, breaks down on about 4 in every 10 days on average (and therefore doesn't on about 6 in every 10).

> *Self-check*
>
> What is the best empirical estimate for the probability that such a machine would not break down in some two-day period?

The 'probability' that this machine will not break down in some two-day period can be found as follows. Imagine a 'long run', say 1000, of such two-day periods, in which the outcomes occur *perfectly as expected*. Then on $1000 \times 6/10 = 600$ of the *first* days, no breakdown would occur. Now consider the *second* days following these 600. If we assume that the fact that the machine did not break down on the first day has *no effect* on what happens on the second day, i.e. that we have *independent* Bernoulli trials, the following reasoning holds. On $600 \times 6/10 = 360$ of the *second* days following the 600 days when no breakdown occurred, no breakdown will occur again. That is, for 360 of the 1000 two-day periods, no breakdown will occur on either day. Thus the relative frequency, and so the probability, of this happening is $\frac{360}{1000} = .36$.

We can calculate the relative frequency (in the 1000 two-day periods) for each other pair of outcomes, e.g. a breakdown on both days, in a similar way.

Self-check

What are these other relative frequencies?

They are shown in table 4, and table 3 shows how they are derived.

TABLE 3. MACHINE BREAKDOWNS IN 1000 TWO-DAY PERIODS

In 1000 periods there are	1000 × 6/10 = 600 first days when no breakdown occurred followed by	600 × 6/10 = 360 second days when no breakdown occurred
		600 × 4/10 = 240 second days on which at least one breakdown occurred
	100 × 4/10 = 400 first days on which at least one breakdown occurred followed by	400 × 6/10 = 240 second days when no breakdown occurred
		400 × 4/10 = 160 second days on which at least one breakdown occurred

Hence the relative frequencies, and so the 'probabilities', for these outcomes are as shown in table 4(a) and 4(b). The latter is a binomial distribution.

TABLE 4. MACHINE BREAKDOWNS IN 1000 TWO-DAY PERIODS

(a)	*Outcome*	*Relative frequency (probability)*
	NN	$\frac{360}{1000} = .36$
	NB	$\frac{240}{1000} = .24$
	BN	$\frac{240}{1000} = .24$
	BB	$\frac{160}{1000} = .16$
		Total 1.00

(b)	*Event*	*Relative frequency (probability)*
	NN	$\frac{360}{1000} = .36$
	NB/BN	$\frac{240 + 240}{100} = .48$
	BB	$\frac{160}{1000} = .16$
		Total 1.00

Key: N = No breakdown on day
B = Breakdown on day

The histograms for these figures are shown in figure 1(a) and 1(b). Notice that these probability distributions are not symmetric, as were all the others we have met so far.

We can carry on this process and calculate the probabilities for the different outcomes when a three-day period is considered.

Self-check

Work out a similar table for three-day periods, and derive the probabilities for the different outcomes.

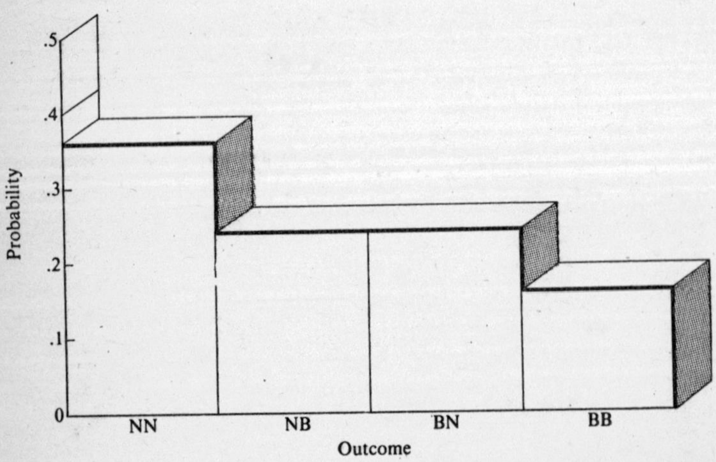

Figure 1(a). Histogram for table 4(a)

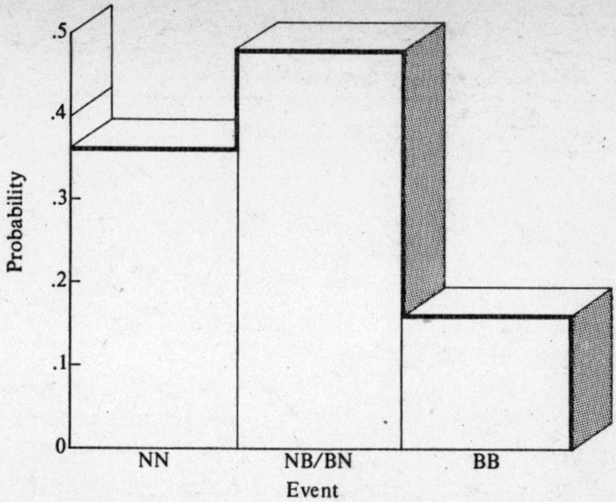

Figure 1(b). Histogram for table 4(b)

The equivalent table is as follows:

TABLE 5. MACHINE BREAKDOWNS IN 1000 THREE-DAY PERIODS

First day	*Second day*	*Third day*
600 with no breakdowns	360 with no breakdowns	360 × 6/10 = 216 with no breakdowns
		360 × 4/10 = 144 with breakdowns
	240 with breakdowns	240 × 6/10 = 144 with no breakdowns
		240 × 4/10 = 96 with breakdowns
400 with breakdowns	240 with no breakdowns	240 × 6/10 = 144 with no breakdowns
		240 × 4/10 = 96 with breakdowns
	160 with breakdowns	160 × 6/10 = 96 with no breakdowns
		160 × 4/10 = 64 with breakdowns

Take care to multiply by the correct factor; 6/10 if there are no more breakdowns and 4/10 if there are.

This gives us the binomial probability distribution shown in table 6:

TABLE 6. MACHINE BREAKDOWNS IN 1000 THREE-DAY PERIODS

Outcome	Relative frequency (probability)	
NNN	$\frac{216}{1000}$	= .216
NNB NBN BNN	$\frac{144 + 144 + 144}{1000}$	= .432
NBB BNB BBN	$\frac{96 + 96 + 96}{1000}$	= .288
BBB	$\frac{64}{1000}$	= .064
	Total	1.000

This distribution, like the one in table 4, is obviously skewed.

Defective items

The occurrence of defective items in a batch can also be regarded as a binomial distribution. Let's see why.

> *Self-check*
>
> What is the Bernoulli trial in this case?

It is that the item is or isn't defective.

> *Self-check*
>
> How many trials are there in the set that generates the binomial distribution?

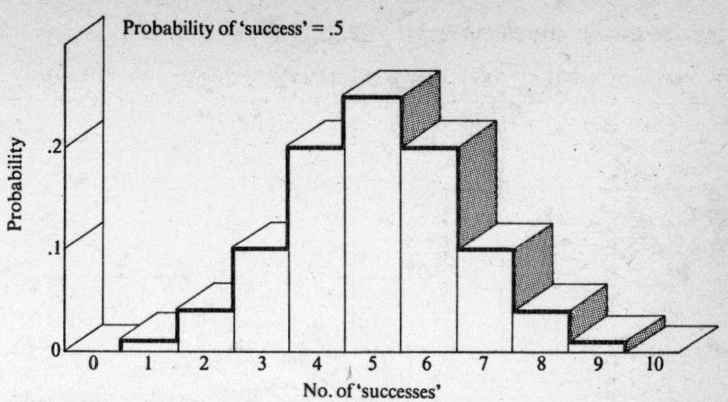

Figure 2(a). Probability of 'success' = .5

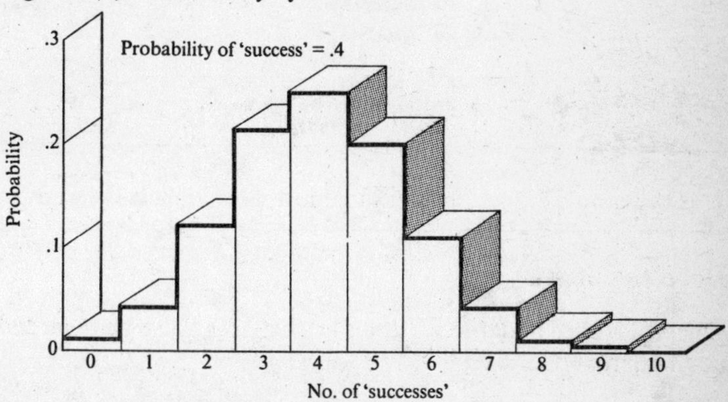

(b). Probability of 'success' = .4

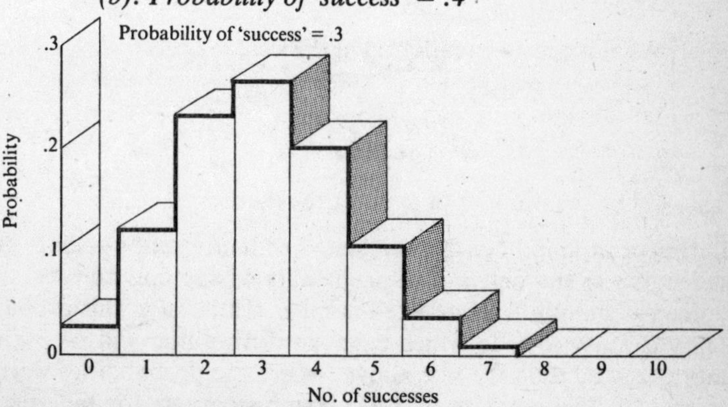

(c). Probability of 'success' = .3

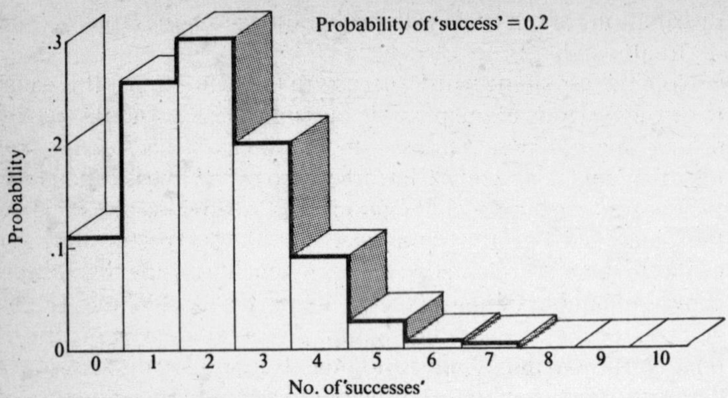

(d). Probability of 'success' = .2

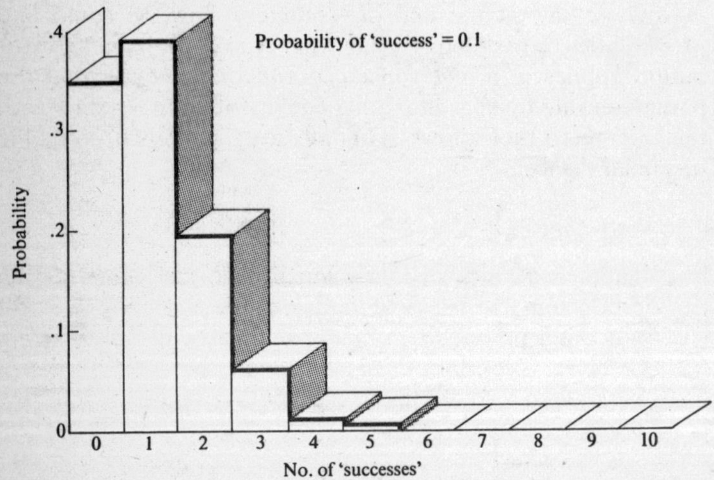

(e). Probability of 'success' = .1

This will be the number of items in the batch.

Different probabilities are associated with different numbers of defectives in the batch. The probability of any one item being defective should be some fixed number. Hopefully, this probability is fairly low, in which case the distribution will be even more skewed than the one above, where the probabilities were .4 and .6. Figures 2(a) to 2(e) show histograms for binomial distributions of ten trials with probabilities ranging from .5 (and .5) to .01 (and .99).

Note the use of the word 'success' in the histograms. It is usual to distinguish one of the possible outcomes in a Bernoulli trial by calling one of them 'success'. In many cases this has no real meaning, and it is purely arbitrary which of the two is called this. Where some meaning can be attached, the obvious one is called the 'success'. For the item quality, the 'success' could, for example, be a non-defective item, in which case the histograms show the number of non-defective items in a batch of ten. If it is, you can see that the later histograms give a rather grim picture of quality. If, on the other hand, the 'success' is discovering a defective item, then the later histograms show a rosier picture of quality than the earlier ones.

Now we saw at the end of Volume *1* how we could find probabilities by first determining what type of probability distribution applies in a given instance and then seeing what the parameters are for that situation. The distribution together with the parameters then allows us to find the probability from a table or similar device.

Self-check

There is a batch of items which have just come off the production line. Some of them are defective and others are not. The probability of any one particular item being defective is constant. What is the type of probability distribution that operates in this case for the number of defective items in a batch?

We have seen above that it is a binomial one.

Self-check

What figures would we need to know so as to be able to calculate the probabilities of the various numbers of defectives in the batch? That is, what are the parameters in this case?

In order to calculate the probabilities we would need to know (a) the numbers in the batch, and (b) the probability of any one item being defective. We could then go through the procedure of calculating the various probabilities. But this is waste of effort if someone has performed these exact calculations before. And *all binomial distributions with this number of Bernoulli trials and this probability for the occurrence of a 'success' are the same*. So statisticians have calculated the probabilities for a great many different parameters and put these into tables. An extract from these is shown below.

TABLE 7. EXTRACT FROM THE BINOMIAL DISTRIBUTION TABLES

Number of trials	*Probability of success*	*Probability of getting the stated number of 'successes'*										
		0	1	2	3	4	5	6	7	8	9	10
10	.1	.349	.387	.194	.057	.011	.001	0+	0+	0+	0+	0+
	.2	.107	.268	.302	.201	.088	.026	.006	.001	0+	0+	0+
	.3	.028	.121	.233	.267	.200	.103	.037	.009	.001	0+	0+
	.4	.006	.040	.121	.215	.251	.201	.111	.042	.011	.002	0+
	.5	.001	.010	.044	.117	.205	.246	.205	.117	.044	.010	.001

(NB: 0+ means too small to record in three places of decimals.)

This extract corresponds to the histograms in figure 2.

Self-check

What, for example, would the probability of getting three defectives in a batch of ten items be if the probability of any item being defective is .3? (Note that this is a very high probability for a defective item, but the realistic values would prove awkward to use.)

From the table above we first find the correct number of Bernoulli trials. (As the extract only shows figures for one number of trials, this step must be imagined to have taken place.) We then find the correct probability of 'success'. Here it is .3, so we take the third line of numbers. Then the number of 'successes' is used to find the correct column on the right. Here it is the column headed '3', since we want the probability of three defectives.

Reading from that row and column we get a probability of .267 for getting three defectives in a batch of ten items when the probability of any one item being defective is .3.

Self-check

Use the extract from the binomial distribution tables, in table 7, to find the probability of:

a getting two defectives in a batch of ten items when the probability of any one item being defective is .4;
b all ten lorries in a fleet being fit for the road, when the probability of any one of them not being so is .1.

ANSWERS

a The answer is .121. If you got .088, you found the probability of getting 4 defectives, where the probability of any one item being defective was .2. That is, you got the two numbers the wrong way round.
b The answer is .349.

Activity

Try this experiment in extrasensory perception (ESP). Find ten objects all of the same size and shape, but which have some marking to identify each one uniquely, e.g. coins of the same denomination, or playing cards. Mix them all up together. Now write down which one of the objects you think is going to be selected and then pick one at random. *Then put it back.* Record both your guess and the actual result – ten times. What is the probability that an individual guess is correct?

There are ten different possibilities, so using the rule found in the last chapter of Volume *1*, the probability is 1/10. That is, there is no reason why any one object should be selected rather than any other. Notice that your guess doesn't really come into it. *Once you have made it*, your guess is fixed and it doesn't matter what it is so long as the selected object matches it: and, out of the ten different possible results, only one will match.

Self-check

What kind of distribution applies to the number of correct guesses in the ten tries?

It is a binomial. The trial is guessing right or wrong, and there are ten of them all independent, i.e. since the selected object is replaced each time, your guess is just as likely to be right one time as any other. The parameters in this case are $\frac{1}{10} = .1$, for the probability of a 'success', i.e. a correct guess, and the number of trials equal to 10.

So now you should be able to find the probability of your result happening *by chance alone*, using the extract from the tables above.

When the author tried this experiment twice, he obtained the following two sets of results, using ten matchsticks with the numbers 1 to 10 written on them.

Guess	*Actual result*	*Guess*	*Actual result*
1	7	6	6
3	10	8	10
5	10	4	3
4	2	2	8
9	6	1	2
10	5	10	1
7	6	9	7
9	1	7	2
5	8	6	10
7	4	10	6

The number of correct guesses is 0 and 1. From the table, the probability of getting such results by chance is .349 and .387 respectively. They are in fact the most likely results. So much for the author's ESP capability! Did you do any better? The more unlikely the result the better from an ESP point of view. Actually, if the experiment was undertaken in seriousness, the technique would be somewhat different. In particular, it would not be the straight probability of getting the specific result that would be used, but rather the probability of getting that *or an even more unlikely one*. However, the experiment here is enough to 'get the flavour'.

Review

1 Writing programs for computers is difficult. In one firm, 20% of the programs written were found to contain *major* errors when tested thoroughly. What are the probabilities that two programs, picked at random from those written, will both contain major errors; will neither contain major errors or will there be one with major errors and one without?

2 An employment bureau finds that 30% of its clients are male (and 70% female). In a random sample of ten of its clients, what are the probabilities for how many of each sex there could be? (Use the table.)

ANSWERS

1 Imagine say 1000 pairs of programs in which the 'defectives' are perfectly distributed according to the probabilities, a defective program being one containing a major error.

Of the 1000 pairs	$1000 \times \frac{20}{100} = 200$ will have the first program defective, of which	$200 \times \frac{20}{100} = 40$ will have the second program defective	*two defectives*
		$200 \times \frac{80}{100} = 160$ will have the second program not defective	*one defective*
	$1000 \times \frac{80}{100} = 800$	$800 \times \frac{20}{100} = 160$ will have the second program defective	*one defective*

will have the first program not defective, of which	$800 \times \frac{80}{100} = 640$ will have the second program not defective	*no defectives*

This gives the following probabilities:

Number of defective programs	*Relative frequency* =		*Probability*
0	$\frac{640}{1000}$	=	.64
1	$\frac{160}{1000} + \frac{160}{1000}$	=	.32
2	$\frac{40}{1000}$	=	.04
	Total		1.00

If you got a different answer, check to make sure that you were consistent with the use of 20% or 80%; that is, that 20% were defective at each stage in the diagram and 80% were not defective.

2 Here the table can be used to find the required probability (since the number of trials is ten, the table covers it).

If 30% of its clients are male, then the chance of any one client selected at random being male is $\frac{30}{100}$ or .3. So whether or not a client is male is a Bernoulli trial with probability of 'success' equal to .3; 'success' being defined as being a male (!).

The probabilities for the different numbers of each sex that there could be can be read straight off line 3 of the table. The results are:

No. of males in the sample	*Probability of occurrence*
0	.028
1	.121
2	.233
3	.267
4	.200
5	.103
6	.037
7	.009
8	.001
9	0+
10	0+

where 0+ indicates a probability too small for three-figure accuracy.

Numbers that vary at random

The previous sections have looked at things like the number of defectives in a sample, which vary from sample to sample in a random rather than a systematic way. That is, we never know for certain what value the variable (e.g. the number of defectives in the sample) will take. Variables like this are called 'random variables'. The discipline of statistics is largely the study of such random variables.

When a discrete random variable is known to be distributed with a binomial or some other probability distribution, we can say what the probabilities are that it will have each of its possible values. This is what we were doing in the preceding part of the chapter. But when we have a continuous variable, there is a problem.

Self-check

What was said earlier in Volume *1* about the accuracy of a continuous variable?

A continuous variable is never 100-per-cent accurate. However fine the measurement, it could always have been finer.

Self-check

So can we ever say that the value of a continuous variable is definitely *equal* to some given value?

No, we can't. The best we can do is to say that it lies between limits; these limits being the absolute error extremes, as defined by the precision with which it was measured.

This means that we cannot talk about the probability of a continuous random variable *equalling* any value: all we can do is to give the probability that it lies within some range of values. This means that the binomial distribution cannot be applied to the values of a continuous random variable. But there are distributions which can be applied to continuous variables, and we will look at one of these now.

What happens when the variable is continuous?

Remember from Chapter 6 in Volume *1*, how a continuous variable can never be said to equal any particular value but only to be within certain limits of it, depending on the precision with which it is measured. This means that we cannot talk about the probability of a continuous variable having some given value either. We can only talk about the probability of its value lying in some given range. But this doesn't stop us from drawing a graph to represent the associated probability distribution. Let's look at an example. Suppose we go out and collect heights of a lot of adult males. We can only measure them to a certain degree of accuracy; say the nearest inch is all we are interested in. If we were to draw the histogram of the results we might get something like figure 3(a).

But we could have measured to, say, the nearest $\frac{1}{5}$ of an inch. The results when plotted may then have appeared as in figure 3(b).

Note that the outside edge of the histogram now looks a little smoother. If we were to measure to the nearest $\frac{1}{100}$ inch we would have an even smoother one, and so on.

If the number of men measured was very large, then the relative frequencies would be very near to the probabilities *for the classes*. Plotting the relative frequencies instead of the fre-

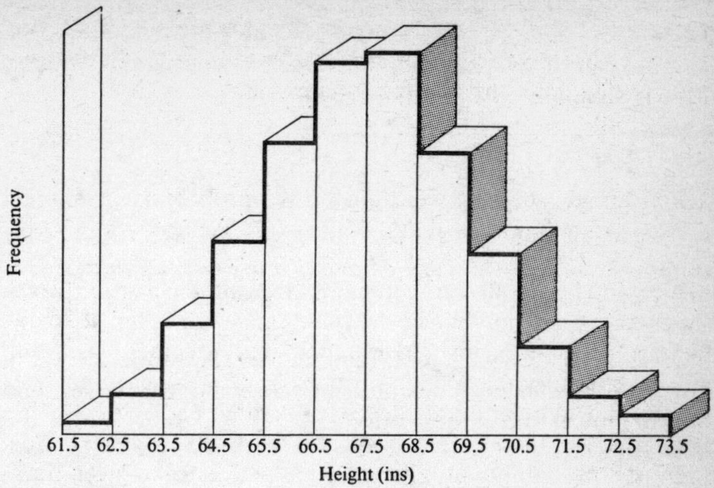

Figure 3a

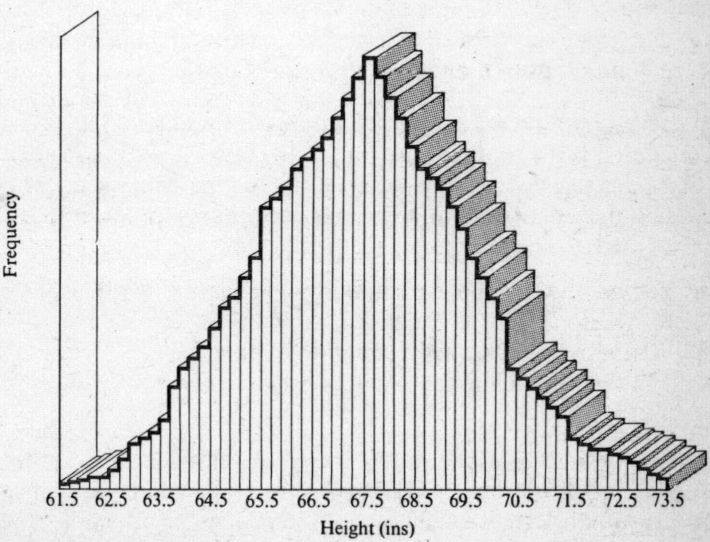

Figure 3b

quencies to get the histogram would not alter its shape, only the heights of the rectangles. Since the class intervals are all the same, depending only on the precision of the measurements, the areas of the rectangles would be proportional to the relative frequencies and so to the probabilities.

> *Self-check*
>
> Can you see how we could get the probability of a height lying in the range of say, 65.5 – 67.5 inches?

We could choose all the rectangles covering this range, two of them, if we are measuring to the nearest inch, ten if to the nearest $\frac{1}{5}$ inch and so on, and add their areas together. The result will be proportional to this probability. As the accuracy gets greater, the number of rectangles in the range 65.5 to 67.5 inches increases, but the above process still works. As a general rule, then, the probability of a height lying between the given limits will be proportional to the area of that part of the histogram between these limits.

The occurrence of errors

The most important distribution where continuous variables are concerned is the 'normal distribution'. This is sometimes called the 'Gaussian distribution' after a famous mathematician who studied the occurrence of errors in observations, processes, etc. His reasoning was something like this: errors will be

- centred on the 'true' (or aimed-for) value, i.e. it will act as a 'balance point';
- distributed symmetrically about this value;
- such that the smaller ones will occur more frequently than the larger.

This would produce a smooth-curve probability distribution for the results of the observations, processes, or whatever, which would look like figure 4. This could represent, for example, the lengths of pipes produced by some machine, the weights of jars of Baby Gourmet food, the length of a plot of land as measured by many different people, and so on. We can even regard the heights of humans as the result of a process, i.e. the 'manufacture' of the bodies, and these are normally distributed.

Another way of approaching the normal distribution is to regard it as being an approximation to the binomial under certain conditions. In this case, all we require is that the number of Bernoulli trials involved is very large. If the probabilities of the two possible outcomes of each trial are equal, i.e. both are $\frac{1}{2}$, there may be less trials before the approximation becomes reasonable. Suppose now we have a binomial distribution from ten tosses of an unbiased coin. Take the random variable, 'number of heads in ten tosses'. It will range from 0 to 10. We can draw the histogram for it as in figure 5(a). Note the distinctive shape again. If we now have 100 tosses of the coin, the histogram becomes more and more to take the shape of a smooth curve, as in figure 5(b). If we raised the number of tosses even higher, we should get an even better approximation to a smooth curve.

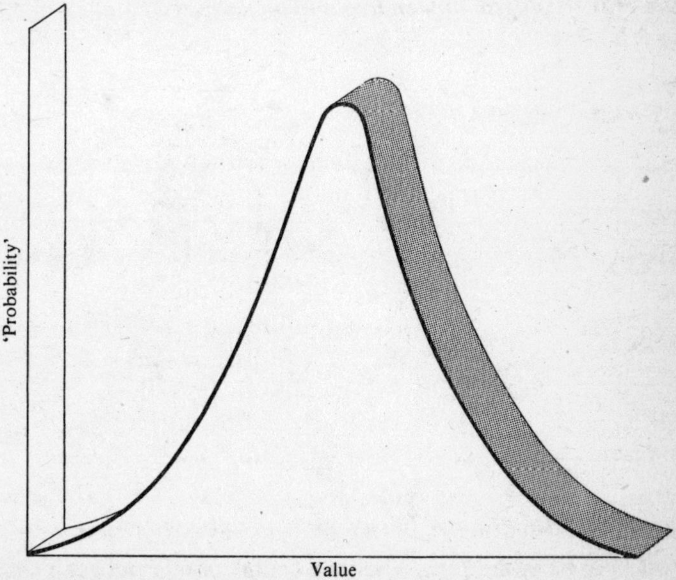

Figure 4. The shape of the normal curve ('probability' is in inverted commas because, strictly, the vertical scale does not indicate probability; a definition of what it is will be given later)

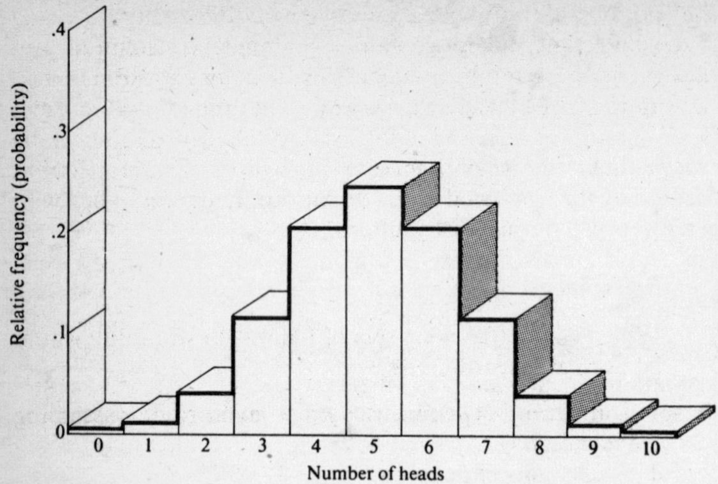

Figure 5(a). Histogram of ten tosses of an unbiased coin

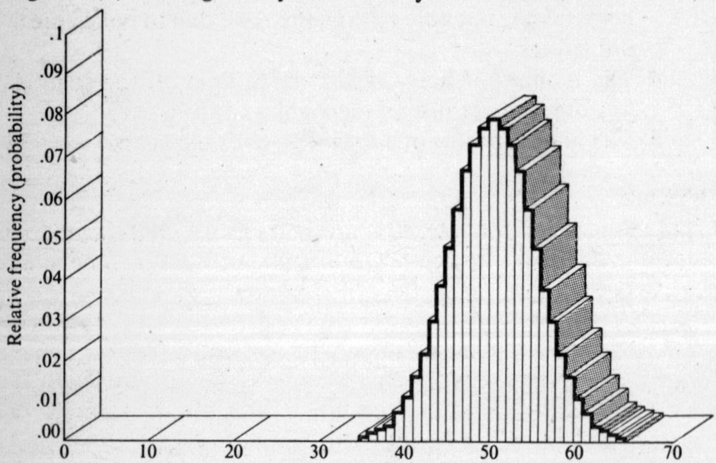

Figure 5(b). Histogram of 100 tosses of an unbiased coin

You may be wondering what the connection is between the approximation to the binomial and the Gaussian study of errors. It can be explained, rather crudely, as follows. The total error is a composite of very many small influences, some of which operate in a given case and some of which do not. 'Operates/

does not operate' situations are effectively Bernoulli trials, and so the collection of these generates a binomial distribution. But with so many different influences, it becomes a normal one. Consider, for instance, the weights of jars of Baby Gourmet food. Though it may say 100 g on the label, it will never be *exactly* that. The weights in each jar will be slightly different because of the combined effect of various influences. They will, in fact, form a normal distribution.

Self-check

Which of the following sets of figures do you think would be normally distributed?

1 The times between buses on a given route (assuming they all run).
2 The lengths of people's feet.
3 The number of days a month that a particular bus in a large fleet is not able to take the road due to mechanical difficulties.
4 The number of buses in that large fleet off the road in any one day because of mechanical difficulties.
5 The annual profits of a business, over the years.

ANSWERS

1 These times are unlikely to be normally distributed. If a bus is early it will wait, but if it is late it will generally be unable to make up the difference. The distribution is likely to be very skewed then.
2 These will be normally distributed because they are a 'product' (of nature in this case) and so subject to 'manufacturing' error.
3 This number is small and is the value of a discrete variable. It cannot, therefore, be normally distributed.
4 While it wouldn't strictly be normally distributed, because it is a discrete variable, it would be approximately normally distributed if the fleet were large enough. If you just said it would be normally distributed, then this is not strictly correct.
5 The annual profits of a business would not in general be normally distributed. Growth could, for example, cause them to rise each year. Any company tries to increase profits: it does

not constantly aim at some fixed value of profits year after year.

In figure 4 the word 'probability' is in inverted commas. The reason for this is the same one as was given for having adjusted frequencies in histograms. Do you remember what it is that really represents the frequencies in a histogram?

Self-check

What is it?

It is the *areas* of the rectangles which are proportional to the frequencies. That was why we had the adjusted frequency.

Now in the probability distributions for continuous variables, the height of the curve cannot be the probability of the variable taking the value at that point, since, as we saw earlier, we cannot talk about the probability of a continuous variable equalling anything. But if you look at the binomial approximations to the normal curve in figure 5, then you can see that the area under the normal curve, as the number of rectangles becomes larger, gets nearer to the total area of these. In those graphs, the frequency is relative and so is equal to the probability. This means that the areas of the rectangles are proportional to the probability. So, in the normal curve, it is *area* that represents probability and not height of the curve, just as in the histogram it is the area of the rectangle and not its height that represents (relative) frequency. Though, of course, *when the class widths are all equal*, the *heights* of the rectangles are also proportioned to the frequencies.

Thus, we can say that the area under the curve, and between two values, gives the probability that the variable will lie between those two values. This is illustrated in figure 6. If suitable units are used for the vertical scale, this area can be made to equal the probability, and this is the way the normal curve is always drawn. The vertical scale is then labelled 'probability density'.

Self-check

What is the sum of all the probabilities in a probability distribution?

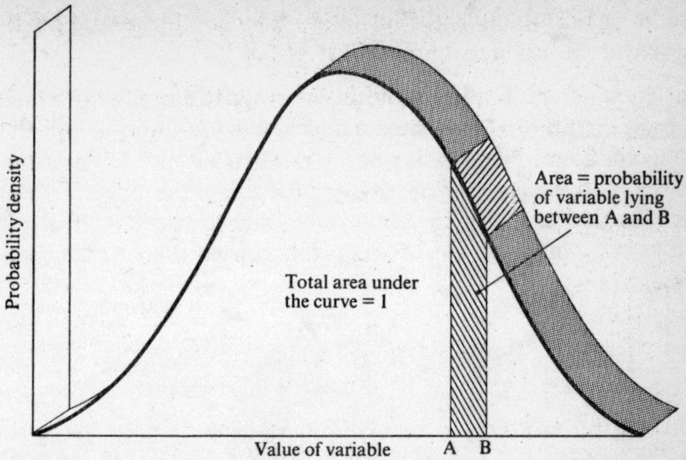

Figure 6. Probability and the normal curve

Since between them they cover all the possibilities, it is 1.

Self-check

So what must be the total area under the normal curve?

This must be 1 too.

Self-check

What is the probability corresponding to the shaded area in the figure below?

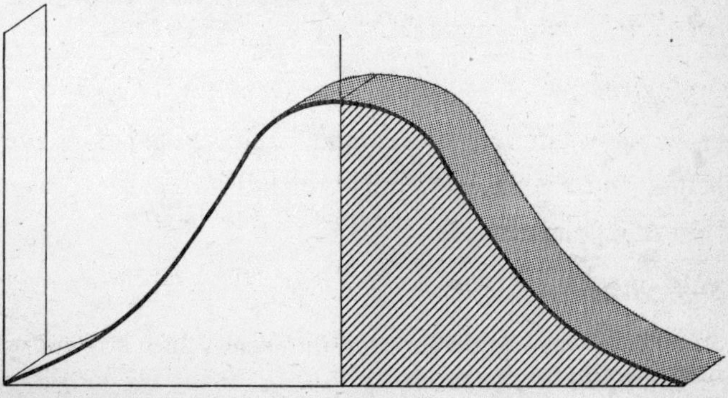

The area represents half that total under the curve and must, therefore, be equal to a probability of $\frac{1}{2}$ or .5.

The parameters that are required in order to say exactly which normal distribution is to be used in any given situation are the mean and standard deviation of the random variable in question. Basically, the mean indicates where the top of the curve lies and the standard deviation indicates how sharp the peak is. Figure 7 shows how the curve varies according to what these parameters are.

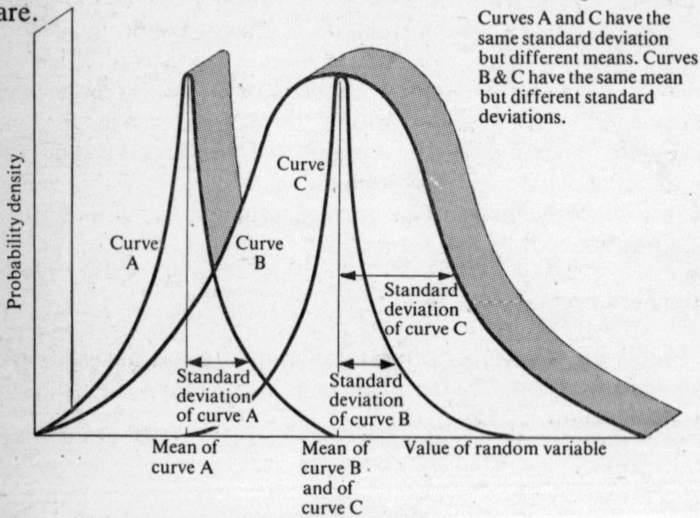

Figure 7. Different normal distributions

Now there is a problem here if statisticians want to provide tables of values of the normal distribution.

> ### *Self-check*
>
> How many different means and standard deviations are there that a normal distribution can have?

There are an infinite number.

> ### *Self-check*
>
> So if there was a table for each different value, how many tables would there need to be?

There would have to be an infinite number. This is obviously impossible.

But there is a way out. What is done is to have tables for just *one* normal distribution. By convention, it is one with mean zero and standard deviation one. When we want to find probabilities for a normal distribution, we have to convert the one we have into this 'standard normal distribution'. This is done as follows.

The characteristic of the normal distribution is that the probabilities depend *solely* on how far away from the mean the values of the variable are. The further away, the less the probability. It is the property of *any* normal distribution that probabilities will depend solely on *the number of standard deviations away from the mean*. For the standard normal curve, which has mean 0 and standard deviation 1, the variable itself is expressed in the number of deviations away from the mean. And note that values to the left of the mean are negative. To convert any other normal distribution to the same form, you must use

$$\text{standard normal form} = \frac{\text{value of variable} - \text{its mean}}{\text{its standard deviation}}.$$

So, for example, if a normal distribution has mean 20 and standard deviation 2, then the value 24 of that variable has a standard normal form of $\frac{24-20}{2} = 4/2 = 2$.

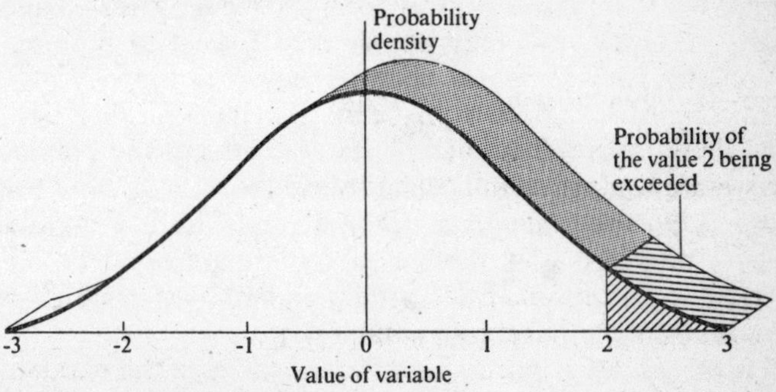

Figure 8. The standard normal curve

The standard normal curve and the probability of the above standard normal value being exceeded are shown in figure 8.

Self-check

Calculate the standard normal equivalents of the following:

1 The value 40 of a normally distributed variable with mean 20 and standard deviation 2.
2 The value 20 of a normally distributed variable with mean 40 and standard deviation 2.
3 The value 90 of a normally distributed variable with mean 80 and standard deviation 1.

Comment on your results.

ANSWERS

1 The equivalent is $\frac{40-20}{2} = -20/2 = 10$.
If you got –10, then you subtracted the wrong way round.

2 The equivalent is $\frac{20-40}{2} = 20/2 = -10$.
Again, if you got +10 this time, you subtracted the wrong way round.

3 The equivalent is $\frac{90-80}{1} = 10/1 = 10$.
Once more, if you got –10, then you subtracted the wrong way round.

All the values are the same except for the sign. They each represent the same distance away from the mean. The first and the last are equal, but they are derived from two different distributions. They are equal because they both represent the same number of deviations from the mean in the same direction.

When we are working with normal distributions, we do not use the area under the standard curve on a graph. Rather, statisticians have prepared a set of tables with these areas, i.e. probabilities, listed for certain values of the standard normal variable. An extract from these is shown in table 8.

The probabilities given are for different values of the standard normal variable being *exceeded*, as in figure 8.

TABLE 8. EXTRACT FROM THE STANDARD NORMAL TABLE

Standard normal value	*Probability of this being exceeded*
2.0	.0228
2.1	.0179
2.2	.0139
2.3	.0107
2.4	.0082
2.5	.0062
2.6	.0047
2.7	.0035
2.8	.0026
2.9	.0019
3.0	.0013

Self-check

What is the probability (from the table) that the value of a standard normal variable will lie between 2.8 and 2.9?

We can see that the probability of the value of a standard normal variable exceeding 2.8 is .0026 and of exceeding 2.9 is .0019. Thus the probability of it lying between 2.8 and 2.9 is .0026 − .0019 = .0007.

Self-check

What is the probability (from the table) that the value of the standard normal variable will be less than 2.4?

The probability that the standard normal variable will *exceed* 2.4 is, from the table, .0082. If you got this answer, you forgot that we want the probability of its being *less*. We can get this by noting that the total area under the curve is 1, so the required probability is 1 − .0082 = .9918.

This can best be seen by reference to a diagram.

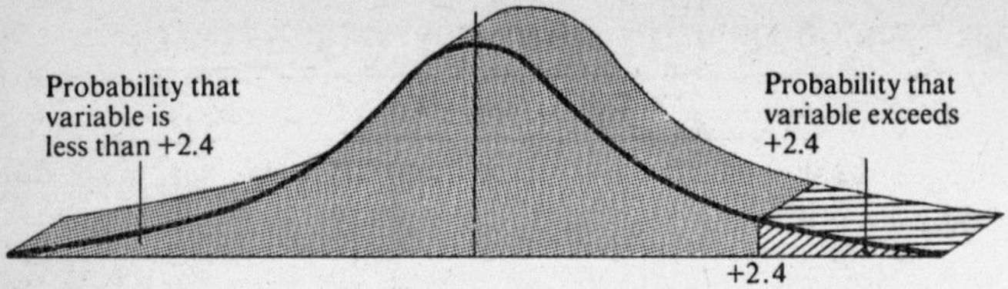

Total area under the curve is thus 1

We never bother with what happens when the continuous variable *equals* the value (here 2.4) as it can never be really said to equal it, as we saw earlier.

But what happens when the value of the standard normal variable is negative? Well, then the symmetry of the distribution is used.

Self-check

Is the probability of the standard normal variable exceeding 2, say, equal to **(a)** that of it exceeding –2 or, **(b)** that of it being less than –2 or **(c)** neither?

To answer this question, let's draw a diagram.

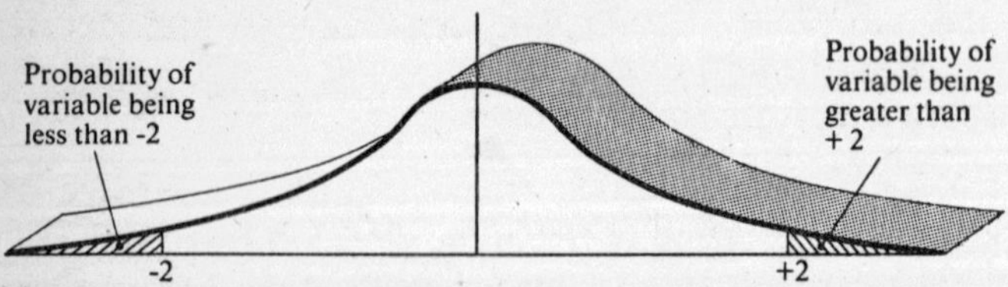

You can see from this that the probability of the standard normal variable exceeding 2 is equal to that of it being less than –2.

Self-check

From the table, what is the probability of the standard normal variable *exceeding* –2.6?

We can find the probability of the variable exceeding –2.6 by looking up the probability of it being less than –2.6 and subtracting this from 1. Remember, the total area under the curve is 1. We can find the probability of it being less than –2.6 by looking up in the table the probability of it being greater than +2.6. By symmetry, these are the same. Doing this we get that the required probability is 1 – .0047 = .9953.

If your answer was .0047, you found the probability of the variable *not* exceeding −2.6 or of it exceeding +2.6.

The diagrams below illustrate this answer.

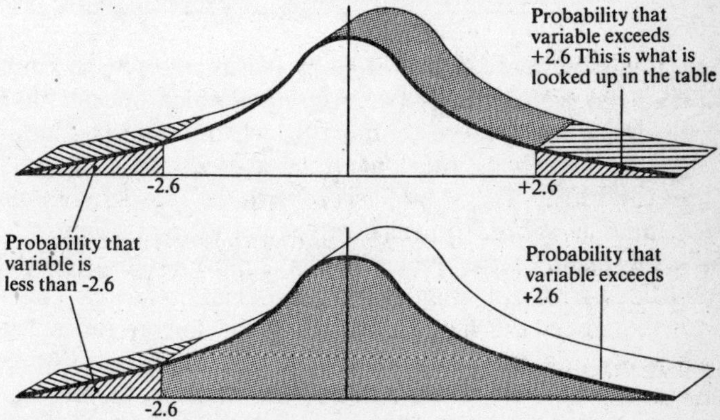

Servicing machine breakdowns

In the scenario at the end of Volume *1*, the plant manager obtained details of the times taken to service the machine that fills the jars with baby food. This is a case where the combined effects of several factors would probably result in these times forming a normal distribution. Suppose the results of that inquiry showed that the service times, including waiting for the engineer to arrive, of the previous five weeks' breakdowns were as in table 9 overleaf.

TABLE 9. SERVICE TIMES FOR BREAKDOWNS OVER FIVE-WEEK PERIOD (NEAREST MINUTES)

6	7	15	8	12	10	8	9	4	7	10	9	10	8	12
7	21	9	7	8	6	10	6	9	6	9	8	23	7	5
8	9	14	7	6	8	10	11	8	9	8	8	9	10	9
7	8	7	8	8	8	8	8	7	7	10	8	6	6	8
9	17	8	8	11	8	13	8	7	5	5	10	8	6	8
7	9	10	7	8	6	8	9	6	7	8	8	8	10	6
8	10	11	6	9	4	21	6	6	7					

Actually, from these figures it looks as if there are two kinds of breakdown, a frequently occurring one which doesn't take long to service and a more serious type which does. The latter seems to be evident in the longer times of 21, 23 17 and 21 minutes (and 15?). This would accord with the reasoning in the scenario that most breakdowns involve readjustments only.

Now the mean of the above figures is 8.6 minutes, and the standard deviation 3.1 minutes (to two decimal places). These are calculated on the figures, including the longer times: we cannot really just arbitrarily leave these out. Since there were, on average, four breakdowns a day of this machine, the average time lost per day can be roughly set at $4 \times 8.6 = 34.4$ minutes, assuming a five-day working week. The point in the scenario is that if it takes only a short while to adjust the machine, the time taken by the service engineer to answer the call becomes significant. Note that it will almost certainly be normally distributed too. Suppose, for example, that the time taken to answer a call averages 4 minutes, then it will account for nearly 50% of all lost time, i.e. 16 minutes a day on average. Over a five day week this mounts up to 1 hr 20 mins. The cost of this time will be quite high, it will have to be made up in overtime, presumably. The cost of reducing it, e.g. by paying overtime to just one service engineer or possibly even by employing another one, may well be less.

The probability of some particular service time exceeding a given value can be found as follows. Standard normal tables are drawn up in terms of numbers of standard deviations from the mean. So suppose we want to find the probability of the service time exceeding 14.8 minutes. The mean service time is 8.6

minutes, so we have a value 14.8 − 8.6 = 6.2 minutes above the mean. The standard deviation of the service times is 3.1 minutes so the value of the standard normal variable is $\frac{6.2}{3.1}$ = 2 standard deviations above the mean. We then look up the standard normal value of 2 and find that the probability of this being exceeded is .0228. This, then, is also the probability of the service time exceeding 14.8 minutes.

Self-check

What is the probability of the service time not exceeding 16 minutes? (Use the nearest value in the table.)

This time is 16.0 − 8.6 = 7.4 minutes above the mean or $\frac{7.4}{3.1}$ = 2.39 standard deviations above the mean. The *nearest* standard normal value in table 8 is 2.4 and this gives a probability of .0082. But this is the probability of a service time *exceeding* 16 minutes. The probability of it being less than this is 1 − .0082 = .9918.

If you got .0082, you forgot to change it from '*exceeding*' to 'less than'.

Review

1 The times taken by coaches to complete a particular journey are normally distributed with mean 4 hours 18 minutes and standard deviation 16 minutes. The scheduled time for the journey is 4 hours 10 minutes. What is the probability that a coach will arrive more than 50 minutes late at its destination? (Use table 8.)

2 A food producer has a product which is sold in cans, labelled '500 grammes'. The canning machine however, produces cans with weights normally distributed with standard deviation .8 g. This machine can be adjusted so that the mean weight can be varied, but the standard deviation remains effectively the same. If the manufacturer wants to make the chances of a customer buying an underweight tin less than 1 in 500, what average weight should the machine be set for?

ANSWERS

1 The mean time is $4 \times 60 + 18$ minutes $= 258$ minutes. If the coach arrives more than 50 minutes late, the journey time will be greater than 5* hrs $= 5 \times 60 = 300$ minutes. We have to find out how many standard deviations this is from the mean. This number is in fact $\frac{300 - 258}{16}$ standard deviations (of 16 minutes) from the mean $= \frac{42}{16} = 2.625 = 2.6$ (to one decimal place).

From the table, the probability of this time being exceeded is thus .0047. If you added the 50 minutes late to the mean time of 4 hrs 18 mins you misread the question. The mean journey time is greater than the scheduled time by 8 minutes.

2 The point here is that if the manufacturer sets the mean weight of the tins at 500 g, 50% of them will be underweight, since the mean of a normal distribution is its mid-point. To make sure that the vast majority of the cans are within the weight limit the manufacturer must set the mean weight a good deal higher than 500 g. We can work out exactly how much higher by finding out how many standard deviations away from the mean 500 g needs to be for the chances of it not being exceeded to be less than 1 in 500. From the table, we can see that a probability of .002, i.e. a chance of 1 in 500, only occurs where values greater than 2.9 deviations from the mean are concerned. That is we use the table 'backwards' by looking up the probability and then finding the corresponding value. If you look at the table you will see that the value of 2.9 is the lowest one with a probability of .002 or less associated with it. That is it is the lowest one which has a probability of less than .002 of being exceeded.

So to ensure that the customer has a lower than 1 in 500 chance of getting an underweight tin, the machine must be set so that a value of 500 g is at least 2.9 standard deviations from the mean. That is, the mean minus 500 g should not be less than $2.9 \times .8$ g $= 2.32$ g. The machine should not then be set for less than $500 + 2.32 = 502.32$ g.

This can be better appreciated by looking at a diagram:

*i.e. the scheduled time of 4 hrs 10 mins plus 50 mins.

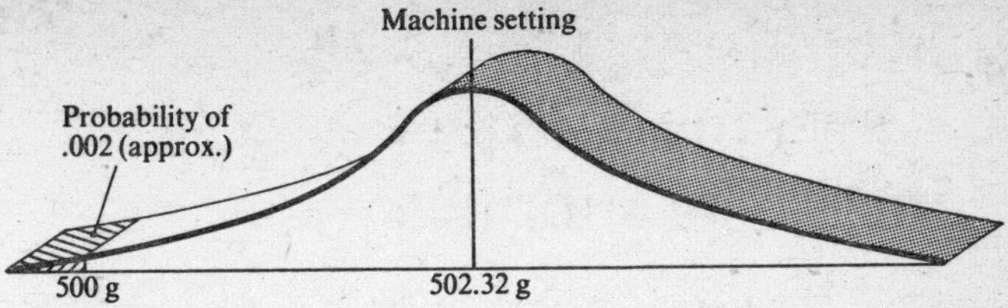

If you got an answer of 497.68 g then you subtracted the wrong way round, i.e. you assumed that 500 g should not be less than 2.9 standard deviations *more* than the mean. Note that, since the normal distribution is symmetrical, the probability of getting more than 2.9 standard deviations from the mean is the same whether this is less than or greater than the mean.

Scenario 1
Checking the quality of incoming supplies

As you read through the following scenario, make a mental note of where and how statistical information is used to make decisions. As you do, think carefully about the kind of data that is required, and what we would need to know about how it was distributed, in order to make these decisions.

Ted Long, the production manager at the Baby Gourmet plant, was in a particularly bad mood. The rather old machinery for putting the baby food into the jars was unreliable enough without having the additional problem of a poor lot of jars. There had been a great many stoppages recently, due to them being smashed in the machine.

Jane Quiller, the chief quality inspector, was only really responsible for the actual baby food, the jars were the responsibility of Len Brown, the head of purchasing at the plant. 'Well, complain to the jar manufacturers' was all he could say. That's all very well, thought Ted, but it was a bit late for that to salvage his schedule. He asked Len why the jars couldn't be examined for flaws, which he thought were the cause of the problem, before they were used.

'We can't examine every single jar,' said Len; 'it would take too much time and money. They have to be quite closely inspected to spot the faulty ones. I suppose that we could check a few of them, though, just to get the picture. We've never had to bother before as we've not had any trouble previously. I reckon it's your machine going wrong again.'

While Ted had to admit that his machine wasn't entirely above suspicion, he still maintained it was the poor quality of the jars. So it was decided that a number of them would be chosen at random from the stock and examined carefully. Ted reckoned that if there were any defective ones found, his suspicions would be borne out.

One hundred jars were subjected to careful testing and it was found that one of them was suspect. 'There you are,' said Ted, 'just as I said, it's the jars.' Len, however, wasn't so easily convinced. 'It could be that this is the only faulty one in the whole lot,' he said, 'and that it was selected for testing by sheer chance.' Ted dismissed this idea right away, saying that with 10,000 jars in stock it was hardly likely that the one faulty one would be included in the 100 chosen.

In the end they decided to check with a statistics textbook. They found that the whole thing was a little more complicated than either of them had imagined. Any conclusion reached had to be qualified by saying how likely it was to be wrong. So Ted and Len agreed that they would apply the techniques described in the book to the problem of the jars.

When they did so, they found that there was a reasonable chance that there were enough defective jars to complain to the supplier about. On the other hand, there was sufficient uncertainty about this conclusion to make Len hesitate from taking that step. They agreed, in the light of this, that they would keep monitoring the situation to obtain confirmation that there was an unreasonably high percentage of faulty jars being delivered.

Situations such as that described in the scenario occur frequently. Whenever goods or materials are purchased in bulk there is always a possibility of defective items being supplied. It is often impossible to test every item. Such a test may, for example, lead to the destruction of the item tested. Even when it is possible it may not be practically or economically feasible. In such cases all that can be done is to test a small number of the items delivered.

Of course, manufacturers generally test their own product for quality. But they, too, mostly have to rely on the same techniques as the customer. That is, they can only test a proportion of the items produced. So it is inevitable that some defectives will get through the checks. This is one of the effects of mass production. Consumers must, then, take account of this.

To carry out this quality checking efficiently and effectively the correct statistical techniques need to be used. These allow us to say what the chances are of various possible conditions holding, for example, that the proportion of defectives in a given consignment of jars is below some given value, based on the evidence obtained from those tested. Thus, though they do not allow us to draw any *firm* conclusions, they do provide measures for the *degree of belief* we can place in a number of possibilities.

But similar techniques are needed in other cases where samples are taken. For example, if we conduct a sample survey on attitudes to advertising we will want to know the likelihood of our findings being applicable to the population generally. Or, again, suppose we send someone on a course to reduce the error rate in their work. We can give them a test before they go and one when they come back. Each test can be regarded as being merely a sample of the employees' work. We then need to find out how likely it is that any improvement in score is due to real gains from the course.

The following chapter deals with the information that can be derived from a sample, and uses quality control to illustrate this. In Chapter 3 the problem of *drawing inferences* from samples in general is dealt with and attention is paid to the points raised in the above paragraph.

When you have finished the next two chapters you should be able to apply your knowledge of probability and probability distributions (which we covered in Chapter 13 of Volume *1* and Chapter 1 of this volume) to the problems of drawing inferences from sample data about the population from which it is drawn. Though Chapter 2 uses quality control as a means of getting over the ideas about making inferences, it does not deliberately set out to teach quality control in any great detail.

2 What can we learn by looking at only a proportion of the available data?

The effects of chance

We saw in Chapter 4 of Volume *1* how we usually take samples rather than collect all the available data. For example, we may examine a sample of a product, or of supplies, in quality testing. But what information can we derive from this? In the scenario, for instance, incoming consignments of glass jars are inspected. What do the results tell us?

> *Self-check*
>
> If in a large consignment of these jars there are 5% defectives, how many of them would you expect to get in a random sample of twenty jars? Does this imply that every time such a sample is taken this same number of defectives would be found?

You would expect to get just one, i.e. 5%. However, it would be possible to obtain a different result. It would even be theoretically possible to have all twenty faulty.

> *Activity*
>
> Collect together twenty 2p coins, one of which has a different date from all the others. This will represent the 5% defective jars. Put all the coins in a bag and shake them up. Pick one at random. Record whether or not it represents a defective (i.e. it is the one with the given date) and replace it. Repeat twenty times to obtain the 'sample'. Do this several times, noting the number of 'defectives' in each 'sample'.

You should find that the values obtained are round about 1, but not necessarily equal to it. The number of defectives in a sample is a random variable in fact. Statistics such as this which are obtained from sample data are called 'sample statistics'. The distributions from which they are drawn are termed 'sampling distributions'. They may be binomial or normal, for instance.

Self-check

What is the 'sampling distribution' in the case above with the coins?

What we have here is a binomial distribution. You should recall this from Chapter 1. The situation roughly models the sampling of the jars, but there is one important difference.

Self-check

What is it?

With the coins, sampling is with *replacement*: i.e. the coin selected is put back in the bag. With the jars, the complete sample of twenty is taken out without replacement. We saw in Chapter 4 of Volume *1* how this affects the probability of getting various results.

Self-check

Suppose there are 10,000 jars in the consignment, of which 5%, i.e. 500, are defective. If the first jar in the sample is defective, what is the probability that the next is?

The probability of selecting a faulty jar as the first one in the sample is $\frac{500}{10{,}000} = \frac{1}{20}$ or .05. But if one of these is selected there are now only 499 of them in the 9999 jars remaining. The chances of the second jar now being defective are 499 in 9999, which is different to 1 in 20.

Strictly speaking, therefore, the number of faulty jars in the sample cannot be said to form a binomial distribution over the samples, as the probability of selection varies. We saw in Chapter 1 how it is part of the definition of a binomial distribution that it should not vary. However, the differences are small enough to enable us to assume a binomial. For example, the worst case (i.e. where the difference is greatest) is if the first nineteen are all faulty. The probability of the twentieth one being also faulty is then $\frac{481}{9981}$. But even this is .0482 (to four decimal places) as opposed to .05. We can thus assume that the number of defectives in the sample of jars forms a binomial distribution over the samples. Use table 10 to answer the following questions.

TABLE 10. BINOMIAL DISTRIBUTION FOR TWENTY TRIALS

Number of 'successes'	*Probability of 'success'*		
	= .01	= .05	= .3
0	.818	.358	.001
1	.165	.377	.007
2	.016	.189	.028
3	.001	.060	.072
4	0+	.013	.130
5	0+	.002	.179
6	0+	0+	.192
7	0+	0+	.164
8	0+	0+	.114
9	0+	0+	.065
10	0+	0+	.031
11	0+	0+	.012
12	0+	0+	.004
13	0+	0+	.001
14	0+	0+	0+
15	0+	0+	0+
16	0+	0+	0+
17	0+	0+	0+
18	0+	0+	0+
19	0+	0+	0+
20	0+	0+	0+

Self-check

What would be the probability of getting **(a)** none and **(b)** all twenty of the jars in the sample acceptable?

The probability of a jar selected at random being faulty is .05. The probability of getting twenty jars in the sample all defective is 0+ in the table. This indicates that this probability is extremely small (it is, in fact, of the order of one in a billion billion billion). Again using the binomial distribution tables, the probability of all twenty jars in the sample being acceptable (i.e. zero unacceptable) is .358 (to three decimal places), i.e. roughly a one-in-three chance. There is thus quite a high chance of this happening.

It would also be quite possible for a sample with no defective in it to be drawn from a population with, say, 30% of the jars in it faulty.

Self-check

What would be the probability of this happening?

Again, we may use the binomial distribution tables this time with the probability of selecting a faulty jar being $\frac{30}{100} = .3$. We thus have a probability of .001 for none of the jars in the sample being defective. That is to say, *by sheer chance alone*, a sample with no defective in could occur about once in a thousand samples, even if the consignment contained 30% defectives.

Deciding on acceptable levels of risk

Now the reason for taking the sample is to check whether the percentage of faulty jars in the consignment is within an acceptable limit.

Self-check

Do you think that it would be required that there be no defectives at all in the consignment?

This condition would be very difficult indeed to check for and would need an inordinate amount of resources to be put into inspection. Normally, a certain percentage of defectives is allowed, say .05%. This percentage is called the 'lot tolerance percentage defective' (LTPD). We shall use higher percentages here to simplify the calculations. Assume then that the consignment will be acceptable if there are no more than 5% defectives in it.

If we take a sample of twenty jars, how many faulty ones do there have to be in it before we reject the consignment? The answer to this is not, as we have seen, straightforward. There is a very small probability that all twenty will be faulty, even if there are less than 5% defective in the consignment. On the other hand there is a possibility that, even with, say 30% defectives, none of them are actually selected for the sample. So what number of defectives in the sample do we accept as a cut-off point, i.e. above which we reject the batch? This figure is called the 'acceptance number', and could, of course, be set at anything from 0 to 20.

Self-check

Suppose we choose an acceptance number of 0 in a sample of twenty jars for an LTPD of 5%. What is the probability of accepting a consignment in which there are exactly 5% defectives?

We will accept a consignment only if there are no faulty jars in the sample. We have seen that the probability of getting no defectives in the sample under such conditions is .358 (to three decimal places). This situation is illustrated in figure 9.

Self-check

Is the probability of accepting a consignment of jars in which there are *more than* 5% defectives less than, equal to, or greater than the figure of .358 above?

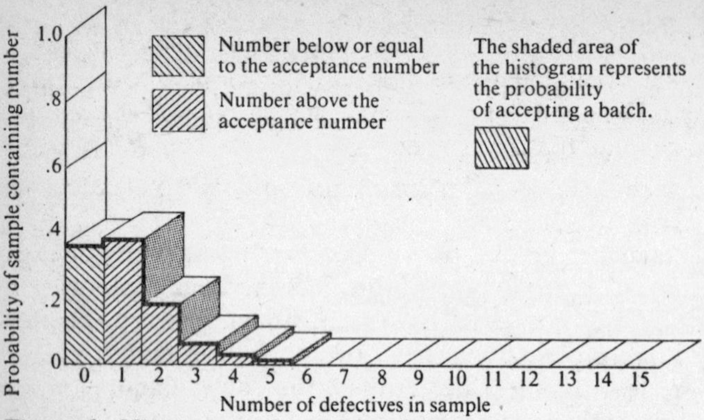

Figure 9. Histogram of number of defectives in a sample of twenty jars drawn from a population in which there are 5% faulty jars

If the percentage of defectives in the consignment is increased they will be more likely to be included in the sample. This is shown in figure 10 for 10% defectives in the consignment. It can be seen that the area of the shaded rectangle here is less than it was in figure 9. The probability of getting no faulty jars in the sample gets smaller then as the percentage of them in the consignment increases and so is always less than .358. This figure is thus an *upper limit* on the probability of wrongly accepting a 'bad' consignment of jars, and is, in fact, called the 'consumer's risk'.

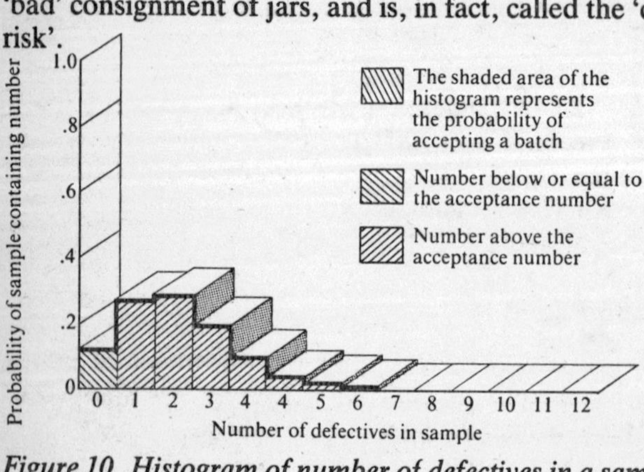

Figure 10. Histogram of number of defectives in a sample of twenty jars drawn from a population in which there are 10% faulty jars

Self-check

What would happen to the consumer's risk if, still keeping an LTPD of 5% and a sample size of twenty, the acceptance number was changed to 1?

Looking at figure 9 we see that the shaded area would be increased by including the rectangle on '1'. So the consumer's risk would become greater. To keep it as low as possible, therefore, we should set a small acceptance number. However, there is another consideration that must be borne in mind. We do not want to reject too many good consignments (i.e. in which there are less than 5% defectives).

Self-check

What happens to the probability of rejecting a consignment with, say, only 1% faulty jars in it if the acceptance number is *increased*?

It becomes less. This situation is illustrated in figure 11. If the acceptance number were increased to 1 or more, the unshaded area of the histogram would be decreased. So, from this point of view, the acceptance number should be as high as possible.

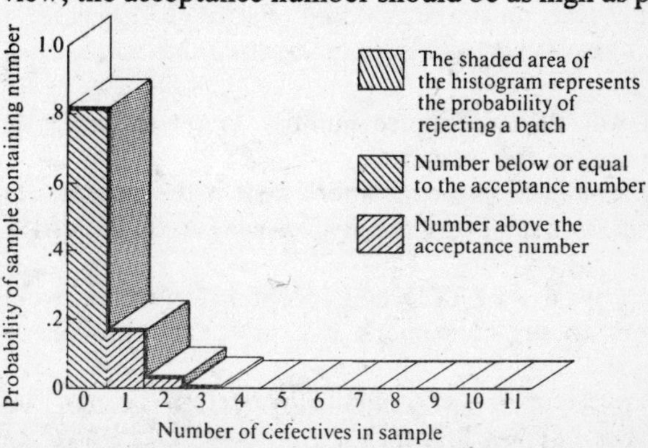

Figure 11. Histogram of a number of defectives in a sample of twenty jars drawn from a population in which there are 1% faulty jars

Thus a balance needs to be struck between these two different requirements and, in order to do this, statistical calculations must be carefully carried out to find the various probabilities involved. In practice, the cost of being wrong would be one of the most important factors in deciding what levels to set. However, as quality control is here only being used as an example of the use of samples, this point will not be pursued further here.

Summary

So we see that the information contained in samples, usually expressed as a sample statistic, can help us to make decisions. Here, it assists us in determining the quality of incoming supplies. But samples introduce uncertainty. We can never be completely sure whether the results obtained are due to the operation of sheer chance or to a characteristic of the population. If this was as far as we could go, taking samples would be pointless. But *if we know the form of the distribution of the sample statistic* (and in this section it was binomial) we can calculate the chances of our being wrong, or at least put a limit on them. This allows us to sample sensibly. For example, we can choose the acceptance number so that the consumer's risk is reasonable and yet does not cause us to reject too many good consignments.

Review

1 What was the acceptance number that was implicitly being used in the scenario?

2 What would be the consumer's risk if the acceptance number for a sample of twenty jars with an LTPD of 1% were 1?

3 With some fixed LTPD and acceptance number, what happens to the consumer's risk as the sample size is increased?

4 A manufacturer has a quality inspection system that produces batches in which the average percentage of defectives – the 'process average' – is 1%. If batches are rejected if there is one or more defectives in a sample of twenty from them, what is the probability of rejecting a batch containing a percentage of defectives equal to the process average? This probability is analogous to the consumer's risk and is called the 'producer's risk'. (Use table 10.)

ANSWERS

1 In the scenario they expect to find no defective jars in their sample, so they are, in effect, setting an acceptance number of 0.

If you said 1, remember the acceptance number is the number of defectives which must not be exceeded for the batch to be acceptable.

2 If the acceptance number is 1, then the batch is rejected if the sample contains two or more defectives. From the tables, the probability of getting 0 defectives is .818. The probability of .01 is used here since 1% is 1 in 100, i.e. a fraction of .01. The probability of getting 1 defective is .165. So the probability of getting either 0 or 1 defective is .818 + .165 = .983. This is also the consumer's risk. It is very high indeed, and nothing even approaching this would be tolerated in practice.

If you said the consumer's risk was 1 − .983 = .017, then you were getting confused about its meaning. It is an upper limit on the probability of wrongly accepting a batch. It is *not* anything to do with there being more than an acceptable number of defectives in the sample.

3 As the sample size is increased, the chances of getting a defective in it must increase too. This will increase the chances of the acceptance number being exceeded. That is, more batches will be rejected. That means that the consumer stands less chance of accepting a 'faulty' batch, so the consumer's risk is *decreased* too.

If you said it would be increased, because the number of defectives in the sample would be greater, think again about the exact meaning of the consumer's risk. It's *not* the risk of getting defectives in the sample but of *not* getting defectives in the sample when there are too many in the batch.

4 The process average is 1%, so we have a probability of .01 of getting a defective in the sample if the process average is being met exactly. A batch will be rejected if the sample contains more than 0 defectives, that is unless it does contain 0 defectives. From the tables, the probability of it containing zero defectives is .818. The probability of it *not* so doing is thus 1 − .818 = .182, and so this is the producer's risk.

If you said the producer's risk was .818, then remember the producer's risk is not passing a batch which is, in fact, within specification; that is, the risk of getting *more* defectives in the sample than are expected if the batch is within tolerance.

How the quality of a product varies

The type of quality testing discussed above, where an item is either defective or not, is called 'attribute testing'. But in some cases it is the value of a variable that is of interest, e.g. the weight of a packet of flour. When this is so the testing is called 'variable testing'. Suppose a manufacturer of ball bearings arranges for a certain percentage of them to be carefully measured after production to check if they conform to specification.

Self-check

Even if the production process is operating correctly, will all the ball bearings of a given nominal diameter be of *exactly* the same size?

No. Small variations in that process will cause corresponding variations in the size of the bearings.

Activity

The following procedure is a simple model of the production process. Take some paper and cut it into thirty strips about 8″ long and $\frac{1}{4}$″ wide. If you use ruled A4 sheets and cut along the lines, this will give you pieces of suitable size. Now take each strip and, measuring *by eye only*, cut off a piece 5″ long. *Do not* measure it after you have cut it, nor compare it with ones produced previously. When all thirty strips have been processed, measure, to the nearest $\frac{1}{10}$″, each of the resultant 5″ long pieces and record the result on the strip itself. (NB: save these strips for later in the chapter when we shall be using them again several times.)

Unless you are extraordinarily consistent at guessing lengths, you will find that these measurements vary.

Activity

Draw up a suitable histogram to display the lengths of the paper strips from the activity above. Calculate and record the mean length of these strips.

It is likely that your histogram will show the characteristics of a normal distribution. That is, most lengths will be near the mean but a certain number will be somewhat further from it and scattered evenly on either side. (This may not come out too clearly since there are only thirty strips.) The average length of the strips is not likely to be 5″ unless you have an excellent eye for lengths, however.

It is, in fact, usually assumed that a production process results in a normal distribution of physical variables such as length and weight (see Chapter 1). Suppose, for example, a batch of 100,000 ball bearings is produced. If every one were measured, and the results recorded in the form of a histogram, it might appear as in figure 12. Note that the mean diameter there is 5 mm and there is a standard deviation of .01 mm.

If the machine for producing ball bearings is set incorrectly it will yield a different distribution of diameters. In general we can assume that it will be a normal one with a standard deviation equal to that for the correct setting, i.e. .01 mm. However, the mean will be different. The strips that you have produced may be regarded as being an example of a process which is set slightly incorrectly. (Unless, of course, you actually managed an average of 5″!) Figure 13 shows the distributions for the correct machine setting for the ball bearings and for one which produces a mean diameter of 5.01 mm.

With the normal setting, virtually all the bearings should lie within the tolerance limits. If they do not we are trying to work to finer limits than the machine is capable of. When it is set incorrectly, however, the machine may well produce a percentage of over- or under-size bearings. If the tolerance limits are 5.0 mm ± .035 mm, for example, then the shaded area of figure 13

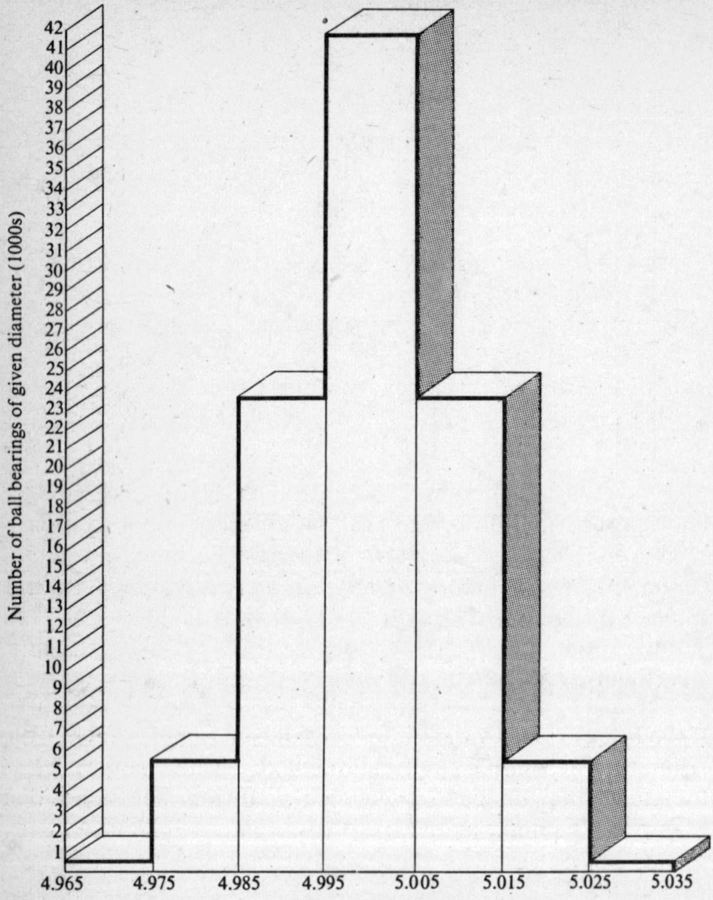

Figure 12. Histogram of diameters of 100,000 ball bearings of nominal diameter 5mm

represents this percentage. With the figures given this is actually about .6%, i.e. 6 in every 1000. As with the jars, whether or not this is acceptable depends on what percentage we are prepared to tolerate.

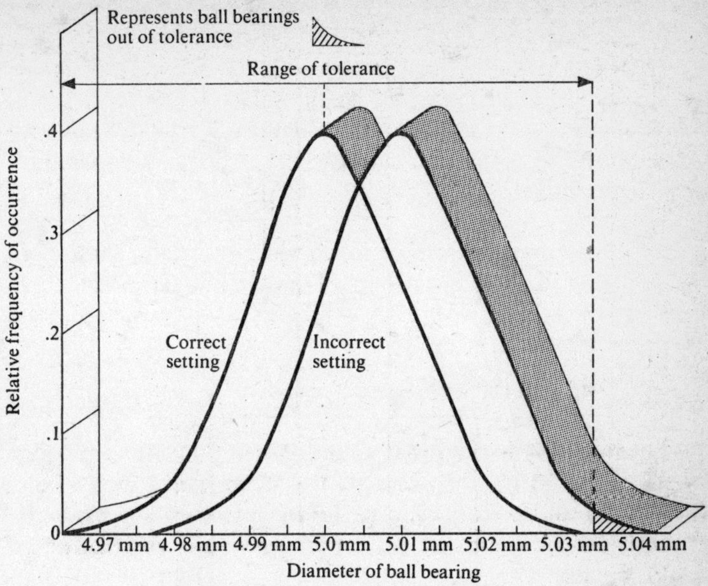

Figure 13. The distribution of ball bearing diameters with correct and incorrect machine settings

Testing just a fraction of production

If the population is variable so too will be a sample drawn from it for quality testing. But we can calculate the arithmetic mean of the measurements taken from such a sample. This is another example of a sample statistic.

Self-check

If the machine is set to produce ball bearings of 5 mm diameter, what would you expect the mean diameter of a random sample of such ball bearings to be? Does this imply that every time such a sample is taken the mean diameter of the bearings in it would take exactly that value?

If the machine was operating correctly you would expect this mean to be 5 mm also. However, the actual value would, in fact, vary.

Activity

Mix up the paper strips produced in the activity on page 62 and, without looking at them, select a sample of five. Calculate and record the sample mean. Compare this with the overall mean obtained earlier. Repeat this procedure several times.

You will find that the sample mean will not be the same each time, nor is it likely to exactly equal the population mean.

Self-check

Why do you think this is so?

It is because, as the sample is a random one, it is quite possible for these five to be unrepresentative of the strips as a whole. They could all be from among the longer ones, for example. Similarly, the samples of ball bearings would yield different sample means.

For instance, if we take a random sample of, say, twenty ball bearings from the population of figure 12, we might not make a 'balanced' selection, i.e. the mean diameter of the twenty bearings might differ considerably from 5 mm. So it would be possible, though improbable, that all of them came from the 5.025–5.035 mm range. Hence the mean diameter of ball bearings in any such sample will not always be 5 mm.

Self-check

Is the probability of the sample mean being near to 5 mm greater than, less than, or equal to the probability of it being further away from 5 mm?

Though the sample mean will not necessarily be 5 mm, we can say that it is more likely to be near it than far away. This is because there are more ball bearings with diameters near to 5 mm than at the extremes, and so these are more likely to be selected. Suppose we now take a sequence of such samples. Their means will differ in general. However, because of what has just been said about values near to 5 mm being more likely to occur, we can say something about what pattern will result in the long run.

Self-check

What pattern will emerge in the long run?

If the machine is working correctly, the sample means should cluster around 5 mm, with more being near than further away. This is illustrated in figure 14(a).

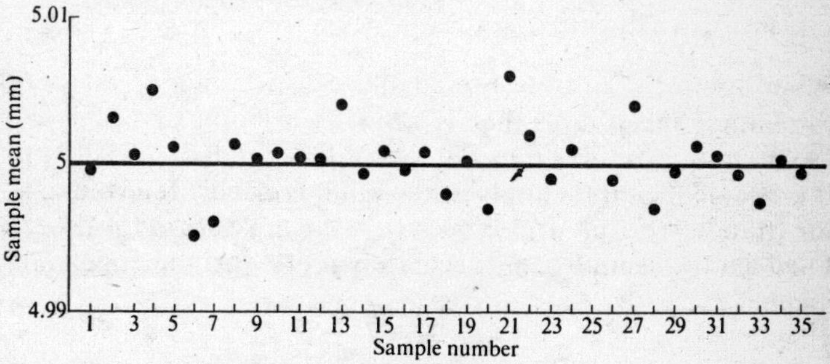

Figure 14. The 'long run' sample means
(a). Sample size 20

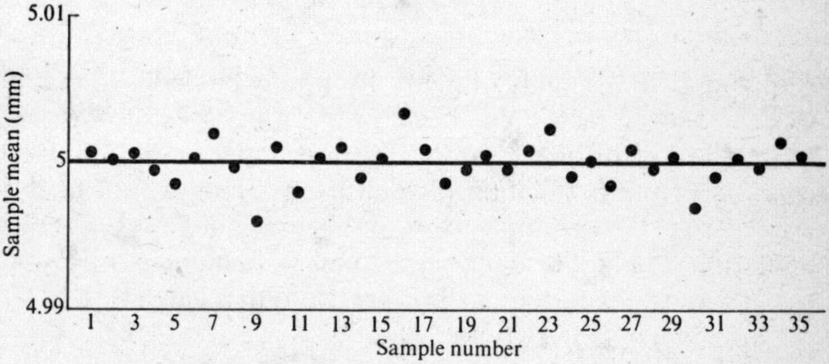

(b). Sample size 50

Now consider the consequences of increasing the sample size. Suppose, for example, we change it to 50.

Self-check

What then happens to the probability of making an 'unbalanced' selection?

Because there are more bearings chosen it will decrease. This is because the chances of having all or most of these at one extreme are less. Hence there will not be as much variability in a sequence of means of samples of this size. This situation is shown in figure 14(b).

It can be seen that the points there cluster more closely around the 5 mm line than do those in figure 14(a).

The error which inevitably occurs when not all available data is utilized

What figure 14 illustrates is actually a distribution of values of the sample mean. This then is a further example of a sampling distribution. We may thus talk about the standard deviation of the sample means themselves, though it is usually referred to as the 'standard error'. This is because it is a measure of the degree to which the sample mean accurately represents the population mean.

Self-check

So what happens to the standard error of the sample mean as the sample size is increased?

From above, and a study of figure 14, it may be deduced that it will decrease. In fact, it can be shown that in cases such as this the standard error of the sample mean is equal to the standard deviation of the population divided by the square root of the sample size. For example, for the figures in figure 12, the population standard deviation is .01 mm. The standard error for the mean of samples of size 100 taken from that batch is thus:

$$\frac{.01}{\sqrt{100}} = \frac{.01}{10} = .001 \text{ mm.}$$

Self-check

What would be the standard error for the mean of samples of size 400 drawn from a population in which the standard deviation was .4 mm?

It would be $\frac{.04}{\sqrt{400}} = \frac{.04}{20} = .002$ mm.

Did you remember to take the square root (of the bottom number only)?

Note that the standard error is completely independent of the size of the population (provided that the sample size does not become a substantial proportion of it). In fact the accuracy with which the sample mean represents the population mean depends only on the population standard deviation and the sample size.

Furthermore, beyond a certain sample size the gain in accuracy if it were increased would not be worth the cost of having to collect the extra data. For example, with the ball bearings of figure 12, a sample size of 1600 gives a standard error for the sample mean of

$$\frac{.01}{\sqrt{1600}} = \frac{.01}{40} = .00025 \text{ mm.}$$

When this result is compared with the standard error for samples of size 100, as calculated earlier, we see that a gain in accuracy of four times is bought at the expense of gathering sixteen times as much data.

Finding patterns

Since the sample mean has a distribution associated with it, we can ask what type it is (see Chapter 1). If the variable in question is distributed normally in the 'parent population', i.e. that from which the sample is drawn, the distribution of the sample mean is normal also. This is, in fact, the case we have been discussing above, and is illustrated in figure 15 for sample size 100. However, in large samples, of the order of thirty or more, the distribution of the sample mean can be taken to be normal for a large number of different distributions of the parent population. This is due to what is known as the 'central limit theorem'. Briefly, this implies that the mean of a large number of independent random variables will be approximately normally distributed.

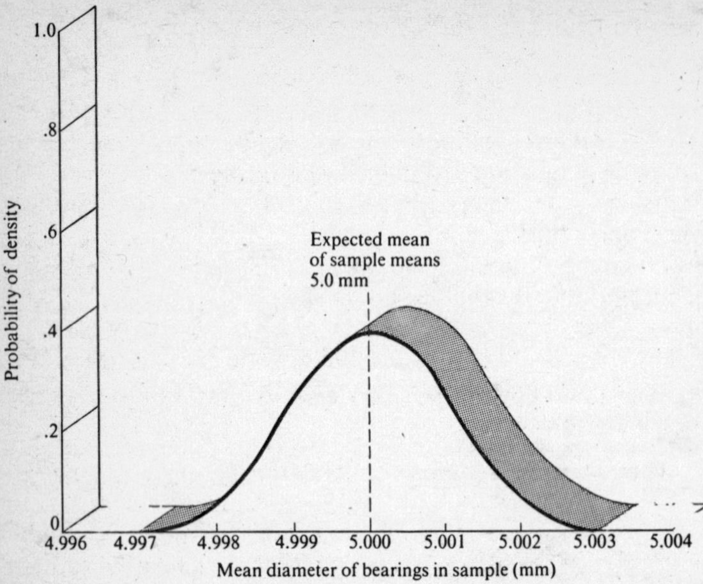

Figure 15. Sampling distribution for the ball bearings: sample size 100

Thus for all large samples, the sample mean can be taken to be distributed normally over the samples. Furthermore, from the last section, we know that the standard deviation (standard error) is equal to the standard deviation of the parent population divided by the square root of the sample size. For instance, suppose the length of the queue at a bank counter is recorded at a large number of times (say sixty-four) over a period and the mean length calculated. If this whole process is repeated, a number of times, further means may be calculated. From above, they will be normally distributed. Furthermore, if the standard deviation of the lengths of the queues is 1.6 say, the standard deviation of the sample mean (i.e. the standard error) will be

$\frac{1.6}{\sqrt{64}} = \frac{1.6}{8} = .2.$

Controlling the quality of a product

Now that we know the distribution of the sample means we can use this to draw conclusions about the quality of a product from samples taken. Suppose we draw a sample of 100 ball bearings from the population described in figure 12.

Self-check

What is the probability that the mean diameter of ball bearings in this sample is greater than 5.002 mm if the machine is set correctly? Use table 11.

TABLE 11. SELECTED PARTS OF THE STANDARD NORMAL DISTRIBUTION

Value of standard normal variable	*Probability of this value being exceeded*
0.0	.5000
0.1	.4602
0.2	.4207
0.3	.3821
0.4	.3446
0.5	.3085
0.6	.2743
0.7	.2420
0.8	.2119
0.9	.1841
1.0	.1587
1.1	.1357
1.2	.1151
1.3	.0968
1.4	.0808
1.5	.0668
1.6	.0548
1.7	.0446
1.8	.0359
1.9	.0287
2.0	.0228
2.1	.0179
2.2	.0139
2.3	.0107

2.4	.0082
2.5	.0062
2.6	.0047
2.7	.0035
2.8	.0026
2.9	.0019
3.0	.0013

A fuller set of tables appears in the Appendix to this volume.

We have seen earlier that the standard error of the mean of samples of this size is .001 mm. We also know that the sampling distribution in this case is normal. We can thus calculate the required probability as follows. First we calculate how many standard deviations away from the mean 5.002 mm is. It is, in fact, $\frac{5.002 - 5.000}{.001} = \frac{.002}{.001} = 2$ standard deviations away from the mean. From the table, the probability of a diameter exceeding 5.002 mm is thus about .023. This means that such a result would be obtained in only 2.3% of the samples.

Suppose, then, we do find a sample mean of 5.002 mm or more when testing a sample of 100 of these ball bearings.

> *Self-check*
>
> What would this tell us about the ball bearings produced?

It would not tell us anything *for certain*. What we could say, however, is that *if* the process was operating correctly, i.e. producing ball bearings of mean diameter 5.000 mm (with standard deviation .01 mm), such a result would happen only 2.3% of the time. But, of course, if the actual mean diameter of ball bearings produced was greater than 5.000 mm the chances of getting a sample mean more than 5.002 mm would be increased.

> *Self-check*
>
> If the machine is incorrectly set and produces ball bearings of mean diameter 5.01 mm, what is the probability that the mean of a sample of 100 exceeds 5.002 mm?

Here the number of standard deviations away from the mean that 5.002 mm is, is $\frac{5.002 - 5.01}{.001} = \frac{-.008}{.001} = -8$. There is thus a virtual certainty that it will be exceeded (look at the highest value in the table to see this). This reflects the fact that, with a sample of 100, the standard error of the sample mean is one tenth of the standard deviation of the population. So although the population mean has only changed by one standard deviation, i.e. from 5.00 mm to 5.01 mm, this moves the expected sample mean through *ten* standard errors.

Because we would normally not know whether the ball bearings would be over- or under-size should the machine be wrongly set, we would look for evidence of either. Thus we would not just test to see if, for example, a sample mean exceeded 5.002 mm, but also whether it was less than 4.998 mm, i.e. .002 mm on the other side of 5.00 mm. This situation is illustrated in figure 16.

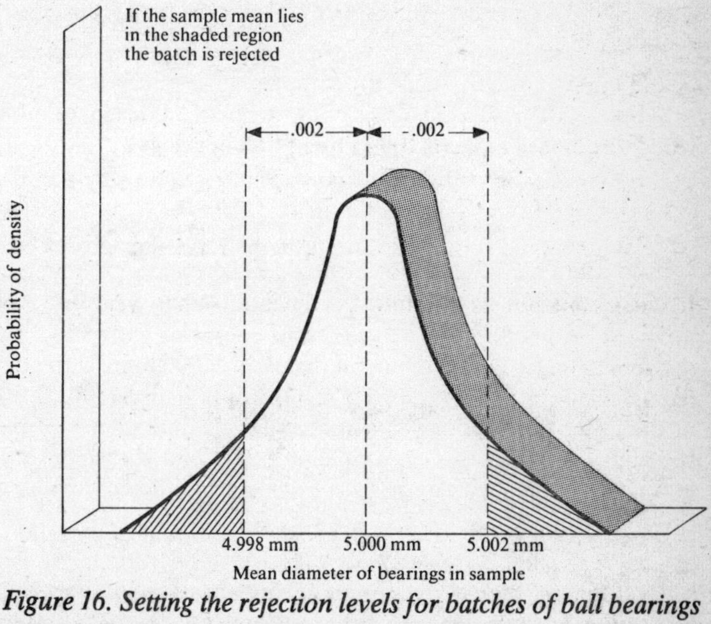

Figure 16. Setting the rejection levels for batches of ball bearings

Actually, in practice, smaller and more frequent samples would be taken so that any deviations could be spotted before too many faulty items are produced. But the principle of looking for values of the sample mean outside some given range would still be used.

Filling in the blanks

In all the calculations on quality testing to date, we have assumed that the standard error is known, either from the standard deviation of the population or because we are dealing with a binomial distribution, where it can be derived from the parameters. While in quality testing it usually is known, in many other cases it is not known. Consider, for example, a sample survey of firms on projected redundancies as a percentage of employees. The only way of finding the population standard deviation, needed to calculate the standard error, would be to actually conduct a census of those firms! We are thus reduced to estimating it.

> *Self-check*
>
> What figure do you think could be used as a *basis* for estimating the population standard deviation using a sample taken from that population?

It would seem sensible to base our estimate of the population standard deviation on the standard deviation of the sample.

> *Self-check*
>
> But can we assume the two are equal? If not, why not?

While we can make the assumption that the population mean is equal to the sample mean, we cannot do the same in the case of the standard deviation. This is because the amount of variation in a sample, except in cases where it is fairly large, is bound to be less, on average, than in the population as a whole, since the less numerous extreme values are not as likely to be selected as ones near the population mean. This does, of course, assume that the parent population is such that there *are* less values near the extremes; an assumption that should be borne in mind, though it is seldom a problem in practice.

There is a rule, developed from theory which is outside the scope of this book, that the best estimate of the population standard deviation is given by multiplying the standard deviation of the sample by the square root of the sample size divided by one less than the sample size.

Self-check

Suppose the sample standard deviation of the expected percentage of redundancies is 5%, and the sample size is 81. What is the standard error for the sample mean?

The best estimate for the population standard deviation is $\sqrt{\frac{81}{80}} \times 5\% = 5.03\%$ (to two decimal places). The estimated standard error is thus $\sqrt{\frac{5.03}{81}} = \frac{5.03}{9} = 56\%$ (to two decimal places).

One important point should be made here. It was pointed out earlier that, provided the variable in question was approximately normally distributed throughout the parent population, the sampling distribution of the mean of *even small* samples was normal. To this should now be added the proviso that the standard deviation of the variable in the parent population should also be accurately known. If it has to be estimated, as described above, this assumption is no longer valid and a distribution known as 'student's t' has to be used. This is not described in this text. For details you should consult a more detailed book on statistics, such as *Statistics for Business: A Course Unit Approach* by P. Taylor and D. Dunning (Polytech Publishers, 1977).

Self-check

The owner of a timber plantation has a plot with trees of all the same age, and he measures a sample of twenty-five of them. The standard deviation of the heights of trees in the sample is 3 ft. What is the estimated standard error of the sample mean?

The estimate of the population standard deviation is $\sqrt{\frac{25}{24}} \times 3 = 3.06$ (to two decimal places). Hence the estimated standard error is $\frac{3.06}{\sqrt{25}} = \frac{3.06}{5} = 0.612$ ft.

Note that for large samples, the above 'correction factor' is virtually 1 and so the standard deviation of the sample may be taken as that of the population.

Review

Use the tables in the Appendix to answer the following questions.

1 a A flour producer sells bags which are nominally 1 kg in weight. If the machine which fills the bags operates with a standard deviation of 1 g, would it actually be set to 1 kg? If not, why not?
b If the producer wants to ensure that no more than 1 in 10,000 bags are under-weight, what weight of flour should the machine be set to deliver? (Hint: use the tables 'backwards', i.e. looking at the entries first.)

2 a If the flour producer set the machine as calculated above, what would be the expected mean weight of bags in a sample of 25 of them? Would this value change if the sample size was increased to 100?
b What would be the standard error of the sample mean in the two sizes of sample above?
c The flour producer wishes to select samples which have a standard error for the sample mean of less than .05 g. What is the minimum sample size that could be used?

3 a The flour producer weighs a sample of 25 of the '1 kg' bags. If the machine is set at 1.001 kg, what is the probability that the mean weight of bags of flour in the sample is less than 1 kg? (Assume the population standard deviation is still 1 g.)
b What would be the effect on this figure of decreasing the sample size to 9?

4 a If, in attribute testing, large samples are used, what distribution may be assumed for the number of defectives in a sample?
b A process for producing integrated circuits yields a very high proportion of defectives, namely 36%. What is

the probability of a sample of 100 such circuits containing more than 45 of them? (Note that the standard error has to be obtained by using the known standard deviation of binomial distribution – in this case it is 4.8.)

ANSWERS

1 a If the flour producer were to set the machine to 1 kg, the customers would not be very pleased. The distribution of the weights of the bags would be normal, as explained in earlier units. So half the bags would be under this weight and half over. What is more, since the standard deviation is 1 g, a reasonable number of the bags could be as much as 3 g light.

b To ensure that no more than 1 in 10,000 bags are underweight, the machine needs to be set for some weight greater than 1 kg, so that the probability of getting a bag of less than 1 kg is at most .0001; i.e. 1 in 10,000. The diagram below shows this:

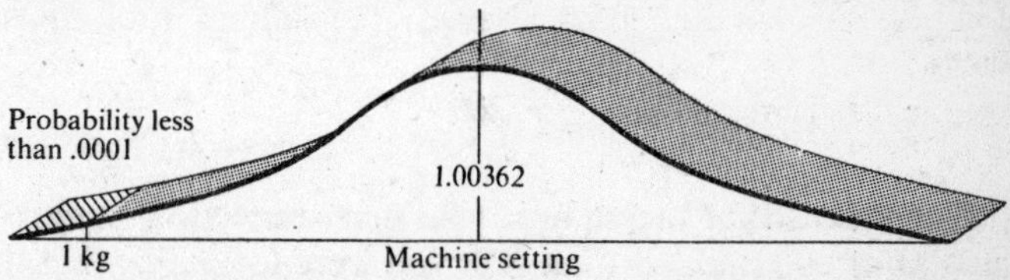

From the tables, the probability of .0001 corresponds to a standard normal value of 3.62, that is a point 3.62 standard deviations from the mean, as shown in the diagram. Note that here, in fact, the 3.62 standard deviations are to the left of the mean. This gives a value for the machine setting of 1 kg + 3.62 × 1 g, since the standard deviation is 1 g.

This comes to 1 kg + 3.62 g = 1.00362 kg. Did you see that you had to set the machine to a value greater than 1 kg?

2 a The sample statistic, 'mean weight of bags in the sample', is normally distributed with mean equal to that of the parent distribution, i.e. 1.00362 kg, in this case. This is independent of the sample size. Did you confuse this with the standard error and say that it would be different if the larger sample were taken? The point is that the population mean is the best estimate of what the sample mean will be, but that the smaller the sample the more likely it is that the sample mean will differ from that value. That is, the smaller the sample, the greater the standard error.

b If a sample is taken, then, the sample statistic, 'mean weight of bags in the sample', is normally distributed with mean 1.00362 kg. But what is its standard deviation, i.e. the standard error? We saw in this chapter how it is given by the expression: $\frac{\text{standard deviation of the population}}{\sqrt{\text{number in the sample}}}$.

Here this gives $\frac{1\text{g}}{\sqrt{25}} = \frac{1}{5} = .2$ g for sample size 25, and $\frac{1\text{g}}{\sqrt{100}} = \frac{1}{10} = .1$ g for sample size 100.

Did you remember to divide by the square root of the sample size?

c If the flour producer wishes to select samples which have a standard error of less than .05 g, then we must have that $\frac{1\text{g}}{\sqrt{\text{sample size}}}$ is less than .05 g. That is, the square root of the sample size is more than $\frac{1}{.05} = 20$.

This means that the sample size must exceed 20 squared, i.e. 400. If you said *less* than 400, you were forgetting that the smaller the sample size, the *greater* the standard error.

3 a If the machine is set at 1.001 kg, then 1 kg is 1.001 − 1.000 = .001 kg from this figure (that is, 1 g).

This is equivalent to $\frac{1}{1} = 1$ standard deviations to the *left* of the mean, since the mean weight of bags produced will equal the machine setting. But if you then used this to look up the probability, and got .1587, *then you made a mistake*. The standard deviation of 1 g applies to the population and *not* to the *sample mean*. You would only have been correct if the question had asked about the weight of *a single bag of flour*. The appropriate measure for the sample mean is the standard error. Now we saw earlier that the standard error with a sample size of 25 was .2 g. 1 g is thus $\frac{1}{.2} = 5$ standard errors from the mean.

The probability of this happening is extremely low; indeed it is so low as to be effectively zero.

b If the sample size is reduced to 9, then the standard error is *increased* to $\sqrt{\frac{1}{9}} = \frac{1}{3}$ g. The 1 g difference is then equal to 3 standard errors. So the weight of 1 kg is 3 standard errors *less* than the sample mean of 1.001 kg. The probability of getting this value is much greater; it is, in fact, .0013. Note that, in both parts of this question, you should be careful about the exact situation for which the probability is being found. If you were not, then you may well have found that your answer was .9987. The diagram below shows what probability should have been calculated:

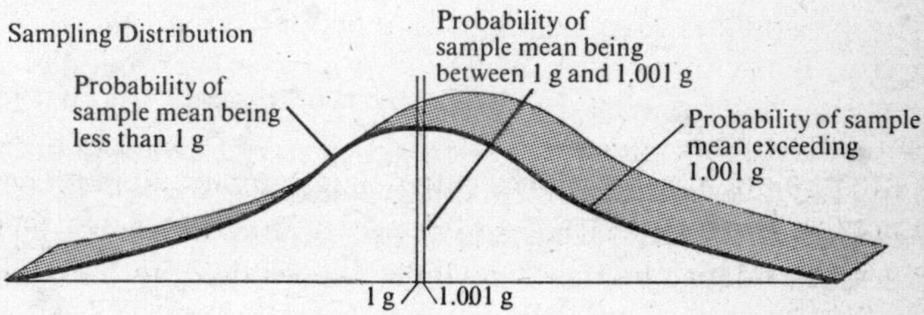

4 a In attribute testing the true sampling distribution is the binomial. But we saw in Chapter 1 that, for large values of observations, this can be approximated by the normal distribution. Note that it is the *sampling distribution* that is binomial *not* the distribution of the attribute throughout the population. The standard deviation of 4.8 (in part (b)) is thus that of the *sample mean*, and so is the equivalent of the standard error.

b If we use the normal approximation, it will have a mean of 36, i.e. 36% of the sample of 100 circuits can be expected to be defective. Its standard deviation will be 4.8

45 defectives represent 9 more than are expected, or $\frac{9}{4.8} = 1.875$ standard deviations from the mean. The probability of this number of defectives being exceeded is then about .03. If you got an answer of .97 then you found the probability of there being *less than* 45 defectives in the sample.

Note that you may have obtained slightly different answers to the probabilities in the above questions because of rounding errors. As long as these discrepancies are not too large, you should not worry about this.

3 Making estimates and testing significance

Trying to find out what is the case

We saw in the last chapter how we cannot draw firm conclusions about a population from sample data taken from it. All we can do is to make inferences, which have a certain probability of being true, but are not necessarily so. For example, whether or not a batch of jars has a higher percentage of defectives than can be tolerated is always problematical, unless every single jar in it is examined. What we have to do is to ensure that we have sufficient evidence to make any inference we do draw 'reasonable'. This chapter basically examines what is meant here by reasonable and how we can ensure that our inference is this.

We are going to start by looking at our old friend the tossed coin. This is so that the concepts that will be treated in a more formal way later in the chapter can be introduced to you now in an informal way. We are going to investigate whether or not a coin is biased; that is, if it is more likely to end up heads than tails, or vice versa.

Self-check

How would you go about doing this?

There is only one feasible way and that is to try it out, i.e. toss it a number of times to see what the results are. Notice that when we do this we are in effect sampling. That is, we are collecting only a proportion of the data available to us. We couldn't collect all the data since it is infinite: we could go on tossing the coin for ever.

Self-check

Take a tenpence coin and toss it twenty times. Record your results.

Now let's look at some results. What were yours with the coin?

When the author carried out the experiment, he obtained 14 heads and 6 tails.

Self-check

Do you think that this proves that my coin was biased? Do you think your results prove that your coin was biased?

You ought not to have said that either your or my results could *prove* that the coin was biased. You saw in the last chapter how, by sheer chance alone, some very unlikely results can be obtained. What we have got to do here is to find out just how unlikely the result we get is.

Now we saw, in Chapter 1, how we could calculate the probability of getting the various outcomes of tossing a coin several times.

Self-check

How can it be done?

It is done by applying the binomial distribution. Each toss of the coin is a Bernoulli trial, and the collection of these, in our case twenty of them, forms the binomial distribution. Remember that the probability of a 'success' does not have to equal .5, so we can deal with biased coins as well as fair ones. But if we are to use the binomial distribution to calculate the probabilities, we will need some information.

Self-check

What information is needed to be able to calculate the probabilities in a binomial distribution?

We saw in Chapter 1 that, in order to use any probability distribution, the parameters applicable to the case in question need to be known. For the binomial, these are the number of trials and the probability of the outcome of a single trial being a 'success'. We know the number of trials here, it is twenty. But we don't know the probability of the outcome of a single trial being a 'success', that is, a tail or a head, whichever we decide to count as a success. It is, indeed, *basically that we are trying to find.*

Now this means that we are forced into making an assumption about this probability.

Self-check

What is a reasonable assumption to make about the probability of a tossed coin being a head, say?

The most obvious assumption would be that the probability of getting a head was .5, that is, that the coin is unbiased, as coins usually are assumed to be. The assumption of a probability of .5

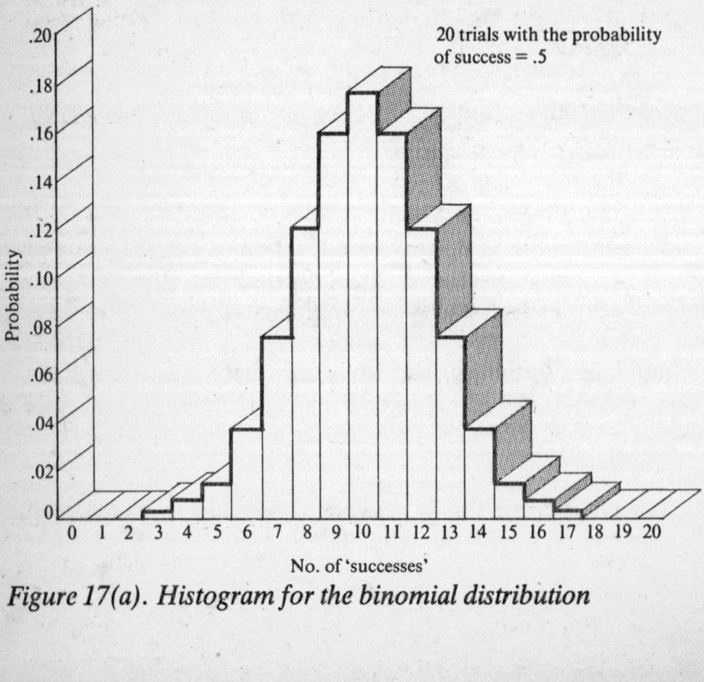

Figure 17(a). Histogram for the binomial distribution

now allows us to specify exactly what binomial distribution we are going to use. Figure 17(a) shows the histogram for it. This is what the probability distribution would look like *if our assumption were correct.*

Now what we want to know is whether this assumption is borne out by the data from the sample or whether the result obtained makes it so unlikely that the assumption is correct that we feel we must reject it.

But just what do we mean by an unlikely result? That is, what event is it that we want the probability of? It *cannot* be the probability of getting the number of heads that we did. To see this let's take an actual number. The author obtained 14 heads in his 20 throws. Let's call heads 'success'.

Self-check

Use table 12 to find the probability that this result could have occurred by chance if the coin was not biased.

TABLE 12. THE BINOMIAL DISTRIBUTION WITH 20 TESTS AND PROBABILITY OF SUCCESS = .5 AND .7

Number of 'successes' in the 20 tests	*Probability of occurrence (to three decimal places)* (a) *With probability of success = .5*	(b) *With probability of success = .7*
0	0+	0+
1	0+	0+
2	0+	0+
3	.001	0+
4	.005	0+
5	.015	0+
6	.037	0+
7	.074	.001
8	.120	.004
9	.160	.012
10	.176	.031
11	.160	.065
12	.120	.114
13	.074	.164
14	.037	.192
15	.015	.179

16	.005	.130
17	.001	.072
18	0+	.028
19	0+	.007
20	0+	.001

It is .037, which is pretty low. But then the probability of the occurrence of a *single* result is seldom high. Even the probability of getting 10 heads in the 20 tosses is only .176, and this is the result you would most expect! So the probability of getting the result obtained is *not* the best guide to the truth, or otherwise, of our assumption, as it can be fairly low even for results which would tend to support that assumption.

But what then do we do? In fact we find the probability of that result, *or an even more extreme one*, occurring: 'more extreme' here meaning more unlikely from the point of view of our assumption.

Self-check

If the assumption that the coin is fair is correct, how many of the possible outcomes are less probable than, or as probable as, the one that was obtained, i.e. 14 heads? (Use table 12 to find out.)

From table 12 the only outcomes with probabilities equal to, or less than, .037 (the probability of getting 14 heads) are:

Outcome	*Probability*
14 heads	.037
15 heads	.015
16 heads	.005
17 heads	.001
18 heads	0+
19 heads	0+
20 heads	0+
6 heads	.037
5 heads	.015
4 heads	.005
3 heads	.001

2 heads	0+
1 heads	0+
0 heads	0+
Total	.116

The sum of these probabilities (that is, .116) is, then, the probability of the result we obtained, or a more extreme one, occurring. It is the probability we need to use to test our assumption that the coin is not biased.

This can best be seen by a diagram. Figure 17(b) shows the probability in question as a shaded area of the histogram of the relevant binomial distribution. Remember that the areas of the rectangles in a histogram are proportioned to the probabilities of the outcome they represent.

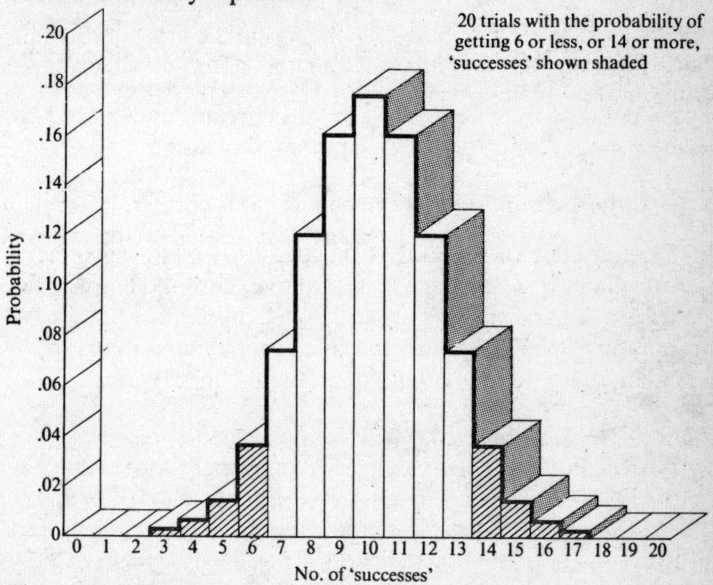

Figure 17(b). Histogram for the binomial distribution

Self-check

So what exactly does this probability of .116 mean? What can we conclude from it about the fairness, or otherwise, of the coin?

Well, it means that, if the coin really were fair, there would be just over a 1-in-10 chance of obtaining the result, or an even more unlikely one by chance. What it tells us about the coin is that it might well be biased. It doesn't tell us that it *is* biased. But it tells us something more. If it didn't then the calculation of the probability would have been a waste of time. It tells us that there is about a 1-in-10 chance that we would be wrong if we were to conclude, on the basis of the results of our sample, that the coin was biased.

Do we wish to take that chance? In this experiment, where there is no real penalty for getting it wrong, there is no great guidance on whether we do or not. But suppose that we were going to use this coin in gambling, and we were going to depend on it being biased; we were going to cheat, in fact! We would want to be fairly sure that it was biased in those circumstances! A 1-in-10 chance may not appeal to us and we might then try to find another coin that showed more evidence of bias.

The point is that we would, in any circumstance, need to decide what level of risk we were prepared to accept.

Activity

Using your own results from tossing a coin, calculate a probability in the same way as above. How likely was your result?

Suppose that . . .

Let's now look at this topic more formally.

Look at the following example. Management at a particular factory wanted to change the system of bonus payments there. When their proposal was put to the vote, the workforce was split fifty–fifty on accepting or rejecting it. Management have now announced a modified version of their plan, which they hope will receive support. Before putting this to the vote again, however, they want to test opinion on it, so as to avoid another inconclusive ballot. They decide to ask a sample of twenty workers what their reactions are to the modified plan.

Now the results from the sample will be used to determine

whether or not any shift in opinion has taken place. But there is always a probability that these will not truly reflect the views of the workforce as a whole. What is really wanted, then, is a way of calculating the probability of an error like that occurring. If this is unacceptably high, no vote would be taken. In order to perform such a calculation, however, some *assumption* has to be made about the *actual* proportion of the workforce that favour the new scheme. This is the first step in all such cases.

Such an assumption is called a 'null hypothesis'. It is that assumption which, in the absence of any evidence *yet* to the contrary, is the simplest or most obvious one to make about the population from which the sample is drawn. A null hypothesis has to be specific and exact, because the probability of getting the particular sample results obtained will need to be calculated from it. In fact, it must define any unknown parameters (see Chapter 13 in Volume *1* and Chapter 1 of this volume) of the sampling distribution of the statistic in question. It should also be formulated *without* taking into account the results of the sample. Indeed, it is usual to state the null hypothesis prior to sampling.

Self-check

What was the null hypothesis in the coin-tossing problem of the previous section?

It was that the coin was *not* biased. If you said that it was that the coin *was* biased, think how impossible it would be to get any parameters for the binomial distribution from that kind of assumption. Only if the *exact* amount of bias was specified could this be done.

Self-check

What should be the null hypothesis in the case of the workers?

If any shift in opinion has occurred, management has no reason to suspect, *before sampling*, that it has any particular magnitude.

Thus, a sensible assumption would be that *no* change has occurred, i.e. that there is still a fifty–fifty split. This was, after all, the known state of affairs beforehand. *After sampling*, we can then calculate the probability of the results obtained having been due solely to chance, *assuming that the null hypothesis were true*. To illustrate this further, let us look at a simple experiment. The same one as you did in the previous section, in fact.

Activity

To model the situation under discussion, take one tenpence coin. This can be tossed to represent the opinion of a worker chosen at random, with heads for 'in favour', say. To obtain the views of the sample of twenty workers the coin must thus be tossed twenty times. Do this and write down the results obtained.

Self-check

In the coin-tossing experiment, what is the null hypothesis corresponding to the assumption that the workforce is split fifty–fifty on the question?

To say that the workforce is split fifty–fifty is to say that the probability of a worker picked at random being in favour of the new scheme is 1/2. The corresponding null hypothesis for the coin is thus that it is unbiased, i.e. that heads or tails are equally likely. The kind of evidence that would cause us to doubt, or to reject, the null hypothesis in the case of the workers is thus precisely equivalent to that which would arouse doubts about whether or not the coin was biased. You do not, for example, expect to get eighteen heads out of twenty with an unbiased coin.

Self-check

So what distribution can be applied to the sample of workers' voting intentions?

Since, from the point of view of probability, the coin experiment and the workers' opinion poll are the same, the results there, too, will have a binomial distribution. If we regard an opinion in favour of the proposal as a 'success', then the probability of a 'success' is .5.

Now, to go back to quality control again.

> *Self-check*
>
> In Chapter 2 the sampling of glass jars was discussed and the concept of a 'lot tolerance percentage defective' (LTPD) introduced. Against what null hypothesis, then, should the results of such a sample be compared?

Given that we have no definite knowledge of the percentage of defectives, we can most simply assume that it is right on the tolerance borderline. That is, we can take it to be equal to the LTPD. This then enables us to use a binomial distribution, with the LTPD, together with the sample size, giving its parameters.

> *Self-check*
>
> What is the null hypothesis in the case of the quality control of the ball bearings of Chapter 2?

With the ball bearings, the most straightforward assumption is that the machine producing them is set correctly. The null hypothesis is then that the mean diameter of the bearings is 5.00 mm. This, together with the assumption that the standard deviation of the diameters is .01 mm, which thus gives the standard error, is sufficient to specify the normal sampling distribution of the mean of the samples.

> *Self-check*
>
> A group of fifty clerks, who make a large number of mistakes in their work, are sent on a special course which it is hoped will reduce their error rate. Their work is sampled before and after the course to see if there is any improvement. As the two error rates may differ by pure chance, depending on the work looked at, etc., a statistical test is to be used. What should be the null hypothesis in this case?

The simplest assumption to make is that there was no improvement, in reality. The null hypothesis would thus be that the difference in error rates before and after the course is zero. If you chose a different answer, think how you could use that to calculate probabilities. It needs to be exact to do that.

What is the alternative possibility?

It is not sufficient merely to specify the null hypothesis. The second step must be to make some statement as to what other possibility we are concerned with. That is, we must state an 'alternative hypothesis'. This hypothesis provides the alternative which will be set against the assumption of the null hypothesis. We then perform a test to see if there is enough evidence to reject the null hypothesis *in favour of the alternative one*.

Self-check

What was the alternative hypothesis in the biased coin problem?

It was that the coin *was* biased. If you said that it was that the coin wasn't biased, then you were confusing it with the null hypothesis. If you said it was that the coin was biased to heads (or tails) then, while this would be a possible alternative hypothesis (see below), it was *not* the one used in the problem as it was looked at.

As another example, look at the glass jars we discussed earlier. In that case we were not concerned with the possibility of there being a lesser percentage of defectives than the LTPD, but only with there being a greater one. The alternative hypothesis is thus that the percentage of defective jars *exceeds* the LTPD. Note that, unlike the null hypothesis, the alternative one does *not* have to be exact. It does, nevertheless, influence the calculations by giving *direction* to the test. We look for results in the sample *which favour the alternative rather than the null hypothesis*.

So, in the case of the jars, we calculate the probability that, *if the null hypothesis were correct*, the actual number of faulty jars in the sample would seem to favour the alternative hypothesis.

That is, we see if there are *more* defective jars in the sample than could reasonably be accounted for on the assumption that the batch contains a percentage of them equal to the LTPD. Figure 18 illustrates this point when the sample size is twenty and it contains two defectives. The shaded area shows the probability that this result, or one *even more favourable to the alternative hypothesis*, could be obtained by chance when the number of defective jars in the batch is equal to the LTPD, here 5%.

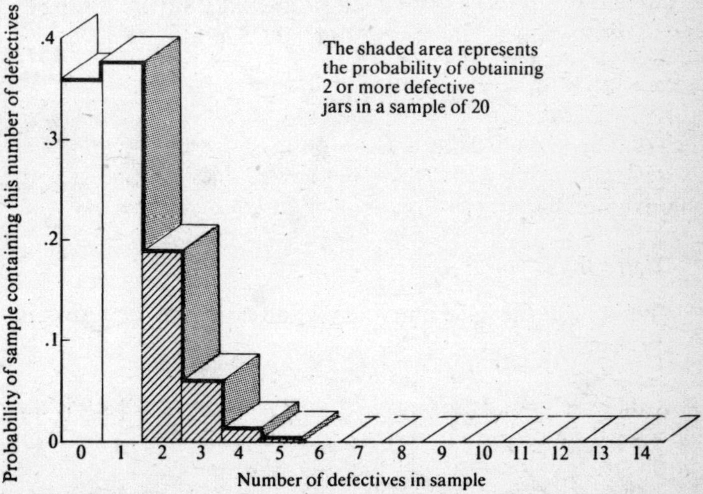

Figure 18. Histogram of number of defective jars in sample of twenty drawn from population in which there are 5% faulty jars

Note that the null and alternative hypotheses between them *need not* cover *all* the possibilities. In the above, for example, the case where the percentage of defective jars in the batch is *less* than the LTPD is not included in either hypothesis. When, as above, we are only interested in differences in one direction, we talk about 'one-tailed' probabilities. 'Two-tailed' probability is involved when differences in both directions are of importance, as they were in the biased coin experiments.

Self-check

What is the alternative hypothesis in the case of the quality testing of ball bearings?

Here we are looking to see if the mean diameter of the ball bearings could reasonably be either greater *or* less than 5 mm. The alternative hypothesis is thus that the population mean is not 5 mm. When performing the calculations, then, we would test whether or not, on the assumption that the mean is 5 mm, the sample results favour rather the alternative hypothesis. That is, we would look to see what the probability was of getting a sample mean further away from 5 mm than this (*either* way). We are thus interested in a two-tailed probability. Figure 19 shows the situation when a sample mean of 5.0025 mm is obtained with a sample size of 100.

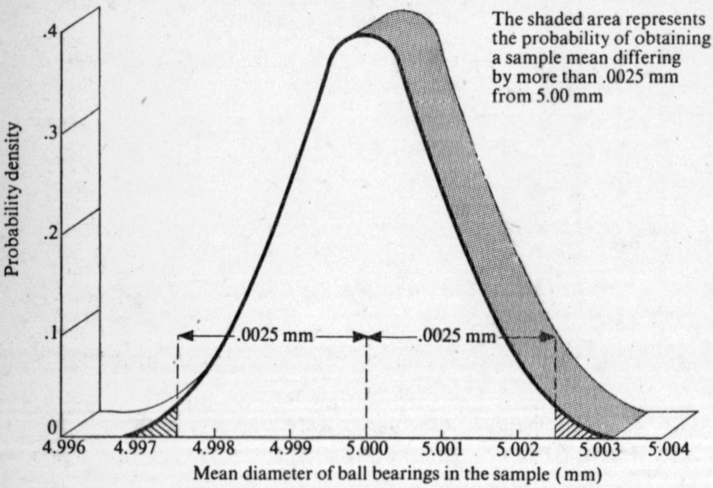

It is generally reasonably easy to see whether we should be using a two-tailed or a one-tailed probability. Consider the previous example of the bonus scheme.

> *Self-check*
>
> What is the alternative hypothesis there?

If we take the problem as given, it is a one-tailed situation. The alternative hypothesis is that there is a majority in favour of the new bonus system. Of course, we can argue that the change may actually be the other way and that the workforce could find the latest proposals even less satisfactory than the original ones. This is *statistically beside the point* if we are testing specifically to see whether or not there was a swing towards acceptance of the new scheme. We would only use a two-tailed probability here if we were interested to see if there had been *any* reaction, *either way*, from the workforce.

Self-check

In terms of the coin experiment in the activity on page 88, what is the equivalent of the alternative hypothesis that there is a majority in favour of the new bonus system?

Well, since a 'yes' vote corresponds to a head on the coin, it would be that the coin is biased towards heads. So trying to find out if the proportion of workers favouring the management proposal is greater than 50% is like trying to find out if the coin is biased towards heads.

So if we wanted to test if the coin were biased, say towards heads, we would use an alternative hypothesis that specified this direction. We would then only look for evidence which favoured this alternative hypothesis as opposed to the null one (which would be the *same* as it was when the alternative hypothesis was merely that the coin was biased, in *either* direction). That is, we would use only outcomes in which the number of heads *exceeded* or equalled the number obtained in the sample.

Self-check

What would be the alternative hypothesis in the self-check on page 89?

The alternative hypothesis would be that the test had improved the error rate. If you said it was that the error rate had changed, and did not specify a direction, then think about whether that is really just all you want to know. Don't you hope that there has been an improvement as a result of the course?

How unlikely does a result have to be to influence our decisions?

In the coin-tossing experiments we ended up with a probability: the probability that, on the basis of the null hypothesis being true, the result that we had would occur, or one equally or even more favourable to the alternative hypothesis. We then discussed just what this probability meant. We saw that it gave us an idea of the chances of being wrong about rejecting the null hypothesis.

After having set up the null and alternative hypotheses, then, we must specify just how unlikely the result of our sampling will have to be, on the assumption that the null hypothesis is true, before we will reject that null hypothesis in favour of the alternative one. Whether we use one- or two-tailed probability depends, as described above, on just what that alternative hypothesis is. Consider the glass jars again. By setting an acceptance number we are, in effect, specifying how improbable a result must be before we will reject the null hypothesis that the percentage of defectives in the batch is greater than the LTPD. This limit is called the 'level of significance' for the test being undertaken and results with probabilities *less* than this are said to be statistically 'significant'.

Thus we need to calculate the probability, on the basis of the null hypothesis being true, that the result obtained in the sample, or one equally or more strongly favouring the alternative hypothesis, would occur. This probability has to be compared with the level of significance we have set for ourselves. If it works out more or equally improbable, the null hypothesis is rejected in favour of the alternative one. If it doesn't, however, *we cannot just accept the null hypothesis*, though we can reject the alternative one.

To see this, let's look at the sample of workers mentioned earlier. Suppose when they are questioned about how they would vote on the new bonus scheme, there is significantly *less* support for it than the old one. We cannot then justify accepting *either* the alternative *or* the null hypothesis (as given earlier). It is for this reason that, when framing the null and alternative hypotheses, we try to arrange it so that *what we want to prove is the alternative one*. Figure 20 shows when we do and do not accept or reject the hypothesis.

		Action on	
		Null hypothesis	Alternative hypothesis
Sample result is	Significant	Reject	Accept
	Not significant	Not proven	Reject

Note that under no circumstances may we assume that the null or the alternative hypothesis is true or false: we may only accept or reject them.

Activity

Take the coin which was used to model the voting on the new bonus system and toss it twenty times. What proportion of heads to tails (yes's to no's) did you get?

Self-check

Use table 12 to find the probability of getting such a result, or an even more unlikely one, on the assumption that the coin is unbiased (the voting intentions are split fifty–fifty), with the alternative hypothesis that the coin is:

a biased towards heads (there is a shift to acceptance of the proposal);
b biased either way (opinion has been changed, one way or another, about the new bonus scheme).

You should have used a one-tailed probability for **a**, but a two-tailed one for **b**. For example, if you had obtained fourteen heads, the probability of getting this number or more is:

$$\begin{array}{ll} \ .037 & \text{(probability of 14 heads)} \\ + .015 & \\ + .005 & \text{(probability of more than 14 heads)} \\ + .001 & \\ \hline = .058 & \end{array}$$

This is the answer to **a**. If, however, we could not assume anything about the direction of bias, we would need to add the probabilities of all those other results which are equally, or even more, favourable to the alternative hypothesis. Now, on the basis of the null hypothesis of an unbiased coin, six heads in the twenty is just as favourable to the second alternative hypothesis as fourteen. Less than six heads would thus be even more favourable. Figure 21 shows the situation for the two-tailed probability of getting either fourteen or more, or six or less, heads. From the symmetry of the figure, the probabilities on either side are thus equal, giving a total of $2 \times .058 = .116$.

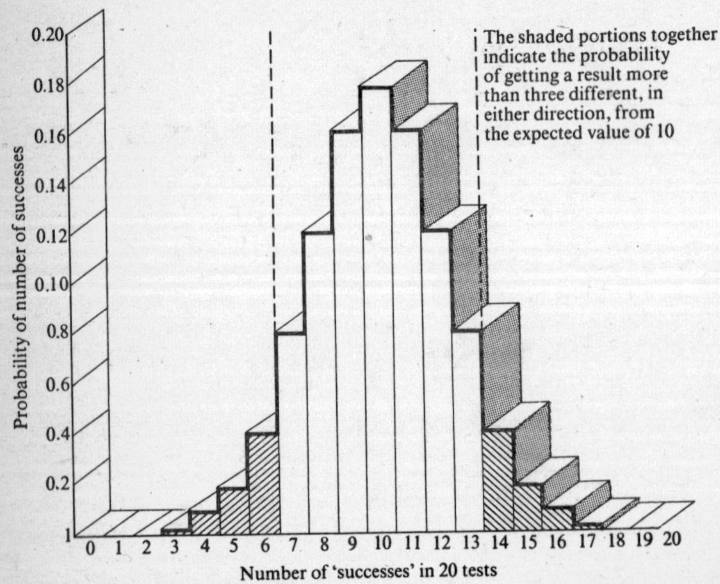

Figure 21. Histogram for table 12(a)

Self-check

Is the result you obtained significant **a** at the 5% level, and **b** at the 10% level?

Now suppose we had set a significance level of 5%, that is, we will reject the null hypothesis if the sample result, or one even more favourable to the null hypothesis, has a probability of occurrence of less than .05. On the basis of the above calculations, in neither case above would rejection occur. If, however, we had set a 10% level, the null hypothesis would be rejected in the first case, but not in the second. In practice, levels above 5% are seldom used. Note that the null hypothesis is the same in both cases, it is the alternative hypothesis that is different and which thus affects our interpretation of the results.

In cases where we are likely to be repeating some test a number of times, calculation time can be saved by working out in advance what the sample results would be if they were on the borderline of significance. Any results actually obtained can then be compared with this. One example we have already seen, of where this is done, is when the acceptance number is set.

Self-check

What would be the number of 'yes' replies required in the sample of voting intentions on the bonus scheme, introduced earlier, if a switch towards favouring the scheme is looked for at a 1% significance level?

From table 12 and figure 21, we can see that for it to be less than 1% likely that the vote is split 50–50, more than 15 'yes' intentions are required in this case. It is one-tailed because we are looking for a swing in favour of the scheme.

In cases where the sampling distribution is, or approximates to, normal, a similar process is gone through.

Self-check

With the ball bearings of Chapter 2, a sample of 100 is taken for quality testing. If the average diameter of ball bearings in the sample is 5.002 mm, is this significant at the 2.5% level, where the null hypothesis is that the population average is 5.00 mm and the alternative is that it isn't? (NB: you can assume that the population standard deviation is .01 mm.)

Here we need the standard error. It was calculated in Chapter 2 as $\sqrt{\frac{.01 \text{ mm}}{100}}$ = .001 mm.

5.002 is thus twice the standard error from the presumed mean. Using table 11, the probability that such a difference is exceeded (this being the direction that favours the alternative hypothesis) is .023 (to three decimal places). Note that a diameter of 4.998 mm would favour the alternative hypothesis equally to one of 5.002 mm and values less than this even more so. Hence we must include these in our considerations too. The probability of getting a value in this range is also .023 (to three decimal places). The total required two-tailed probability is thus .046. Hence our result is not significant at the 2.5% level. Note, however, that it is significant at the 5% level and also that, had we been looking specifically for a mean diameter *exceeding* 5.00 mm, this result would have been significant at the 2.5% level.

Review

1 A company wants to find out what housewives think of its new washing powder. It arranges for two piles of similarly dirty clothes to be washed, one in the company's powder and one in Brand X. Each of a randomly chosen group of housewives is asked to state which powder is the best. (They *have* to choose one or the other.) What would be a suitable null and alternative hypothesis for this test?

If there are twenty housewives in the sample and fourteen of them give the company's new powder as best, is this result significant **a** at the 5% level, and **b** at the 1% level? (Use table 12 to answer this question.)

2 The average wage of manual workers in a particular industry is £110 a week. In a particular factory, which is typical of the industry as a whole (in terms of the types and mix of manual employees) the average wage is £109.05. A statistical test is to be made to see if the workers at the factory are paid significantly differently to those in the industry as a whole. What would be a suitable null and alternative hypothesis for this test?

If the standard deviation of wages in the industry as a whole is £10, are the 400 manual workers in the factory paid significantly differently **a** at the 5% level, and **b** at the 1% level? (Use the Appendix to answer this question.)

3 The rules of a particular club state that a change to the constitution needs the approval of at least 70% of the members. A change is proposed and twenty of the several thousand people in the club are chosen at random and asked how they would vote on such a change. Eighteen say they would favour it. Does this result significantly favour acceptance of the proposal by more than 70% of the club's membership if it were put to the whole membership **a** at the 5% level and **b** at the 1% level? (Use table 12 to answer this question.)

ANSWERS

1 The idea here is to find if the result is significantly different from what would be obtained if the housewives just guessed. If they did this then there should be as many saying that Brand X was better as saying it was worse, or not far off this. The null hypothesis is then that this is the case, i.e. that housewives *as a whole* (given that this is a representative sample of them), would be split evenly as to which powder was best. Note that this is the only reasonable hypothesis that allows us to say what the parameters of the distribution are. (We would otherwise have to assume some proportion favouring one of the two.) So if you chose a different one think about this point.

The alternative hypothesis must reflect what result we are interested in. In this case, we are trying to show that Brand X is not so good as the other powder. So the alternative hypothesis is that Brand X *is* less often chosen as the best. If you said that it was that the housewives did not guess, but showed a distinct preference for *either one* of the powders, then you were forgetting what the purpose of the exercise is.

If fourteen of the twenty vote the company's powder as best, then the probability of this number *or more* happening, if the null hypothesis holds, can be found by using the binomial distribution, with the probability of a 'success' equal to .5. This is because, if the housewives were just guessing, it would be the equivalent of tossing a coin to make the choice. Using table 12, this probability is .037 + .015 + .005 + .001 = .058.

If you just said it was .037, then you were forgetting that results which favour the alternative hypothesis even more should also be included. This result is not significant at either the 5% or the 1% level. If you did only include the .037, you would, of course, have said that it *was* significant at the 5% level! You may have got .058 and said this anyway. If so, you were getting mixed up with what is significant and what is not. A result is significant at a given level if the calculated probability is *less than* that for that level, i.e. 5% or whatever.

2 Here the null hypothesis is that the workers aren't worse or better off. This allows us to assume that really they do conform with the industry as a whole, but that by virtue of the age distribution of the workers in the factory, or some other random factor, the wages at that factory are not entirely representative of that industry. That is to say, it is because the workers in the factory are a *sample* of the industry as a whole that the difference arises (as sampling error), not because they are, job for job, age for age, etc., paid any differently. Again, if you chose differently, think how the probabilities can be calculated, since we need to define the parameters.

The alternative hypothesis must be that the factory workers are indeed paid differently to the industry as a whole. If you chose a different one, look at the question, which states that you are to look for the factory workers being either better or worse off. Remember that the alternative hypothesis must show what supposition we are trying to set against the null hypothesis.

We can make the assumption that the wages are approximately normally distributed in the industry as a whole. As we saw, large amounts of data like this, where there are a number of effects occurring, can usually be taken as normal. The calculation of the probability is then as follows. £109.05 is 95p less than the industry average.

Now we have to find out how many standard errors this is. In this case the standard error is $\frac{10}{\sqrt{400}} = \frac{10}{20} = £.50$ as there are 400 workers.

The 95p is thus $\frac{.95}{.5}$ standard errors from the mean, i.e. 1.9 of them. The *two-tail* probability of getting this number of standard deviations from the mean or more is, from the tables, $2 \times .0287 = .0574$. This is not significant at the 1% level, nor at the 5% level. If you used one-tail probability in error, you would have found a significant result at the 5% level. The two-tail probability is used because either direction is of interest as specified by the alternative hypothesis.

Here the null hypothesis is that the percentage of the club members favouring the change is 70%. It is no use in this case saying that it is that the members are evenly split. This would not help us at all, since 70% is the crucial dividing line here and not 50%. We can then say that the alternative hypothesis is that there are more than 70% of the members in favour of the change. This is, after all, what is of interest. Note that the question does ask specifically if the result favours acceptance.

The sampling distribution here is the binomial: there are twenty trials each with two possible outcomes, with given probabilities of occurrence on the null hypothesis. These probabilities are .7 and .3 for acceptance and rejection respectively. The chances of getting eighteen *or more* members in the sample in favour, on the basis of the null hypothesis, can be found from the binomial tables with the probability of 'success' equal to .7. Success is thus defined as a yes vote. This probability is, from table 12, $.028 + .007 + .001 = .036$.

If you left this as your answer you were correct: there is no need for a two-tailed probability this time. We are only interested in results favouring the plan. This result is not significant at the 1% level, but it is at the 5% one. That is, this probability is between .01 and .05.

If you had a probability of .028, you forgot to take into account any other result even more in favour of the alternative hypothesis.

But we could be wrong

Significance testing is rather like a court trial. The null hypothesis corresponds to the 'innocent until found guilty' rule while samples supply the evidence and 'beyond all reasonable doubt' is an attempt to lay down a level of significance for jurors to work to when weighing this evidence. But, occasionally, the innocent are found guilty or vice versa. We can never be totally certain that we have judged correctly. The same applies in statistical inference. We may reject the null hypothesis when it is, in fact, true or not reject it when it is false. We saw this in the last chapter where we could reject a perfectly good lot of jars, or accept one with a percentage of defectives above the LTPD. These two errors are called 'Type I' and 'Type II' errors respectively, as shown in figure 22.

Null hypothesis is in 'fact'	Null hypothesis is: Not rejected	Null hypothesis is: Rejected
True	Correct	Type I error
False	Type II error	Correct

Think about the following situation. A football fan has moved to a new town and goes to see the local team a few times. On none of these occasions does he think they played well, but he's not sure if they are just going through a bad patch. He wants to make up his mind whether or not to support them as he has been offered a season ticket. Now, though this is not strictly a statistical problem, it has the characteristics of one. We can, for example, see the null hypothesis as being that the team is worth watching. The alternative hypothesis is that it is not. (The situation is one-tailed because, if they are *well* worth watching, he has no problem; he would be only too pleased to support them.)

Self-check

What situations correspond to the types I and II errors here?

If he rejects the offer of the season ticket and the team do well, then a Type I error has occurred. If, however, he goes to the matches regularly and the team play badly then he has made a Type II error.

The probability of a Type I error is equal to the level of significance. This is evident from the definition of the latter. It is, in fact, precisely the probability of such a result (that we reject the null hypothesis) occurring by chance alone despite the null hypothesis being in fact true. In terms of the quality testing of the previous chapter, it is the consumer's risk. The choice of the level of significance will thus depend on what probability of a Type I error occurring we are prepared to tolerate. Generally, this is a matter of looking at the penalties incurred if a Type I error does occur.

The probability of a Type II error cannot be stated exactly as it depends on just how 'far from the truth' the null hypothesis is. Only an 'all knowing' observer with access to the 'truth' would be able to calculate it, though we can generally put limits on it.

Consider the new bonus scheme again.

Self-check

Suppose management decide that if more than fifteen workers in the sample of twenty profess support for the new bonus scheme, they will put it to a vote of the whole workforce. What is the probability of a Type I error?

If the workforce really is split fifty–fifty on the question still, the probability of getting more than fifteen in support in the sample is, from table 12:

```
   .005 (probability of 16 yes's)
+  .001 (probability of more than 16 yes's)
=  .006
```

As this would lead to the null hypothesis being rejected, this must be the probability of a Type I error. It also corresponds to a level of significance of .6%.

Self-check

Suppose there were enough workers in the sample in favour of the new bonus scheme and management, consequently, put the question to the vote. If everyone voted according to their intentions, and there were 70% for the proposal, what was the probability that a Type II error *could* have occurred during the sampling. (Use table 12.)

Now, though a Type II error did not occur, it could have done. Even with 70% of the workers in favour, it would have been possible to have selected a sample in which there were less than sixteen of these included, and, consequently, to have not put the question to the vote. The probability of this happening was:

```
   .001 (probability of less than 7 yes's)
+  .004 (    ,,       ,, exactly  8 ,, )
+  .012 (    ,,       ,,     ,,   9 ,, )
+  .031 (    ,,       ,,     ,,  10 ,, )
+  .065 (    ,,       ,,     ,,  11 ,, )
+  .114 (    ,,       ,,     ,,  12 ,, )
+  .164 (    ,,       ,,     ,,  13 ,, )
+  .192 (    ,,       ,,     ,,  14 ,, )
+  .179 (    ,,       ,,     ,,  15 ,, )
=  .762
```

And so this was the probability of a Type II error.

Self-check

What would have been the probabilities of getting a Type I and a Type II error if the cut-off number had been fourteen not fifteen?

To obtain the answers we can *include* the probability of getting fifteen yes's in a sample in the above calculations for the probability of a Type I error, to give a result of .006 + .015 = .021, and *exclude* it from the calculations for the probability of a Type II error, to give a result of .762 − .179 = .583.

The probability of a Type II error, above, is very high. Unfortunately, if we reduce the cut-off number from fifteen, so as to lower this probability (by taking out one or more of the components in the above sum) we increase the chances of getting a Type I error. This is evident in the case of the last self-check above. The best tests are those which have the lowest probability of a Type II error for a given level of significance. One way of improving a test is to increase the sample size. Let us look at the ball bearings of the last chapter again.

Self-check

Suppose we have a sample of only twenty-five ball bearings. If we set a level of significance of 1%, what is the probability of a Type II error if the machine is, in fact, erroneously set to produce bearings of mean diameter 5.002 mm, but with a standard deviation of .01 mm still? (Use the tables in the Appendix.)

We must first calculate the standard error. It is, in fact, $\frac{.01}{\sqrt{25}} = \frac{.01}{5} = .002$ mm. We are interested in differences either way, so we want a two-tailed probability. Our null hypothesis is that the population mean is 5.00 mm, and a 1% significance level is specified. From the tables, this gives limits for the sample mean of 5.00 mm ± 2.58 × .002 mm (the standard error), outside of which we reject the whole batch. A Type II error will occur then if, despite an incorrect machine setting, a sample mean is obtained *inside* this range.

Now here we know that the machine is, indeed, incorrectly set to 5.002 mm, though the standard deviation, and thus the standard error, is as usual. This situation is shown in figure 23(a).

The probability of a Type II error is represented by the shaded area in the diagram. It is, in fact, equal to the difference between the probabilities, given a machine setting of 5.002 mm, of

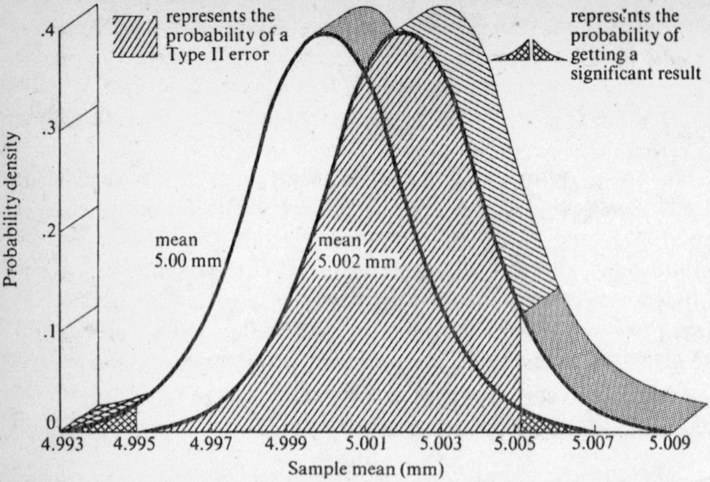

Figure 23(a). Sampling distribution of the mean of samples of twenty-five ball bearings from populations with mean diameter 5.002 mm and standard deviation .01 mm; and with mean diameter 5.00 mm and standard deviation .01 mm

a sample mean being less than 5.00 + 2.58 × .002 mm and of it being less than 5.00 − 2.58 × .002 mm. The number of standard errors that the first figure is from 5.002 mm is $\frac{(5.00 + 2.58 \times .002) - 5.002 \text{ mm}}{.002}$. This works out to $\frac{2.58 \times .002 - .002}{.002}$ = 2.58 − 1.0 = 1.58.

The number of standard errors that the second figure is from 5.002 mm is $\frac{(5.00 - 2.58 \times .002) - 5.002}{.002}$. This works out to $\frac{-2.58 \times 002 - .002}{.002} = -2.58 - 1 = -3.58$.

From the tables, the respective probabilities are .9429 and .0002. This gives the probability of a Type II error with a sample size of 25 as .9429 − .0002 = .9427.

Self-check

What is the probability of a Type II error if, under similar circumstances, a sample size of 100 is used?

A similar calculation can be carried out to the one above, replacing the .002 standard error by .001, as calculated earlier.

The number of standard errors from 5.002 mm then become $\frac{(5.00 + 2.58 \times .001) - 5.002}{.001}$ and $\frac{(5.00 - 2.58 \times .001) - 5.002}{.001}$ respectively. These work out to $\frac{2.58 \times .001 - .002}{.001} = 2.58 - 2 = .58$ and $\frac{-2.58 \times .001 - .002}{.001} = -2.58 - 2 = -4.58$.

The probability of a Type II error is the same as the probability of getting a sample with a mean diameter within these limits, if the population mean is 5.002 mm. From the tables, this is .7190 − 0+, and so is effectively .7190. Thus we have considerably lessened the chances of a Type II error occurring when the machine is set to 5.002 mm, by increasing the sample size, while the *level of significance is unchanged*.

Self-check

What size sample of ball bearings would be required to reduce the probability of a Type II error occurring, under the same circumstances as above, to less than .01? Can the probability of a Type II error ever be less than the level of significance (i.e. the probability of a Type I error)?

From above we see that, for an even larger sample size, we can ignore the lower limit. The other one is always $2.58 - \frac{.002}{\text{the standard error}}$ or, since the standard error is $\frac{.01}{\sqrt{\text{sample size}}}$, it is

$$2.58 - \frac{.002}{\frac{.01}{\sqrt{\text{sample size}}}} = 2.58 - \frac{\sqrt{\text{sample size}}}{5}.$$

From the tables, to obtain the required probability of .01, this needs to be less than −2.33 (note the negative sign), i.e. more than 2.33 standard errors *less* than the mean of 5.002 mm. So $2.58 - \frac{\sqrt{\text{sample size}}}{5}$ is less than −2.33, giving $\frac{\sqrt{\text{sample size}}}{5}$ is greater than 2.33 + 2.58, or sample size is greater than 5 × 4.91 squared.

The sample size must thus exceed $(5 \times 4.91)^2$ or 602.7025, i.e. a sample of 603 ball bearings or over is required. From this calculation we can see that, not only could the probability of a Type II error be less than the level of significance (i.e. the probability of a Type I error), but it can be made as small as we wish by increasing the sample size. This situation is shown in figure 23(b).

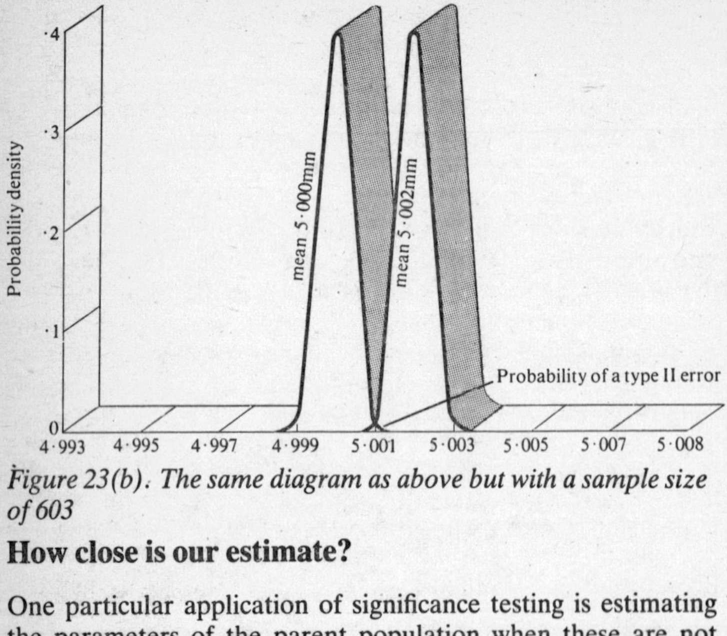

Figure 23(b). The same diagram as above but with a sample size of 603

How close is our estimate?

One particular application of significance testing is estimating the parameters of the parent population when these are not known. Consider, for example, a sample survey undertaken to discover family spending levels on confectionery. We may start off with no idea whatsoever of what this may be. The sample results themselves must be used to *estimate* the value of the average family spending in this area. (It might be useful to recall at this point that, since socio-economic grouping will probably affect this value, we would be dealing with a stratified random sample.) Suppose there are 400 families in this sample and they spend on average, £1.25 a week on confectionery.

> *Self-check*
>
> What would you estimate the average spending per week on confectionery to be in the population as a whole?

We would certainly put this estimate at £1.25, since it is the most sensible course of action given the results we have. Such a procedure is called 'point estimation' and what we get is a 'point estimate'. It is, indeed, usual to use the sample mean as an estimate of the population mean.

But, of course, it *is* only an estimate and, as in many areas of statistics, we really should ask how likely this estimate is to be wrong. We actually approach it in a slightly different way.

Consider, for example, the ball bearings of Chapter 2. Suppose an odd batch of these was found and it was not known exactly what size they were. A sample of 100 of them is taken and measured and their mean diameter is found to be 5.002 mm. We want to know what nominal diameter the batch could be related to, assuming that the standard deviation of the diameters is .01 mm. Now a point estimate would say that it was 5.002 mm. But, of course, this is only one possibility, albeit the most likely one. It could, for example, be 5.001 mm.

Self-check

Suppose we have a null hypothesis that the true population mean was 5.001 mm and an alternative one that it was nearer to 5.002 mm than this. Would this null hypothesis be rejected at the 2.5% significance level on the evidence of the sample?

As we have seen, the standard error of the sample mean is .001 mm. 5.002 mm is .001 mm from the hypothesized mean of 5.001 mm, that is one standard error. From the tables, the (one-tailed) probability of obtaining a difference greater than this is .1587 (to four decimal places). So were the true mean 5.001 mm, the results of the sample would not be significant at the 2.5% level. Were the true value of the population mean 5.003 mm, a similar strategy would show that the sample result would not be unduly improbable there either.

Self-check

But if the null hypothesis was that the population mean were 5.004 mm, what then? Would a sample mean of 5.002 mm be significant at the 2.5% level?

5.002 is $\frac{5.004 - 5.002}{.001} = \frac{.002}{.001} = 2$ standard errors away from 5.004. The (one-tailed) probability of this happening by chance is .0228 (to four decimal places) which *is* significant at the 2.5% level. Similar calculations could be performed with values below 5.002 mm.

There is thus a range of values such that, *if the true mean were to lie within it*, the sample result actually obtained *would not* be significant, while if the true mean *were to lie outside it*, the sample result *would be* significant. The level of significance could be set at any value: here it was 2.5%. This range is called the 'confidence interval'; the 95% confidence interval in this case. The extreme values of the confidence interval are called the (95%) 'confidence limits'. The confidence interval represents a broader estimate of the population mean than the point estimate and is called an 'interval estimate'.

Now you are certainly asking yourself, 'why *95%*?' Well, the reason is as follows. The 95% confidence interval will contain the true mean *95% of the time*, i.e. *not* contain it 5% of the time. This 5% is composed of two 2.5% figures, one for the true mean being greater than the upper 95% confidence limit and one for it being less than the lower one. Each of these corresponds to the one-tailed 2.5% significance levels used earlier, one for hypothesized means less than the sample mean and one for those greater. Figure 24 illustrates this point. The 99% confidence interval is similarly defined, and so on.

To calculate the confidence limits, we note that we want two values, one less than the point estimate and one greater, for which this point estimate is on the very borderline of significance (one-tailed). That is, the probability of a sample mean being less (greater) than the point estimate, on the null hypothesis that the population mean is equal to the lower (upper) limit, is exactly equal to the level of significance. We can find out how many standard errors from the mean a value needs to be if it is significant at some given level by using the tables. Note that for the 95% confidence limits we require 2.5% significance, for the 99% ones .5% significance and so on.

So, for example, the 95% confidence limits in the above case are calculated as follows. For one-tailed 2.5% significance, a

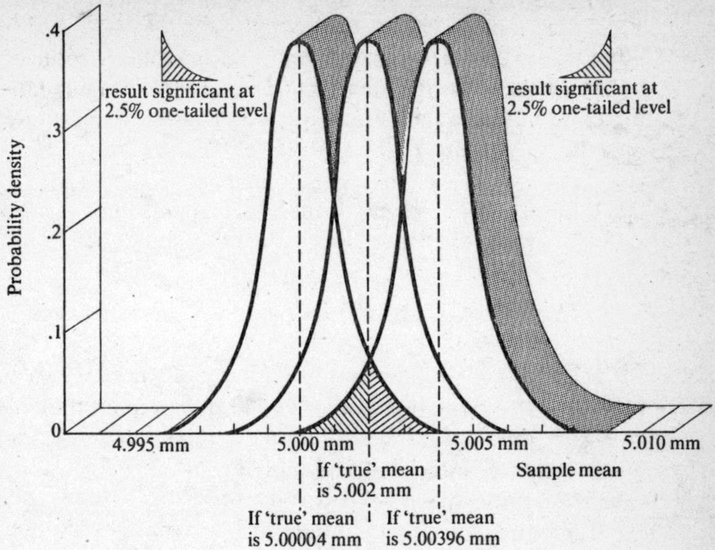

Figure 24. 95% confidence limits for the mean of a sample of 100 ball bearings (with mean 5.002 mm)

value more than 1.96 standard errors from the mean is required. Hence 5.002 mm must be 1.96 standard errors less than the upper confidence limit and the same figure greater than the lower one. The limits are thus $5.002 + 1.96 \times .001 = 5.00396$ mm and $5.002 - 1.96 \times .001 = 5.00004$ mm. It is evident that increasing the sample size, and so decreasing the sample error, will narrow the confidence interval.

Self-check

What would be the 95% confidence limits if the sample of ball bearings, above, were increased in size to 400 and the same sample mean obtained?

The standard error would then be $\frac{.01}{\sqrt{400}} = \frac{.01}{20} = .0005$ mm,

and the confidence limits would be $5.002 + 1.96 \times .0005 = 5.00298$ mm, and $5.002 - 1.96 \times .0005 = 5.00102$ mm.

Self-check

What would be the 99% confidence limits for the sample of 100 ball bearings with mean 5.002 mm above? (The standard normal value you should use is 2.58 instead of the 1.96 with the 95% limits.)

From the tables, the .5% level of one-tailed significance is 2.58 standard errors from the mean. Thus the 99% confidence limits are $5.002 + 2.58 \times .001 = 5.00458$ mm, and $5.002 - 2.58 \times .001 = 4.99942$ mm.

Review

1 What is the probability of a Type I error in the following cases?
a 5% significance level, one-tailed;
b 5% significance level, two-tailed;
c 1% significance level, one-tailed;
d 1% significance level, two-tailed.

2 What would be the true level of support for the proposal in review 3 on page 99 that would give a maximum probability of a Type II error, if a 5% level of significance was looked for?

3 A process to cut bars into lengths yields a standard deviation of .2 cm. A sample of 100 bars from the output is taken and the average length of bars in it is found to be 50 cm. Find the 95% and 99% confidence limits for the estimate of the population mean as 50 cm.

4 A sample of a particular make of car tyre is examined. Each tyre is allocated a number from 0 to 100, representing the percentage of tyre wear. The hundred tyres have all been on similar cars which have done 10,000 miles. The average percentage allocated to them is 30% with standard deviation 9.95%. What are the 95% and 99% confidence limits for an estimate of 30% as the percentage wear such tyres suffer after 10,000 miles on this type of car? (Hint: you will have to estimate the population standard deviation.)

ANSWERS

1 **a** .05, **b** .05, **c** .01, **d** .01. If you had different results for the two- and one-tailed cases, then you were forgetting that the 5% or 1% automatically allows for the difference. That is, it is 5% on the *one* end for a one-tailed test with 5% significance, but 2.5% on *either* end for a two-tailed test with 5% significance, for example.

2 For a 5% level of significance the alternative hypothesis would be rejected – if there were less than eighteen members in the sample in favour of the proposal. The probability of getting, for example, seventeen or more is .072 + .028 + .007 + .001 = .108, which isn't even significant at the 10% level. So, for sixteen, fifteen, etc. it would be even less significant.

What we need to find, then, is what proportion of members in the society as a whole would need to be in favour of the change for the probability of getting less than eighteen of these in the sample to be maximum, while yet being a majority of the society's members. Now, the lower that proportion, the less likely the chances of getting a lot of them in the sample, and so the more likely the chances of getting less than eighteen in it. The proportion we are looking for is thus a fraction over 70%. (It can't be less, otherwise the proportion would not favour acceptance.) Now, from table 12 the probability of getting less than eighteen for a probability of 'success' of .7 – which is the nearest we can get to the 'fraction over 70%' – is .964. This is, then, the answer required.

As this is rather a difficult point, it is worth while going over these steps once more. A Type II error occurs if the alternative hypothesis is wrongly rejected, that is if:

(a) the alternative hypothesis is really true – i.e. there *is* a majority of more than 70% of members of the club in favour of the scheme;

(b) our evidence suggests that it is not – i.e. there are *less than eighteen* in the sample who say they support the change.

The figure of eighteen is arrived at as follows:

(a) We are proceeding on the assumption in our investigation that the null hypothesis is true. (Even though it is not, we do not know this or there would be no point in doing the test.

Don't forget that to calculate the Type II error, we need to be 'all knowing'.)

(b) If it were assumed to start with that just 70% were in favour, then the result of the sample would only be significant at the 5% level if there were eighteen or more in favour of the change in the sample.

(c) If we are going to *reject* the alternative hypothesis, then there must be *less* than eighteen in the sample in favour of the change.

We can look at the *true* situation now, which is that the alternative hypothesis holds (that is, there are more than 70% in favour) but that, through the operation of chance, less than eighteen of those are included in the sample. If we knew the proportion of those in favour of the change in the society as a whole, we could calculate the chances of this happening. The probabilities for various proportions are shown below. The exact proportion will determine the probability of a 'success' in the binomial distribution, where a 'success' is a vote for the proposal.

Proportion	*Probability of success*	*Probability of getting less than 18 successes in the sample of 20*
70%	.7	.9645
80%	.8	.7939
90%	.9	.3231

As you can see, the higher the proportion, the less the chances of getting under eighteen in favour in the sample. The maximum probability for a Type II error thus occurs for a proportion of just a fraction over 70%. The nearest probability we can get for this is, however, for 70%, which is .9645, or .964 when rounded.

3 For the 95% limits, we need to have 1.96 standard errors on either side of the 50 cm. As the standard deviation is .2 cm the standard error is $\frac{.2}{\sqrt{100}}$ cm = $\frac{.2}{10}$ cm = .2 mm. This is 1.96 × .2 mm = .392 mm on either side of the 50 cm. The confidence limits are thus: 50 cm ± .392 mm – that is, 49.9608 cm to

50.0392 cm. Did you remember to use the standard error and *not* the standard deviation? The 99% limits are similarly 50 cm ± 2.56 × .2 mm, that is 50 cm ± .518 mm or 49.9494 to 50.0516 cm.

4 Because there are a large number of tyres and a large range of possible values, we can regard the sampling distribution as being normal. Here the standard error has to be estimated. From Chapter 2, this is done by first of all estimating the population standard deviation. We get: $\sqrt{\frac{100}{99}} \times 9.95 = 10\%$.

The standard error is thus: $\frac{10}{\sqrt{100}} = 1\%$.

The 95% confidence limits are thus: 30% ± 1.96 × 1% = 28.04 to 31.96%.

And the 99% ones: 30% ± 2.58 × 1% = 27.42 to 32.58%.

Did you remember that you could not just use the standard deviation, but had to convert it into the standard error? Did you remember how to estimate the population standard deviation?

Scenario 2
An employee selection test

As you read through the following scenario, make a mental note of any occasion where there are two sets of data which have to be related in some way. Think about what sort of relationships are likely to be looked for; for example, one set of figures being significantly different from another, and so on.

Mary Fletcher, Gourmet Food's personnel director, took a great interest in selection tests, and was helping to develop one for clerical grades. She felt that the reliance placed on academic achievement in filling such posts was resulting in a gross waste of talent. There were plenty of people without good formal qualifications, she believed, who could do such jobs very well.

In conjunction with several others, including a consultant from the nearby university, she devised a test which was felt to cover essential clerical skills. It included both 'pen and paper' questions and a series of practical exercises, based on common clerical tasks like filing. The next stage was to try to prove that the test worked; to validate it.

It was felt that if it was a good test, it should discriminate between those who were currently doing the job well and those who were not. Mary and her colleagues arranged to see if this was the case by giving it to their clerical employees. In addition, some way of grading those clerks had to be established for the purposes of comparison. The error rate of the clerks plus a mark awarded by their immediate superior were used to establish a job performance rating for each clerk.

At the Baby Gourmet plant, ten clerks there were chosen and subjected to the tests by Brian Kelly, the personnel officer at the plant. He then obtained their job performance ratings. Just out of interest, he performed the same calculations on the ten pairs of values he had, that were going to be performed on the whole lot of data when gathered. These revealed the degree of relationship between the two sets of figures, the test results and the ratings. If it was a good test, then high test marks should go with high ratings and low ones with low ratings. He was surprised to find how good the agreement was with his figures.

When all the data had been collected, Mary and her colleagues found that their test seemed to work fairly well with existing employees. The next step was to try it with applicants. This, however, was a fairly long-term project as, obviously, it would be some time before there were a great many new entrants having been at Gourmet Foods long enough to be assessed. Brian Kelly, and all the other personnel officers, were accordingly instructed to make the test the basis of the selection of new clerks, with a view to following up the research.

Mary was also interested in the fact that clerical work, especially at the 'lower' levels, was often regarded as 'women's work', so she took the opportunity to use the results obtained from the trials of her test to examine if there was any marked difference between sexes on the scores. She was actually quite peeved when there did seem to be some significant difference favouring females. This would, of course, mean that use of the test would bias selection towards females also, another point she wasn't too happy about.

This scenario points to the need for statistical tests to discover what relationships exist between different sets of data. The point is that very much of the time we are dealing only with samples and there are bound to be sampling 'errors' which will affect the actual data that is available for analysis. Furthermore, one of the major objectives of statistics is to attach 'degrees of belief', that is, probabilities, in effect, to statements about relationships between data.

Take the point about sex differences in scores on the test, for example. Here, although there may be some difference, without further analysis it is impossible to say whether this is significant, i.e. whether it is unlikely to be a result of chance rather than of any intrinsic difference. In this we see strong connections with the previous chapter and the first half of this chapter develops these. As to the main point in the scenario, the relationship between the test scores and the job performance ratings, what we need here is a method of 'quantizing' such a connection; that is, of arriving at the number by which we may judge the degree of connection. Here, a new statistical technique needs to be introduced, and this is done in the second half of this chapter.

This chapter is probably the most complex in the book. Readers are encouraged to try to familiarize themselves with the broad principles discussed here, rather than with the minute details of the calculations. It is not possible to go into the subject very deeply in an introductory text of this nature, but a sound grasp of the principles outlined should considerably ease the study of these topics, and allied ones, in greater depth.

After studying this chapter you should be able to derive information from two sets of data which will enable you to determine the implications of the relationships between them, whether they are significantly different or not, whether they show some mutual interrelationship or not and so on.

4 Determining the relationship between two sets of data

What kind of data can we deal with?

This chapter deals with problems where there are two sets of data involved. But there are various different ways in which these two sets of data may be related. Before we can start to interpret our results, we must determine which way holds. The first thing to look for is whether both sets of data are from the *same* variable, or whether they are each from *different* ones. To use the terminology introduced in Chapter 9 in Volume *1*, we need to decide whether we have univariate or bivariate data.

For example, in the scenario, the problem of differences in scores on the selection test between men and women applicants involves one type of data, the test scores. That is, we are concerned with one variable only (which is why it is called univariate data). When, however, we are trying to validate the test by using the workers themselves, we are concerned with two types of data, the test scores and job performance ratings. That is, we are dealing with two different variables (which is why it is called bivariate data).

Self-check

Which of the following cases involve bivariate data and which univariate?

1 The performance of firms in Great Britain is compared with that of firms of a similar type in Japan by looking at productivity per employee.

2 The performance of British firms in one year is compared with that in the next by looking at the productivity per employee of several firms; the figures from each firm over two years are taken.

3 The performance of British firms, in terms of productivity per employee, are compared with the size of the firms, to see if there is any relationship between them.

ANSWERS

1 This is univariate data. The only variable involved is productivity per employee. If you said bivariate, because you thought the different firms, or even countries, formed another variable, then you were confusing the *domain* of a variable, which is what the firms are, with a second variable. Remember, from Chapter 6 in Volume *1*, that the domain of the variable is what it varies over, and here it is the firms (and countries).
2 Again this is univariate data. We are again only concerned with employee productivity. If you thought time was a second variable, then this was understandable. But it would only count as a second variable if some number representing time was to be included in the comparison, and it isn't. The only thing to be compared is employee productivity.
3 This is bivariate data. Here the two variables are the employee productivity and size of the firm.

The first question to ask then, when there are two different sets of data to be dealt with is, Do we have univariate or bivariate data? If we have neither univariate nor bivariate data, e.g. we might have three or four variables involved, then the techniques required are outside the scope of first level statistics texts, in general, though a reasonable treatment of this topic may be found in *Facts from Figures* by M. J. Moroney (Penguin, 1969). If we have univariate data, then the appropriate techniques are discussed later in this chapter on page 122. The rest of the chapter deals with the case where bivariate data is involved.

Note that bivariate data must be obtained in pairs, and each pair must contain related data. So, for example, in the scenario the test is administered to workers and information collected on their error rates and so on for job evaluation. But it would be a totally pointless exercise unless the same workers were involved in both cases! The same is not *necessarily* true of univariate data. For instance, comparing men's scores with women's in the scenario does not involve the same people in each set of data, obviously! However, suppose, for example, that what was of interest was whether or not a particular course, which was supposed to improve clerical error rates, actually did so. Here it would be necessary to use the same people and to test their error rates before and after the course. But note that only one variable, the test score, is of interest still.

Self-check

Were any of the cases in the last self-check instances of this type of paired data?

Yes. In **2**, the figures for employee productivity from year to year were paired, i.e. sets of two items of data *for each firm* would be used (the two years' employee productivity figures).

Where such 'paired' observations occur, as opposed to independent samples, we may use the techniques introduced in the last unit to test whether or not the result is significant. We do this by setting up a new random variable, namely the difference between each pair. The null hypothesis in this case will be that its value is zero. Its standard deviation may be calculated from the set of differences, and may then be used as an estimate of the population standard deviation. This, in turn, will give an estimate of the standard error of the sample mean (difference). Suppose, for example, the mean difference in error rates of 400 clerks before and after taking such a course is 1.5% (improvement) and the standard deviation of the differences is 5%.

Self-check

Is this improvement significant at the 5%, 1% or .1% levels?

Since the sample is large, we can use the sample standard deviation as an estimate of that of the population. The estimated standard error is thus $\frac{5\%}{\sqrt{400}} = \frac{5\%}{20} = 0.25\%$. The mean difference of 1.5% obtained is then $\frac{1.5}{0.25} = 6$ standard deviations from the hypothesized mean of zero. Since the alternative hypothesis will be that the difference is negative (if we subtract rates before from those after), we have a one-tailed probability. The value obtained is significant at both the 5% and the 1% level and is also significant at the .1% level. Indeed, it is so significant as to be virtually beyond any possible doubt!

Is there really any difference?

Suppose we want to find out whether there is a significant difference in two sets of independent (i.e. not paired) univariate data, for example, if men really do, *on the whole*, score differently to women on the selection test in the scenario.

> *Self-check*
>
> Say that, in fact, women were generally superior to men on that test. Would this mean that any woman must score higher than any man?

If this were the case it would, indeed, indicate a vast superiority on the part of women. There is bound to be overlap, the best men scoring higher than the worst women. This is, of course, why random samples are important. If we pick a proponderance of low-scoring women and high-scoring men we will get unreliable results.

> *Self-check*
>
> What statistic do you think we could use to compare the two sets of data?

It would seem sensible to average each of the sets of data and compare the results.

> *Self-check*
>
> But, bearing in mind the contents of the two previous chapters, if, say, the mean of the women's scores was higher than the men's, could we just then glibly assume that women in general would score better than men?

Random variations in the two samples would ensure that there was at least some probability of such a result occurring by chance though there was, in fact, no real overall difference. Indeed, it could happen even if men actually scored more than women on the whole.

It is evident, then, that a technique similar to those used in Chapter 3 must be used to test whether or not any such difference between means is, indeed, significant. The problem here is that we have two samples, and not one, to deal with. We get round this by setting the null hypothesis in such a way that we can effectively combine these two samples into one. We do it by considering a new parameter, *the difference between the sample means*. This can then be examined under the null hypothesis that the difference between the population means, i.e. between all men and all women, is zero. If this null hypothesis is correct, this would imply that the mean difference between sample means, taken over all possible samples, would be zero. The actual difference obtained between sample means could then be tested against this.

> *Self-check*
>
> What would be a suitable alternative hypothesis in this case?

It would depend on what we were trying to prove. In the scenario, a difference between men and women in *either* direction is indicated. This argues for the alternative hypothesis that the difference between population means is *not* zero. If we were concerned to show that women scored higher than men, the null hypothesis would be that it was greater than zero (assuming we subtract the mean for the men from that of the women).

Now in order to use the techniques of Chapter 3 we need to know the distribution of this new statistic. Firstly, we can assume it is normally distributed if the conditions specified previously are met. Secondly, we assume a mean of 0, from the null hypothesis. All that is left, then, is to find its standard deviation, i.e. the standard error. In order to find this we need a little piece of theory which states that the 'variance' (i.e. the square of the standard deviation) of the difference (or sum, in fact) of two independent random variables is equal to the sum of their separate variances.

Although this will not be proved here, some indication of why this is so can be given. Look at the following situation, for example. Some metal rods have been cut too long by a machine which cuts with a fixed standard deviation. The same machine is now used to cut these rods back to their proper length. Now we assume that, as shown in figure 25, the bars are placed up against some fixed block on the left and cut to the new length with the same accuracy as they were first cut. The standard deviation of the lengths of the rods will then be the same as before they were cut. But what of the offcuts? We can see from figure 25 that they will vary by more than the actual rods. The errors will, in fact, be cumulative for them. That is, a rod that was towards the shorter end when originally cut may be towards the longer end when cut again, giving a very short offcut, or one that was on the long side when first cut could be on the shorter side when cut again, giving a very long offcut. This just shows, incidentally, that you should never measure the piece *to be cut off*, otherwise the extra variation is on the piece you want!

Self-check

If the standard deviation in lengths cut by the machine is .1 cm, what will be the standard deviation of the lengths of the offcuts? (Use the formula given earlier.)

With the figures given, the actual variance of the offcuts is $(.1)^2 + (.1)^2 = .01 + .01 = .02$.

The standard deviation, which is the square root of the variance, is thus $\sqrt{.02} = .14$ (to two decimal places).

Note that this result is totally independent of the rods' lengths; they could have been 100 cm or 5 cm or any length – in figure 25 they are shown as 5 cm reduced to 3 cm.

Notice that the condition of independence of the two random variables is crucial. For example, suppose we were to pick pairs

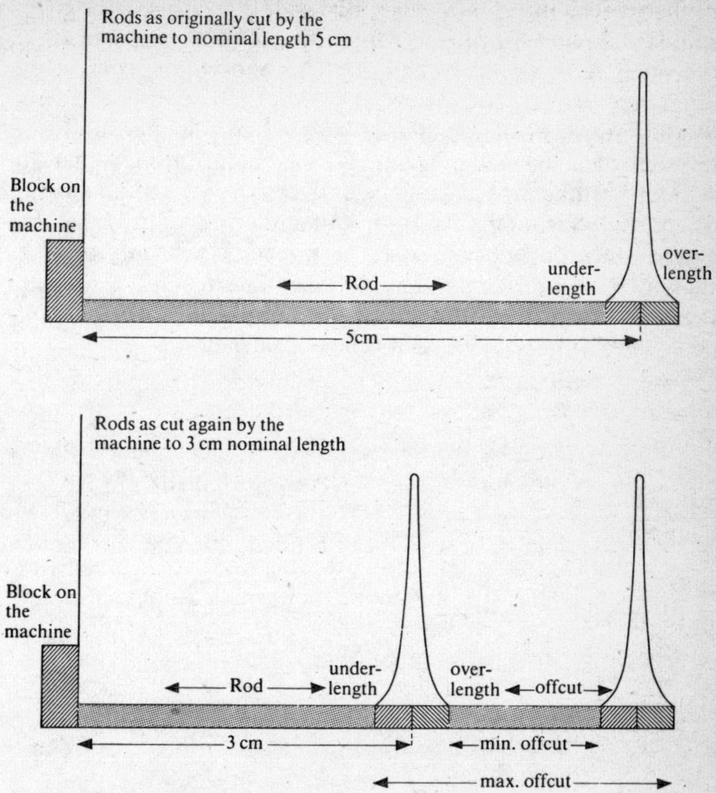

Figure 25. Cutting '5' cm rods down to '3' cm

of offcuts and shortened rods at random and place them together. The variance in the length of the result would *not* be the sum of the separate variances. This is because the two sets are not independent: indeed, the sum of the mean lengths of the two sets should equal 5 cm.

Self-check

What is the standard deviation of the taxable weekly pay of workers in a factory if the standard deviation of their gross wages is £10 and of their weekly tax allowance is £5?

From the formula, it is $\sqrt{(5^2 + 12^2)} = \sqrt{(25 + 144)} = \sqrt{169} =$ £13. If you said £15, you were forgetting to square, add and take the square root. This result about the standard deviation of the difference of two random variables can then be applied to the original problem of calculating whether or not the difference between means was significant. We can deduce from it that the standard error of the difference between the sample means can be calculated from the separate standard errors of those sample means since each of these is, in effect, a random variable. Suppose that 625 women and 400 men had taken the test and that the former scored an average 60% with standard deviation 20%, and the latter 58% with standard deviation 12%.

Self-check

What would be the best estimates of the standard deviations of the scores for *all* women and *all* men?

Since the sample is large, we can estimate the standard deviations for the scores if all women were to take the test as 20%, and if all men were to, as 12% (See Chapter 2.)

Self-check

What, then, would be the best estimates of the standard errors of each of the sample means be?

We can use the estimates for the population standard deviations, to give $\frac{20}{\sqrt{625}} = \frac{20}{25} = .8\%$ for the women's mean, and $\frac{12}{\sqrt{400}} = \frac{12}{20} = .6$ for the men's.

Self-check

What would be the standard error of the difference between sample means?

Using the formula given earlier, it would be $\sqrt{(\,(.8)^2 + (.6)^2)} = \sqrt{(.64 + .36)} = \sqrt{1.00} = 1\%$.

Self-check

Is the stated difference significant at the (a) 1% level, and (b) 5% level?

With the null hypothesis that the difference between population means is 0, 60% − 58% is $\frac{2\%}{1\%} = 2$ standard errors away from the mean. Since we have no reason to suppose either sex superior, we have a two-tailed probability. This result is, from the tables, significant at the 5% level (which would be 1.96 standard deviations from the mean), but not at the 1% level (which would be 2.58 of them).

Self-check

A market research agency wants to find out if there will be any difference in customer reaction to a new product between the north and the south of England. They have reason to suspect the north will offer greater sales resistance. A sample of potential customers from each area is given the product to evaluate. The northern sample of 100 customers rates it on average 15 out of 20, with a standard deviation of 2.0, while the southern one, of 144 customers, gives it an average rating of 15.4 with a standard deviation of 1.2. Is the difference significant **a** at the 5% level, and **b** at the 1% level?

Because the samples are large, we can use the sample standard deviations as estimates of the population ones. This gives standard errors for the sample means of $\frac{2.0}{\sqrt{100}} = \frac{2.0}{10} = .2$ for the north, and $\sqrt{\frac{1.2}{144}} = \frac{1.2}{12} = .1$ for the south.

The standard error of the difference between these means is thus $\sqrt{(.2^2 + .1^2)} = \sqrt{(.04 + .01)} = \sqrt{.05} = 0.22$ (to two decimal places).

The null hypothesis here would be that there was no difference between the mean ratings of northerners and southerners of this product. The number of standard deviations from the zero mean of the null hypothesis of the difference between the means of .4 is thus $\frac{.4}{.22} = 1.82$ (to two decimal places).

Now the alternative hypothesis in this case is that the southerners would give higher scores than northerners (because this is what we suspect). Thus we have a one-tailed probability and it is .0344. On this basis the above result is significant at the 5% but not the 1% level.

Did you remember to phrase the alternative hypothesis in such a way that it indicated the direction of difference we were interested in?

Review

1 Which of the following are univariate and which bivariate data? Of the sets of univariate data, which are paired and which are independent?

a The profits (losses) of a number of companies, some British owned and some foreign owned.

b The sizes of a group of companies in terms of employees, and their gross profits.

c The number of TV licences issued in the UK over a number of years and the number of burglaries reported in the UK during the same years.

d The output of coal from a selected number of UK mines in each of two years.

2 In a factory the productivity per man of the 225 workers in one year exceeds that for the previous year by 200 units on average. The standard deviation of the differences in productivity for each worker between the two years is 2000 units. Is this increase significant at the 5% or 1% levels?

(NB: any worker who left over the period is not included in the figures.)

3 The average wage of the 64 unskilled workers at factory A is £80 a week, with a standard deviation of £2.40. At factory B, 36 similar workers are paid £81, with the same standard deviation. Are the workers in factory B significantly better paid than those in factory A at a 5% level of significance or at the 1% level?

4 A car manufacturer wanted to find out if running a car on lead-free petrol affects engine wear. It obtained details from the USA on the engine wear in 100 cars run on ordinary petrol and 100 run on lead-free petrol after the same number of miles. Engine wear was specified on a scale of 0 to 20 (the more the engine wear the higher the number). For the cars run on ordinary petrol the average wear was 8.58 with a standard deviation of 1.20. For the cars run on lead-free petrol it was 8.20 with a standard deviation of 1.60. Was there any significant difference in engine wear at the 5% level? (This experiment is purely imaginary.)

ANSWERS

1 a Univariate: only profits (losses) are being examined. They are not paired, i.e. we cannot associate one British with one foreign company.

b Bivariate data: the gross profits and the number of employees are the two variables.

c Bivariate: the number of licences and the number of burglaries are the two variables.

d Univariate: only the output of coal is being examined. The data here is paired, though; there are two figures for each mine.

2 In this question we have paired data, the productivity per employee over each of the two years. Thus the differences can be looked at as the values of a variable which, if there were no real difference in productivity from one year to the next, would have a mean of zero. Now, simply from random errors, this difference would not in general equal zero exactly. Here it is 200 units. But is this significant? To see this we have to calculate the standard error. It is $\frac{2000}{\sqrt{225}} = \frac{2000}{25} = 80$ units. The 225 is the 'sample' size, i.e. the number of employees.

How does this compare with the difference of 200 units? Well, it is $\frac{200}{80} = 2.5$ standard errors from the mean (of zero). We can use the normal tables since we have a fairly large 'sample'. Since we want to know if the *increase* is significant, we use one-tailed probability. The probability of getting *more* than 200 units difference is .0062. This is significant at both the 5% and the 1% level.

If you used two-tailed probability in error, you would have said that the result was significant only at the 5% level.

3 The first step is to estimate the standard deviations of the populations. Since the 'samples' are reasonably large, these can be taken to be £2.40 in both cases, i.e. the same as for the 'samples'. The two standard errors are then $\frac{2.40}{\sqrt{64}} = \frac{2.40}{8}$ = £0.30 for factory A, and $\frac{2.40}{\sqrt{36}} = \frac{2.40}{6}$ = £0.40 for factory B.

The standard error of the difference between the means is then $\sqrt{(.3^2 + .4^2)} = \sqrt{(.09 + .16)} = \sqrt{.25} = .5$. Now this difference was £81 − £80 a week. This is $\frac{1}{.5} = 2$ standard errors.

The alternative hypothesis is that the workers in factory B are better paid than those in factory A, so it is a one-tailed probability that is needed. From the tables, the probability of getting a difference greater than £1 in a given direction is .0228. This is significant at the 5% level but not at the 1%.

4 As in **3**, we calculate the two standard errors. Here they are

$\frac{1.2}{\sqrt{100}} = \frac{1.2}{10}$ = .12 for the ordinary petrol,

$\frac{1.6}{\sqrt{100}} = \frac{1.6}{10}$ = .16 for the lead-free petrol.

The standard error of the difference between the means is thus $\sqrt{(.12^2 + .16^2)} = \sqrt{(.0144 + .0256)} = \sqrt{.04} = .2$. Now the difference between the means is 8.58 − 8.20 = .38. This is $\frac{3.8}{2}$ = 1.9 standard errors from zero.

Now here the alternative hypothesis is that there is some difference between engine wear, so it is a case of two-tailed probability. The probability of getting a difference of 1.9 standard errors or more is .0287 + .0287 = .0574. So this is *not* significant at the 5% level. If you forgot and used one-tailed probability, you would have found that it was a significant result at the 5% level.

When figures vary together

If we have bivariate data we are often interested in the degree to which the two sets of figures vary together. For example, in the scenario the question was asked, Does a high score on the selection test indicate that the applicant will do well at the job? Here the two variables are the test score and a job rating.

Self-check

If the answer to the above question is yes, what pattern would you expect to see in the data?

You would expect that high test scores would go with high job ratings and low ones with low ratings. The degree of relationship between the values of two such variables is called the 'correlation'. Conventionally when high values go with high and low with low we speak of 'positive correlation'.

Self-check

Can you think of an example of where high values of one variable go with low ones of the other and vice versa?

There are, of course, many such examples. One of them is the case of the size of a car engine (in cc) and its petrol consumption (in mpg). While there are, of course, variations, the general pattern is that the bigger the engine the less the miles per gallon. Such cases are examples of 'negative correlation'. Not all pairs of variables are correlated, naturally.

Self-check

Can you think of any pairs of variables that should not show any correlation?

We would not imagine that an adult man's height and his expenditure on cigarettes a week were either positively or negatively correlated, for example. Such variables are said to be 'uncorrelated'.

Correlation may be represented pictorially by plotting the bivariate data on what is termed a 'scatter diagram'. The scatter diagrams for the above cases are shown in figure 26. Note that the more highly correlated (either negatively or positively) the two sets of data are, the nearer the points are to lying on a straight line.

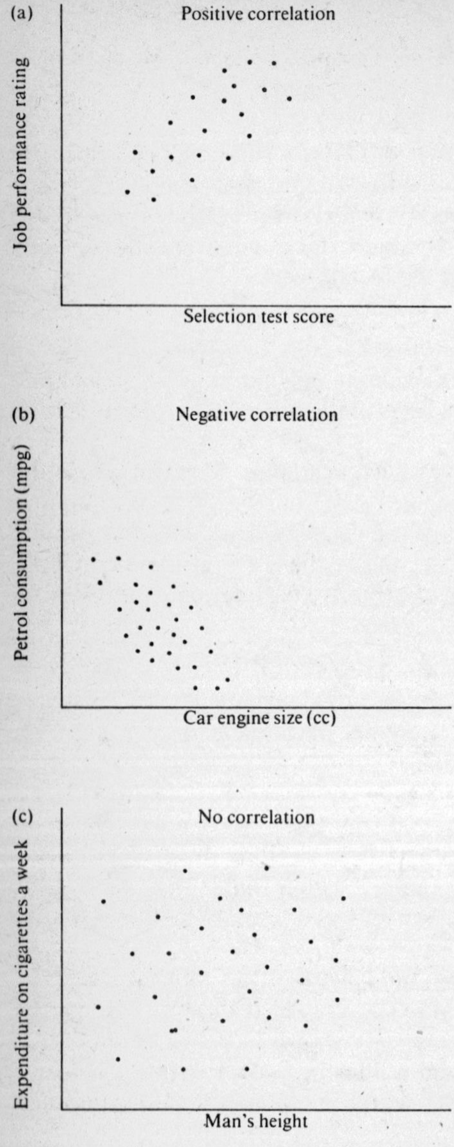

Figure 26. Scatter diagrams

Activity

Ask about ten of your friends and relations what their heights and weights are and plot them on a scatter diagram.

Height and weight are two variables which are fairly strongly correlated. Your scatter diagram should show this. The author performed this same experiment and obtained the results shown in table 13 and figure 27. He was, in fact, somewhat embarrassed by how closely correlated the results were!

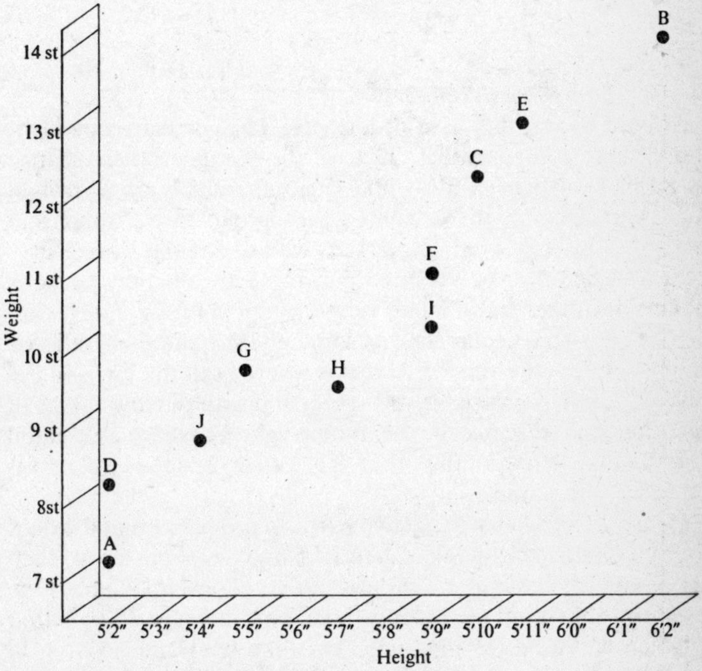

Figure 27. Scatter diagram of table 13 data

TABLE 13. THE HEIGHTS AND WEIGHTS OF TEN OF THE AUTHOR'S FRIENDS AND RELATIONS

Individual	*Height*	*Weight*
A	5′2″	7 st 4 lb
B	6′2″	14 st 5 lb
C	5′10″	12 st 6 lb
D	5′2″	8 st 4 lb
E	5′11″	13 st 2 lb
F	5′9″	11 st 1 lb
G	5′5″	9 st 11 lb
H	5′7″	9 st 8 lb
I	5′9″	10 st 5 lb
J	5′4″	8 st 12 lb

A word of warning is in order here. The correlated patterns above show a *linear* effect. That is, the points on these scatter diagrams (i.e. figure 26 (a) and (b)) fall roughly on a straight line. And, indeed, it is assumed throughout this chapter that these are the only kind of patterns we are dealing with. But it must not therefore be assumed that these are the only patterns that occur. Other 'curvilinear' relationships are reasonably common. One, in particular, merits some interest and that is the U-shaped curve. One version of this is where both the low *and* the high values of one variable are associated with the low values of the other, but in between, the middle values of it are associated with the high values of the other. The other version is where it is the other way round.

Figure 28 illustrates these two cases. It is evident that it would not be suitable to assume a 'straight line' relationship in such cases, nor to assume there was no relationship at all. One instance of the kind of relationship shown in figure 28(a) is that between ambition (as measured by some test) and position in the company. It has been found that ambition is actually low amongst those on bottom rungs of the career ladder, but also amongst those at the top. Ambition is maximum with those in the middle. Care, then, should always be exercised when making assumptions about linear relationships. The scatter diagram is a good way to get some picture of the situation, which will back up the calculations to be outlined later in this chapter.

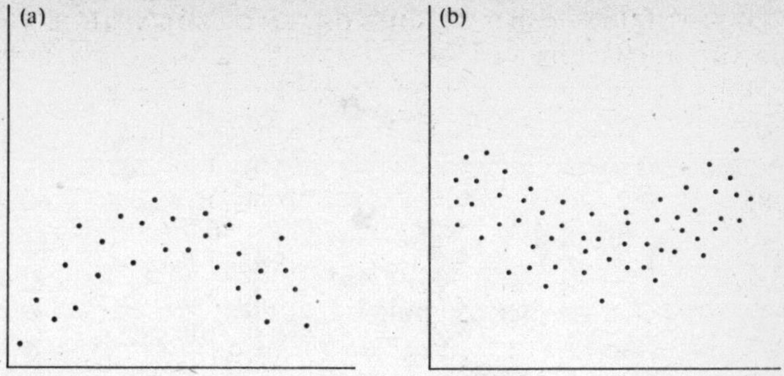

Figure 28. Two curvilinear relationships

Drawing a line to represent the relationship

To illustrate the calculations of the following sections, we will take some test and job performance evaluation figures from the scenario. These are shown in table 14. Note that only ten pairs are shown to simplify the calculations.

TABLE 14. SELECTION TEST SCORES AND JOB PERFORMANCE RATINGS

Employee	*Selection test score*	*Job performance rating*
A	50	11
B	70	12
C	70	11
D	70	13
E	50	9
F	60	11
G	50	10
H	40	9
I	80	14
J	60	10
	600	110

Self-check

Plot the scatter diagram for these figures.

The scatter diagram is as in figure 29(a). What we want to do now is to draw a line through the points so that it fits them as best as we can. The reason for doing this is so that we can predict job performance from the selection test scores. This is, after all, the whole point of them. If we want to do this we thus need a reasonably accurate line. Obviously, it won't be possible for it to pass through all the points.

We should be very clear as to why we are going to use a straight line. What we are assuming is that *there is actually a law* which relates, in this case, the selection test score to the job performance rating. If all the random 'errors' and 'fluctuations' could be eliminated from the figures, on this assumption every point would lie on this line. Such 'errors' and 'fluctuations' would be caused, for example, by prejudice in the ratings, staff not performing work according to their abilities, off-days when taking the tests and so on. The straight line is the graphical embodiment of this law. Once we have this, given the value of one of the variables we can predict the value of the other. Of course, the same 'errors' and 'fluctuations' of above will tend to throw our predication out, but it is, nevertheless, the best one that can be made under the circumstances. That is, it will minimize this difference.

Self-check

How do you think we should try to draw such a line if we were asked to do so by eye?

It would seem sensible to try to keep a balance between the distances of points from the line on one side with those on the other. However, there is one other clue that could help us.

Self-check

Can you think of any one point that such a line ought to go through?

The one point that the line should pass through is that corresponding to the two means. In the case of the data in table 14, this is the point where the test score equals 60 and the rating

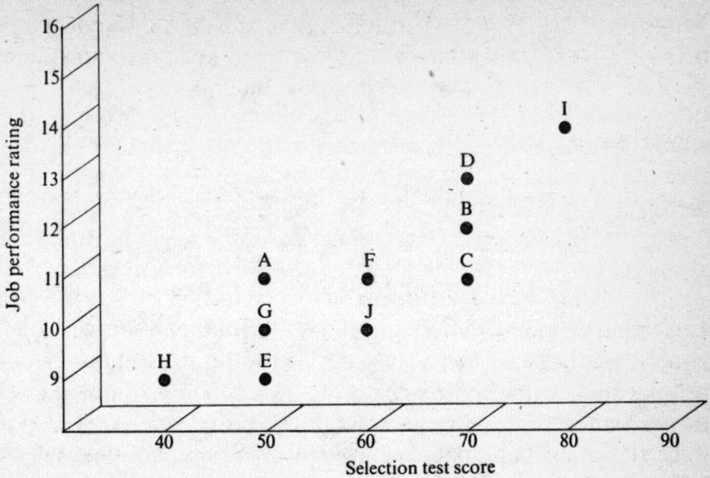

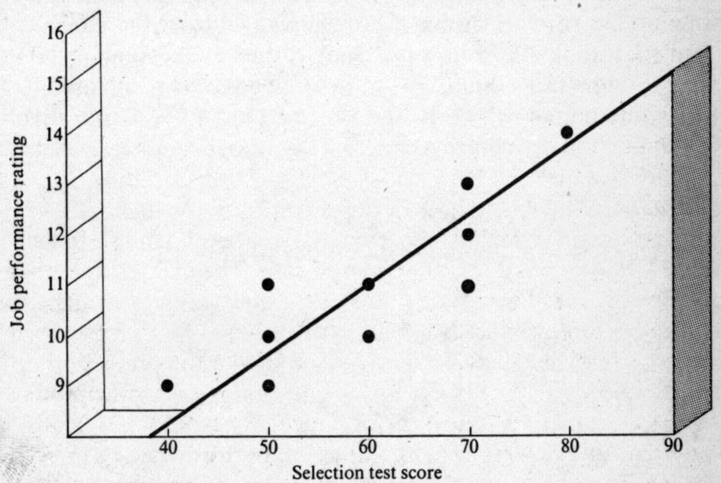

Figure 29. Scatter diagram for table 14 with line of best fit drawn by eye (b)

equals 11. It seems very reasonable that this should be so, since in taking averages we cancel out any random fluctuations because positive and negative ones should balance.

Self-check

Draw in what you think is the line of best fit on your scatter diagram.

The author's attempt at doing this appears in figure 29(b).

Now while this may give a rough guide, it is not very 'scientific'. Statisticians have, in fact, devised a method for calculating how to draw such a line more accurately. While a full treatment of this technique is beyond the scope of this book, some indication of the reasoning behind it can be given. Basically, the idea is that we minimize the sum of the distances of the points from the line. Now you may recall that the standard deviation also deals with a similar sum (of the 'distances' of the values from their mean). There we took the squares of such distances to eliminate the effect of directions. Similarly, here we need to take into account that some points will be below the line, and so be a 'negative' distance from it, while others will be above, and so be at a positive distance. So here, too, we actually minimize the sum of the *squares* of the distances of the points from the line.

Lines drawn in such a way are called 'regression lines'. In fact, there are two such lines for any set of data. The first assumes that any 'errors' or 'fluctuations' are all in one variable, while the second assumes that they are all in the other. Which one is used depends on which way we are trying to make the prediction, as mentioned earlier. In the case in question we want to predict from the test scores to job performance. We would thus assume here that the 'errors' were all in the job performance rating. To get this line, called the regression line of job performance *on* the test score*, we minimize the sum of the squares of the distances indicated by the vertical lines in figure 30. These lines indicate the 'error' component in each job performance rating when compared to the test score. Because they are vertical they

*Or, in general, the regression line of y on x.

contain no such 'error' component for test scores, which are thus assumed to be 'given'.

When this minimization is carried out mathematically, it yields the 'slope' of the regression line, that is, it tells us how much the line rises, or falls, for every unit of test score. So, for example, a line which rose 2 rating points for every 10 'marks' on the test would have a slope of $\frac{2}{10} = .2$. Conventionally, if it fell by 2 points, instead of rising, the slope is $\frac{-2}{10} = -.2$.

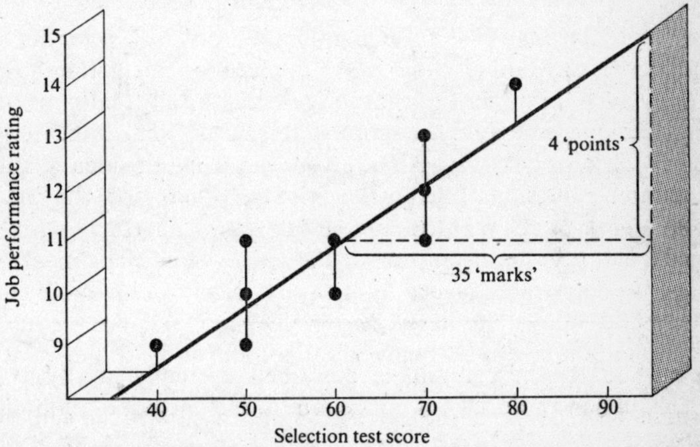

Figure 30. Regression line of job performance rating on test score

Self-check

If the line rose 6 points for every 30 marks on the test, what would be its slope?

It would be $\frac{6}{30} = .2$ as before. If you said 5, you were looking at it the other way round; that is, the increase in test score for every unit of performance.

In order to calculate this slope, a table has to be prepared which shows, in columns, the squares of the test scores and of the ratings for each employee, together with the product of the test scores and the ratings. Each column is then totalled.

Self-check

Construct such a table with the figures of table 14.

TABLE 15. CALCULATIONS OF SUMS FOR USE WITH FINDING THE REGRESSION LINE OF JOB PERFORMANCE ON TEST SCORE

Column 1 *Selection test score*	*Column 2* *Performance rating*	*Column 3* *(Column 1)²*	*Column 4* *(Column 2)²*	*Column 5* *(Column 1) × (Column 2)*
50	11	2500	121	550
70	12	4900	144	840
70	11	4900	121	770
70	13	4900	169	910
50	9	2500	81	450
60	11	3600	121	660
50	10	2500	100	500
40	9	1600	81	360
80	14	6400	196	1120
60	10	3600	100	600
600	110	37,400	1234	6760

Table 15 shows the columns as described. Actually strictly for the task in hand column 4 is not required. It is included for later use.

Using this table, the next step is to calculate the 'covariance' of the test scores and the ratings. This quantity is a measure of how these two variables vary together. To do this we need to evaluate:

$$\frac{\text{the sum of ((variable 1 − mean of variable 1) × (variable 2 − mean of variable 2))}}{\text{the number of values of the variable}}.$$

You can see that this expression is very similar to the one for the variance of a single variable. In fact, variance is just the covariance of a variable *with itself*. Now there is a way of calculating the covariance which is simpler to use than the one above. For the figures in question the expression is

$$\frac{\text{total of col. 5}}{\text{number of employees}} - \text{mean selection test score} \times \text{mean rating.}$$

The mean selection test score, from Chapter 10 in Volume *1*, is

$$\frac{\text{total of col. 1}}{\text{number of employees}} = \frac{600}{10} = 60$$

and, similarly, the mean rating is

$$\frac{\text{total of col. 2}}{\text{number of employees}} = \frac{110}{10} = 11.$$

What, then, is the covariance? It is $\frac{6760}{10} - 60 \times 11 = 676 - 660 = 16$.

In general, the covariance of two sets of figures is given by

$$\frac{\text{the sum of the products of each pair of figures}}{\text{the total number of pairs of figures}} - \text{the product of the means of the two sets of figures.}$$

To obtain the slope of the required regression line we simply divide the covariance by the variance of the test scores. Now, from Chapter 11 in Volume *1*, this variance is

$$\frac{\text{the sum of each (value} - \text{mean)}^2}{\text{the number of values}}.$$

In fact, from a calculation point of view, it can be shown that an easier, yet equivalent, expression for the variance is

$$\frac{\text{the sum of each (value)}^2}{\text{the number of values}} - \text{(the mean value)}^2.$$

Here this is $\frac{\text{col. 3}}{\text{number of employees}} - \text{(mean test score)}^2$,

which is $\frac{37{,}400}{10} - (60)^2 = 3740 - 3600 = 140.$

The slope of this regression line is thus $\frac{16}{140} = .114$ (to three decimal places).

Recalling that this means that the line rises .114 rating points for 1 test mark, we can rewrite this as 1.14 rating points for every 10 test marks or, even more useful for drawing the line, 4.00 points in 35 marks exactly.

Self-check

Draw this line, remembering that it goes through the point corresponding to the mean of each variable.

The line is as appears in figure 30, in fact. The slope is also shown.

Now we can look at the variables the other way round. We could, in fact, say that, because the test is being validated, we can assume the job performance ratings as given and that the 'errors' occur in the test scores. That is we are now attempting to predict the test score from the rating and not vice versa. The appropriate regression line here is that of the test scores on the ratings.* Figure 31 shows horizontal lines indicating the distances whose squares are now to be minimized. Note that this line too goes through the mean point. The calculation of the slope proceeds similarly to above except that the covariance is divided by the variance of the performance rating rather than of the test score and the result is upside down; that is, variance on the top, and covariance on the bottom.

Self-check

What is the slope of this other regression line?

The variance of the ratings is given, from table 15, by

$$\frac{\text{col. 4}}{\text{number of employees}} - (\text{mean rating})^2$$

which is $\frac{1234}{10} - 121 = 123.4 - 121 = 2.4$.

The slope is thus $\frac{2.4}{16} = 0.15$.

It is actually easier to use if we say it is exactly 3 rating points for every 20 marks. This is shown in figure 31.

Self-check

Plot this regression line on the same graph as you did the other one.

The regression line of the test score on the job performance rating is shown in figure 31. Figure 32 shows both regression lines, together with the author's guess. Note that the guess, because it tries to take into account fluctuations in *either* set of data, lies in the middle.

*Or, in general, the regression line of x on y.

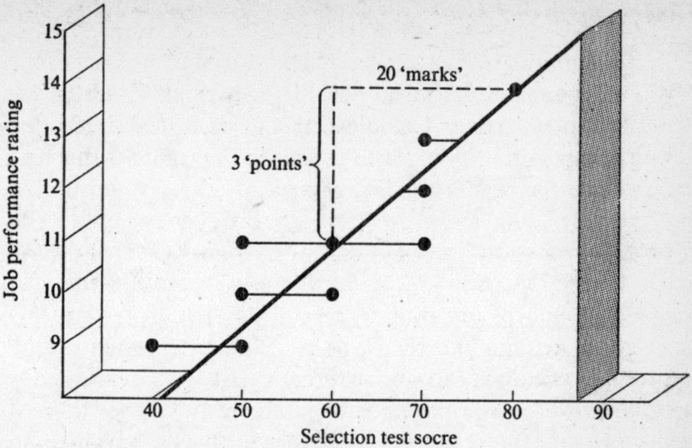

Figure 31. Regression line of test score on job performance rating

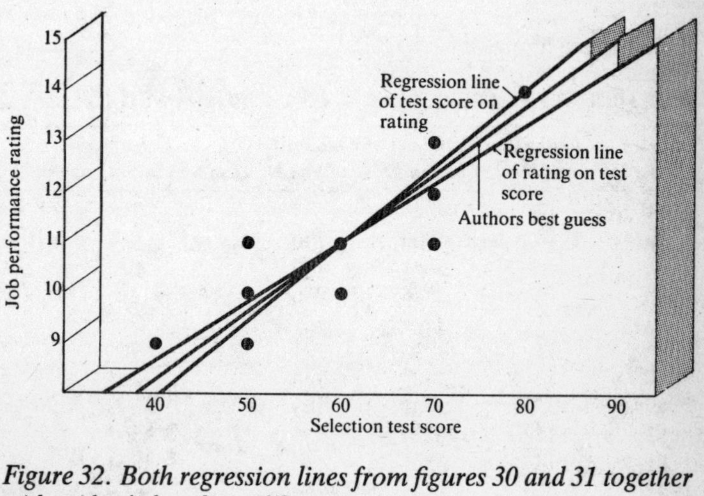

Figure 32. Both regression lines from figures 30 and 31 together with author's best line of fit

Self-check

A consumers' panel awarded marks out of 20 to each of ten different makes of battery of a given type. Their prices were also recorded. Calculate the slope of the regression line of marks on price. Plot the scatter diagram for this data and draw the regression line on it.

Battery	*Price (p)*	*Mark*
A	64	12
B	70	14
C	62	10
D	76	16
E	65	11
F	64	11
G	67	12
H	69	13
I	82	17
J	81	14

What mark might you expect a battery priced at 75p to get on these figures?

TABLE 16. DATA FOR SELF-CHECKS ON PAGES 144 AND 150

Column 1 Price	*Column 2* Mark	*Column 3* (Column 1)^2	*Column 4* (Column 2)^2	*Column 5* (Column 1) × (Column 2)
64	12	4096	144	768
70	14	4900	196	980
62	10	3844	100	620
76	16	5776	256	1216
65	11	4225	121	715
64	11	4096	121	704
67	12	4489	144	804
69	13	4761	169	897
82	17	6724	289	1394
81	14	6561	196	1134
700	130	49,472	1736	9232

Table 16 shows the required columns and their totals. From this the covariance is $\frac{9232}{10} - 70 \times 13 = 923\ 2 - 910 = 13.2$, while the variance of the price is $\frac{49{,}472}{10} - 70^2 = 4947.2 - 4900 = 47.2$.

The slope of the required regression line is thus $\frac{13.2}{47.2} = .28$ (to two decimal places).

This is best written, for drawing the line, as 2.8 marks in 10 pence. Figure 33 shows the scatter diagram and regression line. This line passes through the point where mark equals 13 and price 70.

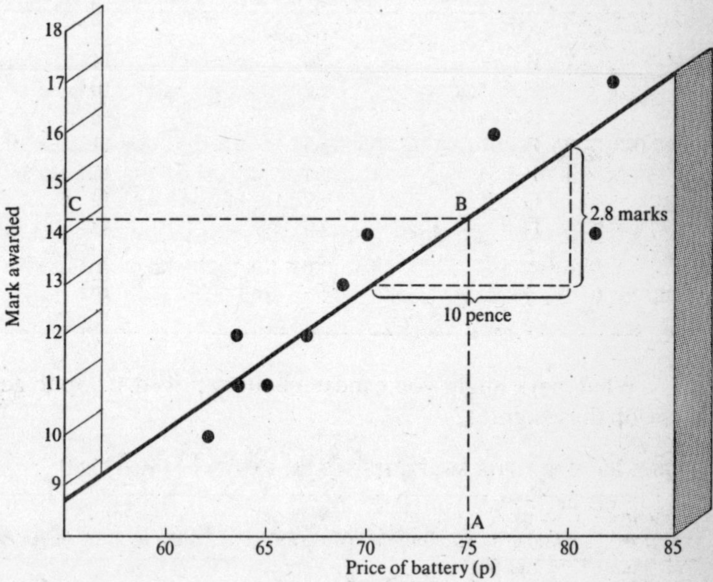

Figure 33. Scatter diagram and regression line of mark awarded on price of batteries in table 16

Looking up 75p along the horizontal axis, drawing a line up to meet the line (AB in figure 33) and then looking at the corresponding reading on the vertical axis (using line BC), we get a mark of 14.4.

Calculating the degree of relationship

It was shown in the last section how the slope of both regression lines depended on the covariance. This figure does, in fact, reflect the degree of relationship between the two sets of data. But it is not suitable for general comparisons because it is not dimensionless. That is to say it is in units which depend on the two variables. To remove these dimensions we can divide by the standard deviations of both sets of data. If we do this we end up with something called the 'product–moment coefficient of correlation'. Hence this coefficient is given by

$$\frac{\text{covariance}}{(\text{standard deviation of first set of data}) \times (\text{standard deviation of second set})}.$$

It is a mathematical fact that this coefficient cannot lie outside of the range -1 to $+1$. But what interpretation do we put on its value?

In order to see, let us look at the slopes of the two regression lines. Remember that they each pass through the point corresponding to the means of both sets of data and that their slopes are given by

$$\frac{\text{covariance}}{\text{variance of variable 1}} \quad \text{and} \quad \frac{\text{variance of variable 2}}{\text{covariance}}$$

Self-check

What could we conclude about the two regression lines when, if plotted on the same graph, their actual slopes would be the same?

Since they both pass through one common point, corresponding to the two means, if their slopes are the same they must be identical lines. So we conclude that if

$$\frac{\text{covariance}}{\text{variance of one set of data}} = \frac{\text{variance of other set of data}}{\text{covariance}}$$

then there are not two regression lines but one. The condition is equivalent to $(\text{covariance})^2 = (\text{variance of first set of data}) \times (\text{variance of second set})$ or

$$\frac{(\text{covariance})^2}{(\text{variance of first set of data}) \times (\text{variance of second set})} = 1.$$

Given that the variance is equal to the square of the standard deviation, the expression on the left is equivalent to the *square of the product–moment coefficient of correlation*.

Self-check

So if we get a product–moment coefficient of correlation whose square is 1, what does it mean?

It means that there is only one regression line, and hence that the *correlation is perfect*; that is, there are no errors and the scatter diagram itself forms a straight line.

Self-check

But there are two different values that the product–moment coefficient of correlation can have if its square is 1. What are they, and what do you think is their meaning?

Well, they are +1 or −1. The plus 1 implies perfect positive correlation and the minus 1 perfect negative correlation. That is, in the second case we have a *negative* slope to the line, since one variable's values get bigger as the other's get smaller. Figure 34 illustrates this. The figures there are taken from the following examples.

As an instance of perfect positive correlation, consider the case of the costs of production as shown in figure 34(a). There will be certain fixed costs, e.g. of plant and machinery, but there will also be a variable cost of so much per unit of production. Here the production costs and the number of units produced will be perfectly, positively correlated. It is interesting to note that this straight line relationship only holds over a certain range: eventually the production capacity of the machine would be exceeded. This is often the case, and we should always be careful as to the range we assume the relation to hold over. Perfect negative correlation can be seen in figure 34(b). Here we have the amount outstanding on a loan plotted against the total

(a) Product-moment coefficient correlation = +1

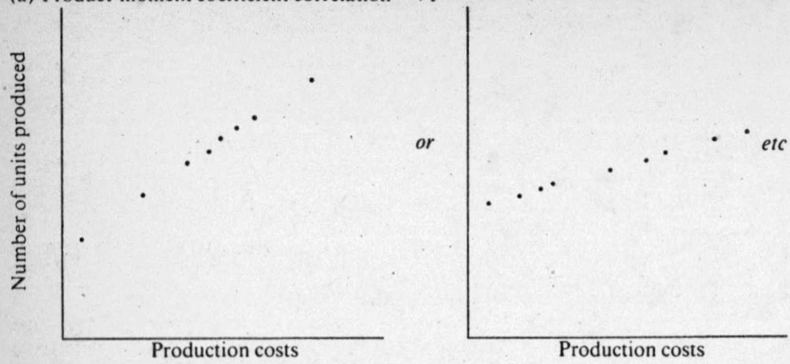

(b) Product-moment coefficient of correlation = -1

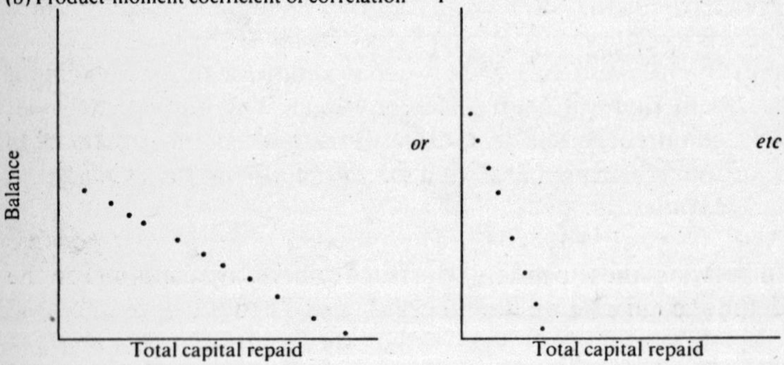

(c) Product-moment coefficient of correlation = 0

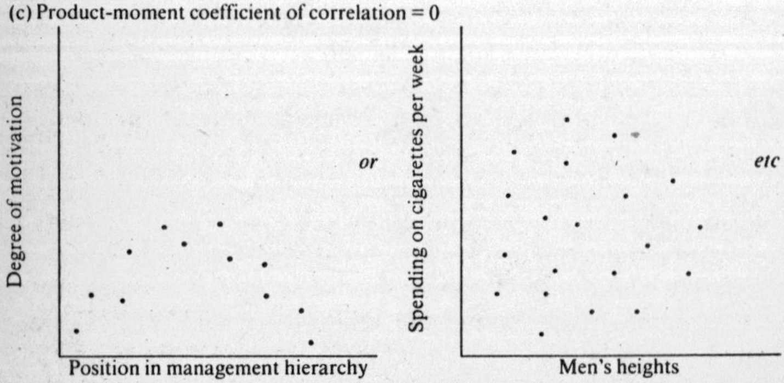

amount of capital repaid. Note that in neither case is the slope itself of any significance for the value of the coefficient of correlation, it is purely whether or not the points in the scatter diagram lie on a straight line and whether this slopes to the right or to the left.

Self-check

What do you think it means when the product–moment coefficient of correlation is zero?

When the coefficient of correlation is zero, there is no correlation between the two sets of data. That is there is no *linear* relationship between them. This is shown in figure 34(c). Notice, however, that in the leftmost of the two examples in figure 34(c) there *is* a relationship. It is the (upside-down) U-shaped relationship, mentioned earlier, between position in the management hierarchy and the degree of motivation. The second example, also given earlier, is of a case where there is no relationship whatsoever, that is between a man's height and his expenditure on cigarettes per week.

In between these possible values, of course, are cases where the degree of correlation is neither −1, nor 0 nor +1.

Self-check

What, for example, is the product–moment coefficient of correlation between the test scores and the job performance ratings of table 14?

Table 15 already contains the required totals, and we have, indeed, already calculated the covariance as 16, and also the

Figure 34. Scatter diagram for different values of the product–moment coefficient of correlation

(a). Product–moment coefficient of correlation = +1
(b). Product–moment coefficient of correlation = −1
(c). Product–moment coefficient of correlation = 0

variance of the two sets of data. That of the test scores was 140 and that of the ratings 2.4. The product–moment coefficient of correlation is thus $\frac{16}{\sqrt{140} \times \sqrt{2.4}} = \frac{16}{11.83 \times 1.55} = .87$ (to two decimal places.

> *Self-check*
>
> Calculate the product–moment correlation for the data in the self-check on page 144.

We have already calculated the covariance as 13.2, and the variance of the price as 47.2. The variance of the marks awarded is, from table 16, $\frac{1736}{10} - 13^2 = 173.6 - 169 = 4.6$.

So the coefficient of correlation is $\frac{13.2}{\sqrt{47.2 \times 4.6}} = \frac{13.2}{6.87 \times 2.14} = .90$ (to two decimal places).

How do we interpret our result?

So we find that the product-moment coefficient of correlation between the selection test scores and the job performance ratings is .87, what does this mean? Well, obviously, it does not mean that there is perfect correlation, either negative or positive. But neither does it mean that there is none.

> *Self-check*
>
> What interpretation would you put on the result?

It would seem that this result is near enough +1 to warrant assuming that there is quite a good positive correlation between the two sets of figures. Actually, for the application concerned it would be amazingly good. We can assume that the nearer to + or −1 the higher the degree of correlation. But there are problems.

The actual interpretation of the product–moment coefficient of correlation should really be made with scientific vigour. We should, and in practice do, set up a null hypothesis that its 'true' value is zero, and that the one obtained was merely a result of chance fluctuations. For this, of course, we need to know its sampling distribution. Details of this would lead us beyond the scope of this book. However, one point should be mentioned and that is that, with a small sample, we would require the coefficient to have a considerably higher value before we were convinced that there was any real effect, than if the sample were a large one.

But even if we do find a very high correlation between two sets of data, what does it tell us? One thing it most certainly does *not* tell us is that we are observing a cause and its effect. We are not likely to make this error in the case of the test scores and performance ratings. But there are cases when the temptation is there. For example, correlations between the amount of tobacco smoked and the incidence of lung cancer led to claims that smoking *caused* lung cancer. On the evidence as stated this conclusion is entirely unwarranted. It might well be, for example, that people who are prone to develop lung cancer are also the very type who would smoke a great deal. Such a factor is called a 'hidden correlate'. Another example of this is that the number of storks nesting in Sweden and the birthrate there are positively correlated. It would, however, be wrong to assume that the tale of storks bringing babies is therefore true! In fact, the hidden correlate here is the weather!

A high degree of correlation, therefore, does not imply causation. If this question of cause is to be investigated, it must be done by other experiments. For example, in the case of smoking, the effects of inhaling tobacco smoke over long periods of time on normal non-smokers may be studied. Indeed, some experiments of this nature were performed on dogs. Here, of course, moral questions arise as to the right of scientists to conduct such experiments. In most cases, however, where businesses are concerned, this problem does not arise. Instead there is the practical problem of getting a company to do something purely to test a theory and regardless of economic consequences. For example, there may be a high correlation between a company going bankrupt and some variation that it adopts on normal business practice. In order to prove causation, perfectly healthy firms would need to be persuaded to adopt this practice just to see if they went bankrupt!

What a high correlation does tell us is that, in the normal run of things, we should expect to see high or low values of the two variables in question being associated with each other, for positive correlation, of low values of one with high values of the other, for negative correlation. What causes the association need not be known, and certainly cannot be inferred from the correlation alone. In particular, knowing the value of one of the variables involved we should be able to use one or other of the regression lines to predict, with some reasonable degree of accuracy, the value the other variable will take. The greater the degree of correlation, the greater the accuracy of the prediction.

A few words are in order about the kind of data that is used with the techniques described in this chapter. Both sets of data should be representative of the populations from which they are drawn. If they are not then, strictly, the techniques described in this chapter may not properly be applied. For example, in the scenario, the selection test was validated against a biased sample of workers; that is, those who had already performed the job for some time. In practice, a correction to the calculations, not covered in this chapter, is made to compensate for this. Ideally, the samples should be random ones, therefore.

In addition, problems may arise if the samples are too small. Up to now we have not bothered too much about sample size, except in connection with the standard error of the sample mean. This is because we have been dealing, generally, either with parent populations which could be assumed to be normally distributed and with known standard deviation or with binomial sampling distributions. While there are specific techniques for dealing with small samples when such conditions do not hold, their introduction in an introductory book such as this was not felt appropriate. If details of these are required, standard texts should be referred to.

All of the techniques described in this chapter are 'distribution' ones (they are sometimes rather loosely and, in fact, erroneously, called 'parametric'). That is, we can make certain assumptions about the parent and sampling distributions. One crucial such assumption is that we are dealing with 'interval' (or 'ratio') scales of measurement. Broadly speaking, this means that a given interval (ratio) between two values of the variable in question has a constant meaning regardless of what those values are. For example, if there are three salesmen, A, B and C, who have sold £507, £483 and £459 worth of goods respectively, then A achieved £24 more sales than B who, in turn, sold £24 more than C. Thus A bettered B by exactly the same amount that B bettered C.

But suppose we know merely that, in rank order of sales, A came first, B second and C third. We cannot then assume that A outsold B by exactly the same amount (or even proportion) that B outsold C. The variable here is neither interval nor ratio but what is known as 'ordinal'. That is, we can, at most, assume some order in our results. In such cases we have to use 'distribution free' techniques (they are sometimes loosely and, in fact, erroneously called 'non-parametric'). Again, coverage of these is not attempted in this book. If you would like to know about them a good book to refer to is *Statistics for Business: A Course Unit Approach* by P. Taylor and D. Dunning (Polytech Publishers, 1977).

As far as this chapter is concerned, then, the general assumption is that we are dealing with reasonably sized samples, randomly selected from normally distributed parent populations. In practice, these strict conditions can be stretched a little. But a statistical knowledge of techniques not covered in this text is really required if you deal with situations which do not reasonably approximate to the conditions described here.

Summary

Bearing in mind the reservations expressed in the last section, then, the techniques discussed in this chapter can be applied to various problems as illustrated in the chart of figure 35 below.

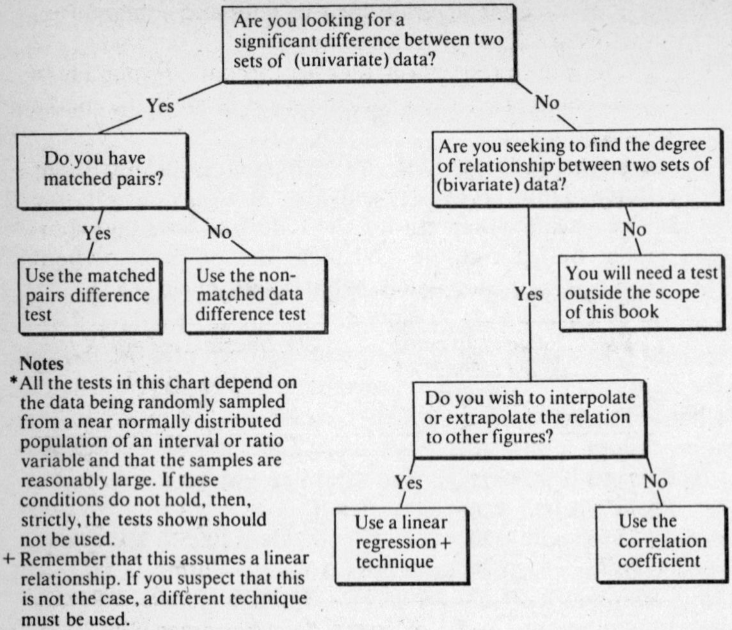

Figure 35. Which test do you use?

Review

1 The following data relates to the net profit per employee and number of employees in ten firms operating within a particular industry.

Number of employees (10s)	*Net profit per employee (£1000)*
5	25
16	26
25	20
38	22
42	18
49	19
54	16
60	22
68	17
73	15

a Plot a scatter diagram for this data and comment on the result.
b Draw both regression lines for this data. Explain how you could use each of them separately to make predictions.
c Calculate the product–moment coefficient of correlation and interpret your result.

2 Plot a scatter diagram for the following data and comment on your result. Calculate the product–moment coefficient of correlation. What does it mean?

Year	*Value of 1p coins issued to the UK* (£100,000)*	*% Unemployed in UK as of 1 Jan. in the period†*
72/73	18	3.5
73/74	27	2.7
74/75	26	3.3
75/76	23	5.5
76/77	26	6.1

*Source: *Royal Mint Report* 1976/77.
† Source: *Dept of Employment Gazette*.

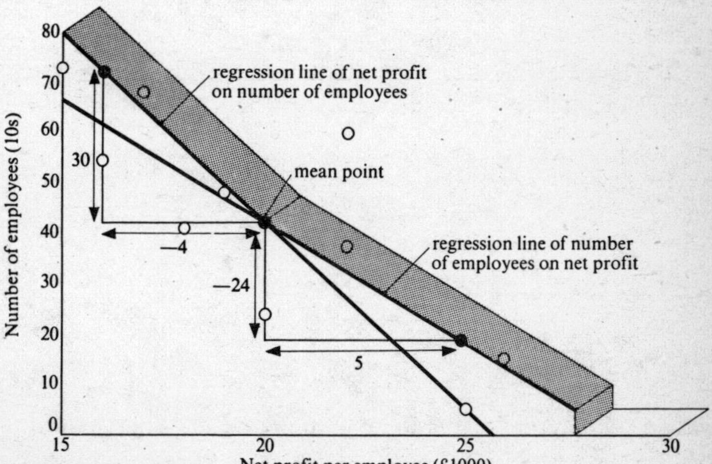

Figure 36. Scatter diagram for review 1 (page 154)

ANSWERS

1 a The scatter diagram is shown in figure 36. It shows that there is a tendency for higher productivity to be associated with the smaller firms.

b To see the connection, the regression lines can be drawn. In order to find out their exact nature, some calculations have to be made. First we need to calculate the two means. These are as follows.

Mean number of employees is (in 10s) = 43.

Mean net profit per employee is (in £1000) = 20.

That is, the ten figures are totalled up and divided by the number of them; that is, 10.

Now the covariance must be calculated. This has the value

$$\frac{5\times25+16\times26+25\times20+38\times22+42\times18+49\times19+54\times16+60\times22+68\times17+73\times15}{10}$$

$$-\ 43\times20 = \frac{125+416+500+836+756+931+864+1320+1156+1095}{10}$$

$$-\ 860 = \frac{7999}{10} - 860 = 799.9 - 860 = -60.1.$$

The next step is to calculate the two variances. These are

$$\frac{5^2+16^2+25^2+38^2+42^2+49^2+54^2+60^2+68^2+73^2}{10} - 43^2$$

$$= \frac{25+256+625+1444+1764+2401+2916+3600+4624+5329}{10}$$

$$-\ 43^2 = \frac{22{,}984}{10} - 43^2 = 2298.4 - 43^2 = 449.4$$

$$=2298.4 - 1849 = 449.4$$

and $\dfrac{25^2+26^2+20^2+22^2+18^2+19^2+16^2+22^2+17^2+15^2}{10} - 20^2$

$$= \frac{625+676+400+484+324+361+256+484+289+225}{10} - 20^2$$

$$= \frac{4124}{10} - 20^2 = 412.4 - 20^2$$

$$= 412.4 - 400 = 12.4.$$

The slope of the regression line of net profit on number of employees is either $\frac{-60.1}{449.4} = -.134$ or -4 in 30 approximately or $\frac{1}{-.134} = -.746$, while that of the number of employees on net profit is $\frac{-6.1}{12.4} = -4.847$ or approximately -24 in 5, or $\frac{1}{-4.847} = .206$.

Which pair of slopes is chosen will depend on which way round you put the axes, i.e. number of employees along the bottom or up the side. In figure 36, they are shown up the side, so the slopes are –.746 and –4.847 respectively.

Now the regression lines both pass through the point corresponding to the mean of the two sets of figures. So they appear as shown in figure 36. Did you get the regression lines round the right way?

To predict the values of the net profit given the number of employees, the regression line of net profit on number of employees would be used, and for the other way round, the other regression line would be used. In both cases interpolation would be used or extrapolation, though the latter is a more dangerous practice.

c The coefficient of correlation is calculated by
$$\frac{-60.1}{\sqrt{449.4} \times \sqrt{12.4}} = \frac{-60.1}{21.2 \times 3.52} = .81 \text{ (to two decimal places).}$$

This result shows that there is some degree of correlation between these two sets of figures and that it is negative; that is, the bigger the profit the less the number of employees that go with it. What it does *not* show is that it is because there is a small number of employees that the profit per employee is high.

2 The scatter diagram for this data appears in figure 37. You should have said that it indicated that there was little relationship between the two sets of data.

The coefficient of correlation is calculated as follows. The two means are $\frac{120}{5} = 24$ and $\frac{21.1}{5} = 4.22$.

The covariance is
$$\frac{18 \times 3.5 + 27 \times 2.7 + 26 \times 3.3 + 23 \times 5.5 + 26 \times 6.1}{5} - 24 \times 4.22$$
$$= \frac{63 + 72.9 + 85.8 + 126.5 + 158.6}{5} - 101.28 = \frac{506.8}{5} - 101.28$$
$$= 101.36 - 101.28 = .08.$$

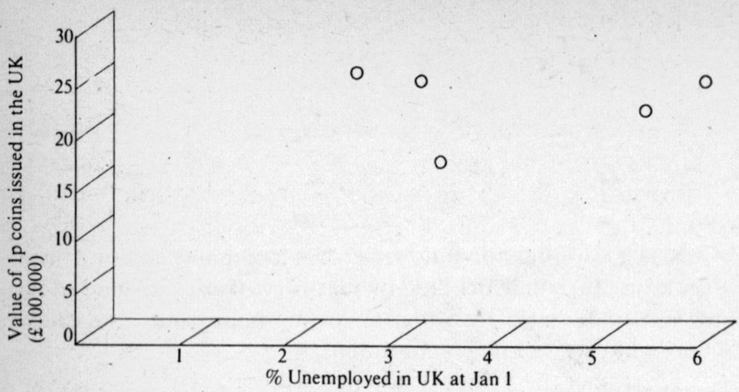

Figure 37. Scatter diagram review 2 (page 155)

The next step is to calculate the two variances. These are

$$\frac{18^2 + 27^2 + 26^2 + 23^2 + 26^2}{5} - 24^2 = \frac{324 + 729 + 676 + 529 + 676}{5} - 576$$

$= \frac{2934}{5} - 576 = 586.8 - 576 = 10.8$ for the coins and

$$\frac{3.5^2 + 2.7^2 + 3.3^2 + 5.5^2 + 6.1^2}{5} - 4.22^2 =$$

$$\frac{12.25 + 7.29 + 10.89 + 30.25 + 37.21}{5} - 4.22^2 = \frac{97.89}{5} - 17.8084 =$$

$19.578 - 17.8084 = 1.7696$ for the unemployed.

So the coefficient of correlation is $\frac{.08}{\sqrt{10.8} \times \sqrt{1.7696}} = \frac{.08}{3.29 \times 1.33}$

$= .02$ (to two decimal places).

This confirms both the scatter diagram and common sense; there is no relationship between these two sets of data.

Scenario 3
Forecasting sales

As you read through the following scenario, make a mental note of the occasions on which figures that vary over time need to be analysed to abstract information from them; and note, too, exactly what kind of information that is.

The board of Gourmet Foods Ltd had been dissatisfied with company performance for some time and so had decided to produce a company plan. This was to be based on a full investigation of the company's performance and potential. The marketing director, Roger Court, was given the responsibility of looking at possible new products and of estimating future sales of current ones.

Roger passed the job of forecasting future sales of Baby Gourmet products on to Ken Collier, the brand manager. The first thing he did was to collect statistics on yearly sales of these products over the previous twenty or so years and on monthly sales over the previous five years. This would at least give him some hard evidence on which to base his forecasts.

Looking back over the years, it was evident that sales had fluctuated. It looked as though there was some sort of pattern, too. But it was also clear that the sales performance at present was particularly poor. In order to see how poor, though, Roger needed to process the data to iron out all those fluctuations. He knew there was a particular statistical technique for doing this, so he looked it up in his books. His calculations showed that the sales of foods under his brand were, indeed, poor when considered over the long term.

But what of the short term? The monthly figures that he had collected also showed some fluctuations. These seemed to be seasonal; sales seemed to depend on what time of the year it was. This was no real surprise to Roger: they geared their production to this assumption anyway. Births followed a seasonal pattern, for one thing. And for another, mothers seemed to buy more jars of baby food at certain times of the year.

In order to see clearly what the trend in sales was, Roger performed the same analysis for the monthly figures as he had for the yearly ones.

Once again, the results were none too encouraging. The trend was markedly downward. By now, indeed, Roger was getting quite depressed. However, he thought he found one ray of hope. When the figures for the last few months were examined, they did reveal that the trend had turned upwards. Since Roger had been with the company for a couple of years only, he liked to think that this may have been due to his efforts.

So what forecast could Roger make then? Well he plumped for the more optimistic one. To back him up in this he also had evidence of increasing orders from the sales representatives and some indication, from the birth rate, that the market would cease to contract for a while. He predicted, then, that the latest upward trend would continue. He fervently hoped that he was right.

Business abounds with figures collected over a period of time. Their analysis is one of the most important aspects of business operation. In the past lie at least some firm clues to the future, if not any direct indications. In particular, of course, any company needs to do business, and most companies want to do more business. Thus they need to sell goods, services or whatever. In order to do this effectively, some idea of future possibilities is required.

It is important, however, to distinguish between predictions of demand and of sales. The former can be estimated from statistical surveys or from sales representatives' reports, but it is difficult to get accurate past details on which to make forecasts of the type described in this chapter. We have records of past *sales* but very seldom do we have records of past *demands*. Sales predictions can become self-fulfilling prophesies. If there is, in fact, a large and unsuspected demand and production is geared to sales forecasts, then such forecasts will, naturally, be met! The fact that the sales could have been a great deal more may never be known.

But suppose, now, we do wish to get some indication of sales performance from past sales figures. We do have to be careful not just to take them at face value. Look at the following data for a firm for some given year:

Quarter	*Sales*
1	21
2	22
3	23
4	24

We might naïvely suppose that the sales are very gradually improving. But suppose we are then given the previous year's figures:

Quarter	*Sales*
1	22
2	24
3	26
4	28

We can now see that, for each quarter, the sales in the given year are below those for the previous year. Even worse, the difference increases from quarter to quarter. Thus, what at first seemed a mild improvement is now seen to be a disastrous decline (at least over the previous year's performance). Of course, this is a very extreme case, but it does illustrate the dangers of not carrying out a thorough analysis.

Just how this analysis is performed is the subject of the next chapter. It will allow us to appraise figures and to make informed forecasts. What it will not do, however, is 'tell the future'. Statistics, as has been stressed, deals mainly with uncertainty, and there is nothing more uncertain than the future.

5 Determining the trend

Figures which change over time

One type of bivariate data which is of particular importance to business is that in which one of the variables is time. The other variable is then said to form a 'time series'. In general figures are given for regular time intervals.

Self-check

What data in the scenario forms a time series?

TABLE 17. QUARTERLY SALES FIGURES OF BABY GOURMET FOOD FOR 1978–80 (£1000)

Year	*Quarter*	*Sales*
1978	1	100
	2	100
	3	94
	4	86
1979	1	88
	2	84
	3	79
	4	72
1980	1	73
	2	65
	3	63
	4	56

In the scenario, the company's monthly or yearly sales form such a series. A time series can be most clearly exhibited by drawing a graph, as outlined in Chapter 9 in Volume *1*. Note that, conventionally, we always put time along the bottom. For example, suppose we had figures for quarterly* sales of Baby Gourmet foods as shown in table 17.

Self-check

Draw a *scatter diagram* of this data.

Such a scatter diagram appears in figure 38(a). If we want simply to display these figures, it is usual merely to join adjacent points by straight lines, so forming a graph.

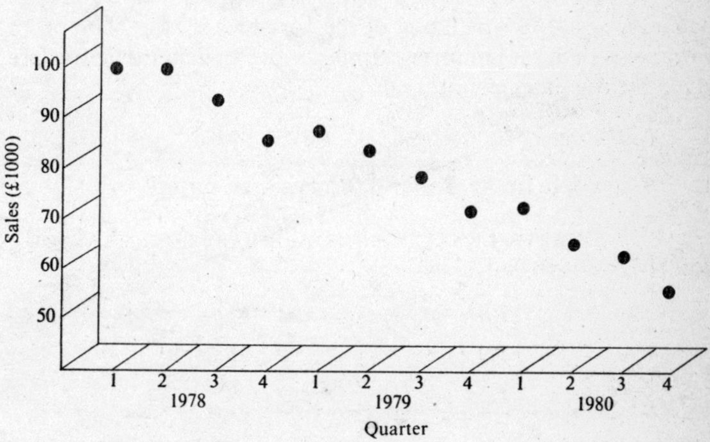

Figure 38(a). Scatter diagram for table 17

Self-check

Do this to the points in your scatter diagram.

*Quarterly figures are used instead of monthly ones to simplify the calculating.

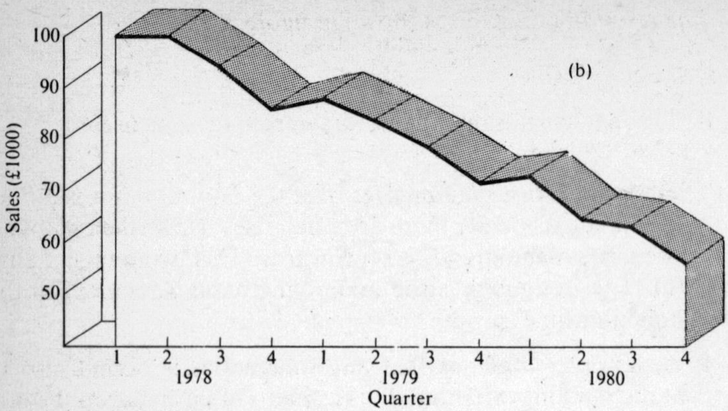
(b)
Sales (£1000)
100
90
80
70
60
50
1 2 3 4 1 2 3 4 1 2 3 4
1978
1979
1980
Quarter

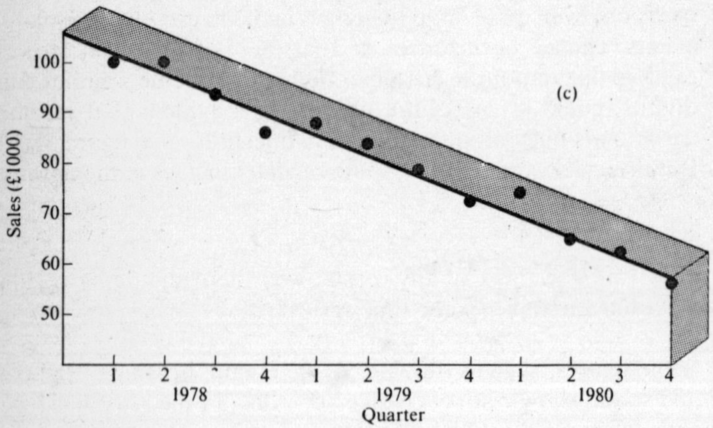
(c)
Sales (£1000)
100
90
80
70
60
50
1 2 3 4 1 2 3 4 1 2 3 4
1978
1979
1980
Quarter

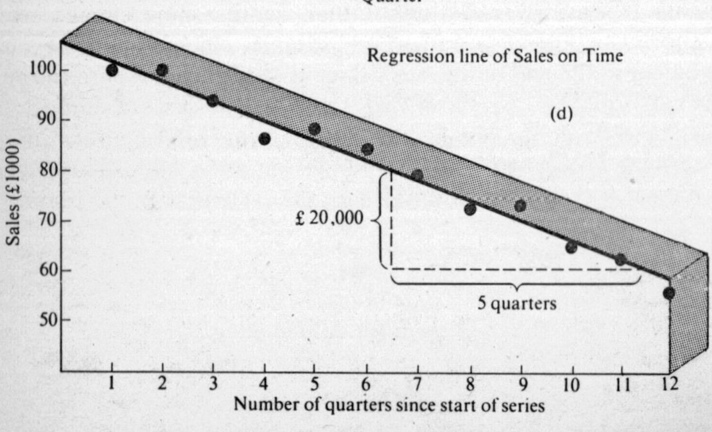
Regression line of Sales on Time
(d)
Sales (£1000)
100
90
80
70
60
50
£ 20,000
5 quarters
1 2 3 4 5 6 7 8 9 10 11 12
Number of quarters since start of series

The result of doing this is shown in figure 38(b).

Self-check

What conclusions can we draw from these figures?

There is an obvious fall in sales over the period, but it is not an even one; occasionally there are small rises. Nevertheless, overall we can say the 'trend' is downwards. This is shown in figure 38(c). The trend is thus the underlying basic movement of the figures over time.

It is, however, obvious that any time series is bound also to contain 'random variation' that is small – or perhaps, on the odd occasion, even quite large – changes in the figures due to isolated events, chance occurrences and so on. For example, strikes, random fluctuations in customer demand, extreme weather conditions, could all affect the figures. It is evident that random variation is present in the figures in question – see figure 38(b). But there also appear to be some *regular* changes in the figures.

Self-check

Can you think of any reason why there should be regular fluctuations in some time series?

Some figures, such as the sales of ice cream, heating oil, gloves and so on, show distinct change according to the season. This is called 'seasonal variation'. Other figures show change over shorter or longer periods. For example, cinema audiences are higher at the end of the week than at other times. There is some evidence, also, to show that some businesses are subject to changes over 'cycles' lasting several years. In general, this is termed 'cyclical variation'. Seasonal variation is thus the special name for cyclical variation, where the cycle time is one year.

Figure 38(b). Graph of data in table 17
Figure 38(c). Line of best fit for data in table 17
Figure 38(d). Regression line of sales on time

Let's go over what different basic components of a time series we have identified, with the help of figure 39.

First we start with the raw figures. Figure 39(a) shows these, where the heights of the bars represent the monthly figures. From even a casual look it seems that there is a general increase over the year, but there are fluctuations.

If the yearly total is averaged out over each month, this would give the figure represented by the dotted line. This gives us a base from which to work, and on top of which we can superimpose the components of the time series. It is these components which you will be shown how to calculate in the rest of this chapter. But the rest of figure 39 can give you a general picture of what they are.

The first is the trend, shown in figure 39(b). This shows a steady increase over the year. The figures it gives can be taken to be the basic, underlying ones to which we can add the other components.

The second is the seasonal variation, shown in figure 39(c). This is drawn as a set of differences from the mean. Where the bar goes below the dotted line, it is to be subtracted from the trend. Where it goes above it is to be added. So, here, the seasonal effect reduces the figures in summer and raises them in winter.

Note that there may be more than one cycle involved. For example, cinema audiences in the evenings are lower in the summer as well as being higher at the weekends.

The last component is the random variation. This is also shown as differences from the mean – as in figure 39(d). Unlike the seasonal variation, it shows no particular pattern. There would be something wrong if it did. Here, too, when it is shown above the dotted line it is to be added and when it is below it is to be subtracted.

Adding (or subtracting) the seasonal variation and the random variation to the trend gives the raw data of figure 39(a).

Figure 39. Components of time series (with seasonal variation) over one year

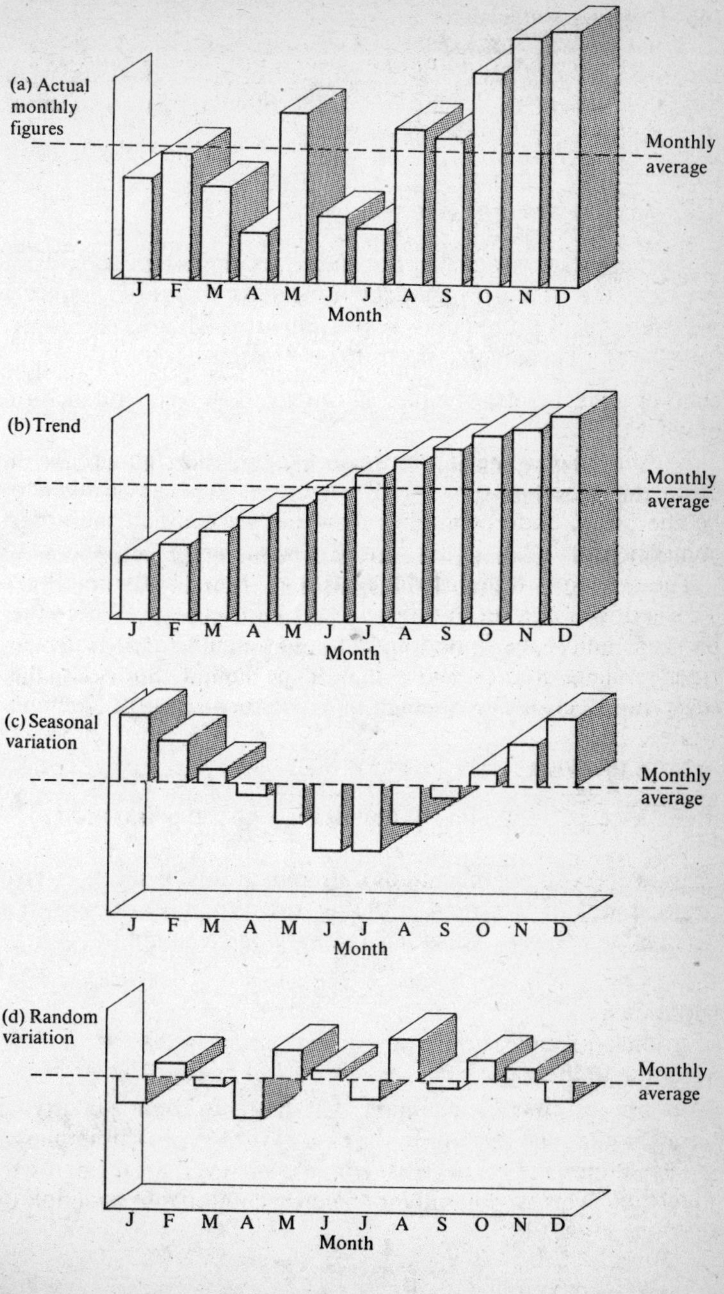

(a) Actual monthly figures
Monthly average
J F M A M J J A S O N D
Month
(b) Trend
Monthly average
J F M A M J J A S O N D
Month
(c) Seasonal variation
Monthly average
J F M A M J J A S O N D
Month
(d) Random variation
Monthly average
J F M A M J J A S O N D
Month

What we want to do is the reverse; we want to take the raw figures and *break them down* into the trend, seasonal variation and random variation. This process is called 'time series analysis', and it is what this chapter is about.

Drawing a straight line

Now there is no reason why bivariate data of this type should not be treated as the bivariate data in the second part of Chapter 4 was. That is, we could draw regression lines. There is, however, one point especially that needs to be stressed.

Self-check

Would it be sensible to draw the regression line of time on the sales figures?

We can safely assume that there will be no 'error' component in the time values. March 1979 is, after all, March 1979 and that's all there is to it, for example. The sales figures, on the other hand, would certainly be subject to random 'fluctuations' from a variety of causes, as noted earlier. Thus the only regression line that could sensibly be drawn is that of sales on time.

Self-check

By eye, draw a line of best fit through the points plotted.

Figure 38(c) shows the author's attempt at this. It seems to give a good idea of the trend in the figures. When we draw such a line, however, we are making a rather large assumption.

Self-check

What is it?

We are, of course, assuming that there is some underlying straight line relationship. In the case of time series this implies a constant increase, or decrease, or an even level, for the figure in question. This is generally a somewhat untenable assumption over the long term, though it may hold better over the short term.

Self-check

Can you think why, after removing all cyclical, seasonal and *random* fluctuations, what is left may not be a straight line?

There is no reason for sales to increase or decrease steadily. They might well be expected to correlate fairly highly with the birthrate, which itself fluctuates, a sales drive may increase the market share, competition may 'hot up' and reduce the market share, and so on. There are thus many reasons, on the other hand, why we should be careful of assuming a linear relationship.

While of limited use, linear regression techniques are employed to obtain the trend where, over the period of time concerned, it is not an unreasonable assumption that it is a linear one. Plotting the graph gives a guide as to whether or not that is so. The regression line, as seen in Chapter 4, will remove the random variation; but what about cyclical variation?

Self-check

What effect do you think assuming a linear trend will have on any cyclical variation present in the figures?

The effect is that it will be treated just as if it was random variation. In practice, this is perfectly satisfactory as this has the desired effect of removing it from the figures.

There is, however, a particular problem in drawing the regression line with time series and that is one of giving values to the time variable. We cannot use the quarter numbers, as they repeat themselves. What we do in such cases is to number the quarters, from the start, 1, 2, 3 . . . 12. Thus we are in effect establishing a new variable, 'the number of quarters since the start of the series'. (Note that there are other ways of allocating values to the time variable, but we shall only use this one here.)

Self-check

Bearing this in mind, draw the regression line of sales on time for the figures in table 17 and comment on the result.

TABLE 18. TOTALS FOR CALCULATING THE SLOPE OF THE REGRESSION LINE FROM THE FIGURES IN TABLE 17

Column 1 *Time (Number of quarters since start of time series)*	*Column 2* *Sales*	*Column 3* *(Column 1)²*	*Column 4* *(Column 2)²*	*Column 5* *(Column 1) × (Column 2)*
1	100	1	10,000	100
2	100	4	10,000	200
3	94	9	8836	282
4	86	16	7396	344
5	88	25	7744	440
6	84	36	7056	504
7	79	49	6241	553
8	72	64	5184	576
9	73	81	5329	657
10	65	100	4225	650
11	63	121	3969	693
12	56	144	3136	672
78	960	650	79,116	5671

The totals required to calculate the slope of this regression line are shown in table 18. The covariance is

$$\frac{\text{col. 5}}{12} - \frac{\text{col. 1}}{12} \times \frac{\text{col. 2}}{12} = \frac{5671}{12} - \frac{78}{12} \times \frac{960}{12}$$

$= 472.6 - 6.5 \times 80 = 472.6 - 520 = -47.4$ (to one decimal place).

The variance of 'time' is

$$\frac{\text{col. 3}}{12} - \left(\frac{\text{col. 1}}{12}\right)^2 = \frac{650}{12} - \left(\frac{78}{12}\right)^2$$

$= 54.2 - 6.5^2 = 54.2 - 42.3 = 11.9$ (to one decimal place).

The slope of the regression line is thus

$\frac{\text{covariance}}{\text{variance of time}} = \frac{-47.4}{11.9} = -3.98$ (to two decimal places). That is, a decrease of about £20,000 in sales over five quarters.

Furthermore, we know that this regression line passes through the point corresponding to the two means, which are $\frac{78}{12}$ and $\frac{960}{12}$, i.e. 6.5 and 80. The regression line thus appears as shown in figure 38(d). Note that it is actually fairly near to the author's guess. The interpretation of this line is the same as that for the guess: it shows a steady loss of sales revenue.

Self-check

For the figures in table 19, find the slope of the regression line of value of output on time and the two means.

TABLE 19. VALUE OF CONSTRUCTION OUTPUT IN THE UK (£ TEN MILLION) 1974–6

	Quarter			
Year	*1*	*2*	*3*	*4*
1974	233	254	264	253
1975	261	286	300	295
1976	296	312	320	325

(Source: *Monthly Digest of Statistics*, December 1977)

Using the totals as shown in table 20 the covariance is

$$\frac{\text{col. 5}}{12} - \frac{\text{col. 1}}{12} \times \frac{\text{col. 2}}{12} = \frac{23{,}230}{12} - \frac{78}{12} \times \frac{3399}{12}$$

$= 1935.8 - 6.5 \times 283.3 = 1935.8 - 1841.5 = 94.3$ (to one decimal place).

The variance of 'time' is

$$\frac{\text{col. 3}}{12} - \left(\frac{\text{col. 1}}{12}\right)^2 = \frac{650}{12} - \left(\frac{78}{12}\right)^2 = 11.9 \text{ (as earlier).}$$

The slope of the regression line is thus $\frac{94.3}{11.9} = 7.92$ (to two decimal places).

The two means are $\frac{\text{col. 1}}{12} = \frac{78}{12} = 6.5$ for the 'time' and $\frac{\text{col. 2}}{12} = \frac{3399}{12} = 283.25$ for the value of output (in £10,000,000).

TABLE 20. TOTALS FOR CALCULATING THE SLOPE OF THE REGRESSION LINE FROM THE FIGURES IN TABLE 19

Column 1 Time (number of quarters from start)	*Column 2* Value of output (£10,000,000)	*Column 3* (Column 1)^2	*Column 4* (Column 2)^2	*Column 5* (Column 1) × (Column 2)
1	233	1	54,289	233
2	254	4	64,516	508
3	264	9	69,696	792
4	253	16	64,009	1012
5	261	25	68,121	1305
6	286	36	81,796	1716
7	300	49	90,000	2100
8	295	64	87,025	2360
9	296	81	87,616	2664
10	312	100	97,344	3120
11	320	121	102,400	3520
12	325	144	105,625	3900
78	3399	650	972,437	23,230

Looking into the future

One of the main tasks of statistics is to make forecasts. When we take a trend and assume it will continue into the future we are doing just that. In this case, however, we give it a special name, 'extrapolation'. This was explained in Chapter 9 in Volume *1*. Basically, we can only extrapolate if we have got a regular pattern for the trend. A straight line is such a pattern and is, indeed, the simplest one. For this reason it is the one most often used.

Straight line extrapolation involves continuing the regression line, or whatever, on into the future. Take the line in figure 38(d) for example.

Self-check

What would be the value of the trend line forecast for the quarterly sales values in 1981?

If the trend line in figure 38(d) is assumed to continue unchanged, then each quarter will see a drop of 3.98 (£1000) which we have rounded to 4 (£1000): this is, in fact, the (negative) slope of the line. Now the value on the trend line at the end of 1980 is, from figure 38(d), 58 (£1000). The projected quarterly trend line figures for 1981 are thus (in £1000):

1st quarter	58 − 4 = 54
2nd quarter	54 − 4 = 50
3rd quarter	50 − 4 = 46
4th quarter	46 − 4 = 42

Self-check

Use the results of the self-check on page 171 to forecast the quarterly trend values of output for 1977.

The first part could be done by drawing the trend line and projecting it forwards. We will use the figures themselves here. We know the trend line passes through the point corresponding to the two means, which are 6.5 and 283.25. The slope (upward) is 7.92 (£10,000,000) per quarter. We are interested in 'time' values of 13, 14, 15 and 16. These are at $13 - 6.5 = 6.5$, $14 - 6.5 = 7.5$, $15 - 6.5 = 8.5$ and $16 - 6.5 = 9.5$ quarters from the mean point respectively. Because the slope is 7.92, the corresponding values of output must be 283.25 plus 6.5×7.92 for the first quarter of 1977, 7.5×7.92 for the second, 8.5×7.92 for the third and 9.5×7.92 for the fourth. These come out to (to the nearest £10,000,000), 335, 343, 351 and 358.

Now if all the variation away from the trend line in the figures of table 17 can be accounted for by random fluctuations, these figures are the best guess that can be made for the actual quarterly sales figures in 1981. By their very nature, random variations cannot be predicted. If, however, we have any reason to suspect seasonal variation in the figures, these forecasts would need modification.

Calculating the seasonal effects

So what we need, then, is a way of calculating how much we should add to, or subtract from, these figures to take into account seasonal variation. In order to see how we can do this, let us examine the differences between the values on the trend line and the quarterly sales figures themselves.

> *Self-check*
>
> Read off and record the figures from the trend line corresponding to the twelve quarter ends from your regression line for the Baby Gourmet sales figures.

The author's estimates for these figures are shown below, together with the actual sales and the differences between them.

Year	*Quarter*	*Sales figure (£1000)*	*Estimated trend figure (£1000)*	*Difference*
1978	1	100	102	− 2
	2	100	98	+ 2
	3	94	94	0
	4	86	90	− 4
1979	1	88	86	+ 2
	2	84	82	+ 2
	3	79	78	+ 1
	4	72	74	− 2
1980	1	73	70	+ 3
	2	65	66	− 1
	3	63	62	+ 1
	4	56	58	− 2

The differences, *on the assumption of a linear trend*, must be due to either random or seasonal variation or a combination of both.

As was indicated earlier, there is very little that can be done about the random component as it is unpredictable. But the seasonal variation, by definition, behaves regularly. Look at figure 40. This shows a time series with zero trend and strong seasonal variation. The average figure per quarter is 3.25 and is shown as a dotted line. Since there is zero trend, this is the trend line (as it passes through the point corresponding to the two means). On the first quarter of every year the actual figure is 1.75 higher than the trend figure, on the second, .25 lower, on the third 2.25 lower and on the fourth .75 higher.

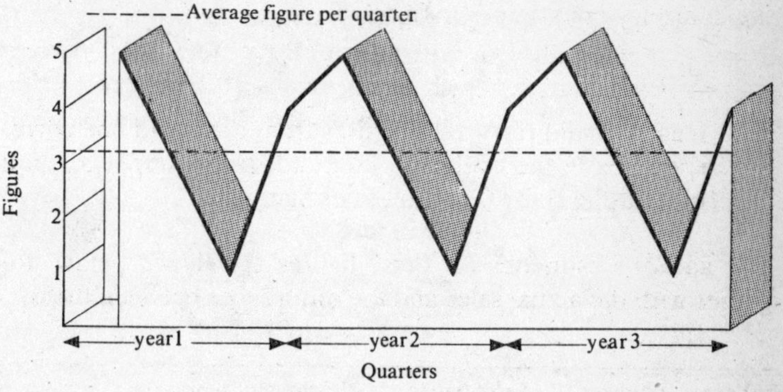

Figure 40. Quarterly figures with zero trend and strong seasonal variations

Self-check

If 'lower' values are negative, and 'higher' positive, add up these differences. What do you find?

Adding them up we get 1.75 − .25 − 2.25 + .75 = 0. So the differences between the actual and trend figures will add up to zero over *any* yearly period; that is, starting at any quarter.

This result will remain true in all cases where the additions and subtractions due to seasonal variations are constant. In practice this is only true for cases where the trend is not very pronounced. For example, the seasonal variation on ice-cream sales will not be an 'additive' constant if sales rocket; it will generally be proportional to those sales. That is, the greater the sales the greater the value of the seasonal variation (and vice versa), though it may stay at a constant *proportion*. The techniques described in this chapter will not deal with cases other than the simple 'additive' model.

What we need to do, then, is to separate out the seasonal from the random variation in the differences, above, for the Baby Gourmet sales figures. If we assume the additive model, we can take it that, over any yearly period, these differences will add up to *zero*, and will be the same for each corresponding quarter. Now this is obviously not true of the differences as they stand. This is because they also contain the random variation. The first step in removing this is to average out the differences over the years for each quarter, which should remove a great deal of the random variation. The calculations for the Baby Gourmet sales figures are:

Year	*Difference for quarter* 1	2	3	4	
1978	−2	+2	0	−4	
1979	+2	+2	+1	−2	
1980	+3	−1	+1	−2	
Totals	3	3	2	−8	
Average	1.00 +	1.00 +	.67 +	−2.67	= 0

These averages add up to zero as they should for seasonal variation.

Such averages do not always add up to zero, because of rounding errors and so on, particularly when the other methods of estimating the trend are used as described later in this chapter. Look at the following set of differences obtained from some other sales figures (£1000).

Year	*Difference for quarter* 1	2	3	4	
1978	−1	+3	+1	−3	
1979	+3	+2	+1	+2	
1980	+3	−1	0	−3	
Totals	5	4	2	−4	
Average	1.67 +	1.33 +	.67 +	−1.33	= 2.34

Since they do not add up to zero, we cannot take these figures to be the seasonal adjustments. We must remove some more random variations from them. To do this we subtract (or in other cases, add) some number to each of them so as to make their sum zero.

Self-check

What would this need to be here?

Because they add up to 2.34, we must subtract $\frac{2.34}{4}$ = .585 from each. This gives average differences for the four quarters:

	1.67	− .585	=	1.085
	1.33	− .585	=	.745
	.67	− .585	=	.085
	−1.33	− .585	=	−1.915
Totals	2.34	− 2.340	=	0.000

We can use the seasonal variation to predict future figures of the projected values for 1981 for other sales figures using the projected trend figures below:

Quarter in 1981	*Trend*
1	55.2
2	51.4
3	47.6
4	43.8

Now the trend, by definition, does not take into account the seasonal variation.

Self-check

How do you think we could do so?

To obtain the forecast sales figures for the four quarters of 1981, we need to add these 'adjusted' differences, above, to the trend line estimates obtained previously. We thus get:

Forecast sales figures for 1981 (£1000)

1st quarter	55.2 + 1.085 = 56.285 (56)
2nd quarter	51.4 + .745 = 52.145 (52)
3rd quarter	47.6 + .085 = 47.685 (48)
4th quarter	43.8 − 1.915 = 41.885 (42)

The figures in the brackets are to the nearest £1000.

Self-check

Find the amounts of quarterly seasonal variation in the figures given in table 20. Use this, together with your trend forecasts, to produce estimates of the values of quarterly output in 1977.

The trend line values for the twelve quarters in 1974–76 can be obtained in a similar way to the projections for 1977. The trend line value of output changes by 7.92 (£0,000,000) per quarter and it is 283.25 (£0,000,000) at 'time' 6.5. At 'time' 1 (the first quarter of 1974), then, it was 283.25 − 5.5 × 7.92 = 283.25 − 43.56 = 239.69 (£0,000,000) or 240 (to the nearest £10,000,000). At each successive quarter this will be 7.92 (£0,000,000) more. The quarterly values together with the differences from the actual values and the means of such quarterly differences are:

	Value of output − trend line value = difference for quarters			
Year	*1*	*2*	*3*	*4*
1974	233 − 240 = − 7	254 − 248 = 6	264 − 256 = 8	253 − 263 = −10
1975	261 − 271 = −10	286 − 279 = 7	300 − 287 = 13	295 − 295 = 0
1976	296 − 303 = − 7	312 − 311 = 1	320 − 319 = 1	325 − 327 = − 2
Total diff.	−24	14	22	−12
Average diff.	− 8	+4.7	+7.3	− 4

Here the mean differences add up to zero as they should to give the seasonal variation (note that your results may, through different methods of calculation giving different rounding errors, be slightly different and have needed adjustment). If we add this seasonal variation to the trend line forecasts already found for the 1977 figures, we get the following estimates:

Quarter	*Estimate*
1	335 − 8 = 327
2	343 + 4.7 = 348 (to nearest £10 million)
3	351 + 7.3 = 358 (to nearest £10 million)
4	358 − 4 = 354

Compare these estimates with the actual figures for 1977 which were:

Value of construction output in the UK (£10 million) 1977

1st quarter	313
2nd "	338
3rd "	359
4th "	360

To summarize then, to calculate the seasonal variation:

1 Calculate the differences between the trend and the raw figures, i.e. raw data – trend, making sure to record when they are negative.
2 Average out these differences over the number of corresponding months/quarters for which data is available, taking into account sign.
3 Add up these averages, taking into account sign. If they come to zero you have found the seasonal variation.
4 If they do not, divide the sum obtained by 4 (for quarters) or 12 (for months) and subtract the result from each of the figures calculated in 2, taking into account sign. The resultant figures then give the seasonal variation.

Review

The following figures are for the quarterly* unemployment percentages in the UK 1973–6 (source: *Monthly Digest of Statistics*):

Year	*Quarter**			
	1	*2*	*3*	*4*
1973	3.1	2.5	2.4	2.2
1974	2.7	2.3	2.8	2.9†
1975	3.4	3.7	4.9	5.1
1976	5.5	5.6	6.2	5.8

1 Draw a graph for these figures. What do you think the general trend is? Can you detect any evidence of seasonal variation? If so, what do you think causes it?
2 Draw the regression line of unemployment percentage on time for the data. Using this regression line, determine the seasonal variation.
3 Using your answers, produce forecasts for the first two quarterly unemployment rates in 1977. The actual figures were 5.9 and 6.2. How do the two sets compare? Why don't they necessarily agree?

ANSWERS

1 The graph for these figures is shown in figure 41. The general trend is obviously upward, so much so that it is difficult to see if there is any seasonal variation. There does, however, appear to be some. Winter seems, on the whole, to be a worse time than summer. This, presumably, reflects the fact that many jobs are seasonal, e.g. the building trade, with more of these in summer than in winter.
2 The regression line is calculated as follows:

Mean 'time' value is $\frac{1 + 2 + 3 \ldots 14 + 15 + 16}{16} = \frac{136}{16} = 8.5.$

*Figures actually as of about the tenth day of last month in the quarter; that is, March, June, September and December.
†Estimated (because of industrial action).

While the mean percentage unemployment is

$$\frac{3.1+2.5+2.4+2.2+2.7+2.3+2.8+2.9+3.4+3.7+4.9+5.1+5.5+5.6+6.2+5.8}{16}$$

$= \frac{61.1}{16} = 3.82$ (to two decimal places).

The covariance is thus

$$\frac{1 \times 3.1 + 2 \times 2.5 + 3 \times 2.4 \ldots 14 \times 5.6 + 15 \times 6.2 + 16 \times 5.8}{16} - 8.5 \times 3.82$$

$= \frac{612.6}{16} - 32.47 = 38.29$ (to two decimal places) $- 32.47 =$ 5.82.

To get the regression line of *percentage unemployed on time* we have to calculate the variance of the 'time' variable. (Did you remember that this was the one that was required?)

The variance is

$$\frac{1^2+2^2+3^2+4^2+5^2+6^2+7^2+8^2+9^2+10^2+11^2+12^2+13^2+14^2+15^2+16^2}{16}$$

$- 8.5^2 = \frac{1496}{16} - 72.25 = 93.5 - 72.25 = 21.25.$

The regression line, then, passes through the mean point, 8.5 and 3.82, and has a slope equal to $\frac{5.82}{21.25} = .27$ (to two decimal places) or 1.35 in 5.

This line is shown in figure 41.

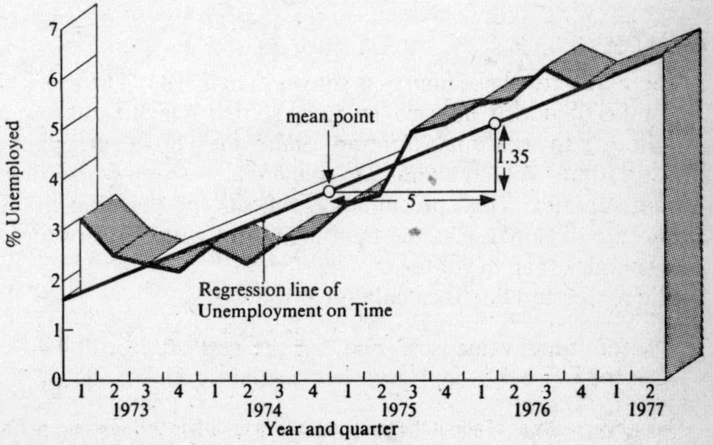

Figure 41. Graph of figures for review on page 180

From the graph, the differences between the regression line and the raw data are:

Year	Quarter 1	Quarter 2	Quarter 3	Quarter 4
1973	3.1	2.5	2.4	2.2
	−1.8 = 1.3	−2.0 = 0.5	−2.3 = 0.1	−2.6 = −0.4
1974	2.7	2.3	2.8	2.9 +
	−2.9 = −0.2	−3.1 = −0.8	−3.4 = −0.6	−3.7 = −0.8
1975	3.4	3.7	4.9	5.1
	−4.0 = −0.6	−4.2 = −0.5	−4.5 = 0.4	−4.8 = 0.3
1976	5.5	5.6	6.2	5.8
	−5.0 = 0.5	−5.3 = 0.3	−5.6 = 0.6	−5.8 = 0.0
Quarterly total	1.0	−0.5	0.5	−0.9
Average per quarter	0.25	−0.125	0.125	−0.225

Since this total does not add up to zero but to 0.025, we must adjust each average by $\frac{0.025}{4} = 0.00625$.

The adjusted seasonal variation is then

$$\begin{aligned} 0.25 - 0.00625 &= 0.24375 \text{ for quarter 1} \\ -0.125 - 0.00625 &= -0.13125 \text{ for quarter 2} \\ 0.125 - 0.00625 &= 0.11875 \text{ for quarter 3} \\ -0.225 - 0.00625 &= -0.23125 \text{ for quarter 4} \end{aligned}$$

You will note that these now add up to zero.

Did you remember to make the adjustment to the figures so that the seasonal variation added up to zero?

3 The regression line gives values of 6.1 and 6.4 for the unemployment percentages for the first two quarters of 1977, respectively. To get the forecast figures we have to add on the seasonal variation. For the first quarter this is 0.24 (to two decimal places) and for the second it is −0.13 (to two decimal places). The forecasts are then, for the first quarter of 1977: $6.1 + 0.24 = 6.34$; and for the second quarter of 1977: $6.4 - 0.13 = 6.27$.

The figure for the second quarter is, in fact, remarkably accurate. That for the first is not so good. We would not expect to get a very good prediction using this method as the underlying trend in the figures is very unlikely to be linear. Government policy and world economic conditions will, amongst other factors, have a strong effect on unemployment, and these will cause sudden changes in the trend, so as to make forecasting very difficult.

Smoothing out the fluctuations supposing there were no trend

If we are not convinced that the trend is linear, we need either to use more complex regression techniques to fit to the curves, 'curvilinear regression', or to smooth out the variation in some other way. Most commonly, this would be by summing the figures over a period of time. Just for the purpose of illustration, suppose that we have available a set of figures for which (a) there is zero trend; that is, no steady increase or decrease; (b) there is a large and regular seasonal variation; and (c) random variation has been eliminated somehow.

Figure 40 shows such a set of figures (which we have used before).

Self-check

If you were to add up the figures in figure 40 for each year what would you find?

You would find that they would be the same for each year. This is because the same figures are repeated each year.

Self-check

Would we have got the same result for the totals of every three successive quarters?

No we wouldn't. Suppose, for instance, that the actual figures for the quarters in each year were 5, 3, 1 and 4. Then successive three-quarterly totals would be:

$$5 + 3 + 1 = 9$$
$$3 + 1 + 4 = 8$$
$$1 + 4 + 5 = 10$$
$$4 + 5 + 3 = 12$$
$$5 + 3 + 1 = 9$$

and so on.

Self-check

Would we get a similar effect if we totalled *not* over calendar years but over some other four-quarterly period, e.g. quarters 3 and 4 of one year and 1 and 2 of the next?

Using the same figures as above, and actually doing the totalling as in the examples, we get

$$1 + 4 + 5 + 3 = 13$$
$$\text{and } 1 + 4 + 5 + 3 = 13,$$

so we do get the same figures each time. Of course, we do not get so many totals, since we have to ignore the end figures. Thus we see that, if we add up the figures *for the period of the cycle* (in this case a year), we smooth out the cyclical (or seasonal) variation.

What is less obvious is that the same process should also remove the random variation. In order to see this we need to examine a little closer what we mean by random variation. It is, in fact, part of its essence that it should be unbiased; that is, it should not tend, over any long period of time, to either increase the figures more than decrease them, or vice versa. Thus, if we add up the figures over a reasonable period, *the sum of the random variations should be zero*. Since this is precisely what we were doing above, it should have this effect. Of course, in practice, there is always the odd bit of random variation left over on any occasion, but the probability of this having any great effect is very low.

Smoothing out the fluctuations when there is a trend

Now there is no reason why the process above should not be used where there is a trend. Of course, we should not then expect to get the same total for each period, but the random and cyclical fluctuations should be removed. Take the figures in table 19, for instance. When the graph of these is plotted it looks as in figure 42. There is an obvious upward trend in these figures, and also some evident seasonal variation.

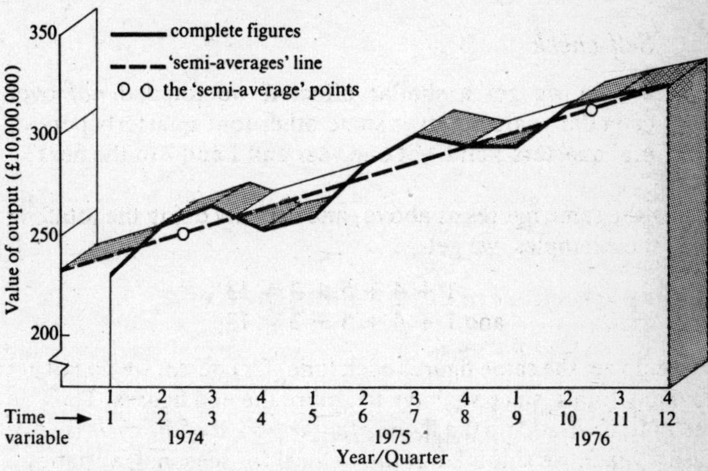

Figure 42. Graph of figures in table 19

Self-check

What are the totals for the three years and the quarterly averages? What do you notice about them?

The totals and quarterly averages are (in £10,000,000):

1974	233
	254
	264
	253
	1004/4 = 251

1975	261
	286
	300
	295
	1142/4 = 285.5
1976	296
	312
	320
	325
	1253/4 = 313.25

These show an increase over the three years, but not a constant one. The quarterly averages thus do not fall on a straight line.

A simple method of determining the trend

Now we could plot these quarterly averages on the graph and join the three points. This would, however, be very unsatisfactory: it would be neither a good straight line nor a clear indication of the detailed trend. The crudest solution is to ignore the middle average and join up the other two. This line is also shown on figure 42. Since this technique is *similar* to one called 'the method of semi-averages', it is labelled 'semi-average' line. In the semi-averages method *proper*, the values in any centre period are split between the two halves and included in their average. Note that, since the two values of output figures represent *averages*, they must be plotted against the average time of the period for which they are the average. In this case we would, as earlier, have to allocate values of 1, 2, 3. . .12 to the time variable. The time average would then be $\frac{1 + 2 + 3 + 4}{4} = 2.5$ for the left half and $\frac{9 + 10 + 11 + 12}{4} = 10.5$ for the right.

The general application of this method to cases where there are more than three cycles merely involves averaging over a longer period. In fact, the cycles are split into two complete halves. The average figure (per quarter or month or whatever) for *each half* is then calculated. These results are then plotted and a line drawn joining them. For example, suppose the figures for 1977 are added to table 17 and that these are 107, 109, 100 and 96 for the four quarters. The two averages are then (in £1,000):

	107	
1977	109	
	100	
	96	1st half
	100	
1978	100	
	94	
	86	
	792/8	= 99
and	88	
1979	84	
	79	
	72	2nd half
	73	
	65	
1980	63	
	56	
	580/8	= 72.5

These values would be plotted on a graph, against the average 'times' of each half and joined by a straight line.

Self-check

Suppose that, in addition, the 1981 figures for table 17 are:

Quarter	*Sales (£1000)*
1	60
2	52
3	48
4	43

What two points would be used to draw the proper semi-averages line for the 1977–1981 figures?

As there are now five years, the middle one (1979) is split while 1977 and 1978 form one half and 1980 and 1981 the other. The two averages are:

	107		79
	109	1979	72
1977	100		73
	96	1980	65
	100		63
	100		56
1978	94		60
	86	1981	52
1979	88		48
	84		43
	964/10 = 96.4		611/10 = 61.1

These two figures are then plotted against the average 'times' for each half. These are $\frac{1 + 2 + \ldots 10}{10} = 5.5$ and $\frac{11 + 12 + \ldots 20}{10} = 15.5$.

Of course, we are back to the straight line again, and one not as accurate as the regression line either though it may be used to give rough predictions. We were trying to find a non-linear trend, so the next section deals with just that.

Running annual totals

We saw in the last section how adding up the figures over a complete cycle 'irons out' both cyclical and random variation. It was also pointed out that it did not matter where the start and end of the cycle were positioned. For example, seasonal variation need not be looked at from 1 January to 31 December, this is a purely arbitrary span as far as the figures themselves are concerned. We could thus obtain a number of different 'annual' totals of the figures in a time series, depending upon where we started the year. Let's look at the figures in table 19 again. We have, in the last section, already calculated the January–December totals. These are shown in table 21, together with the three other period totals possible with quarterly figures, namely April–March, July–June and October–September. It also shows the yearly cumulative totals, which will be used later.

TABLE 21. ANNUAL TOTALS (WITH VARIOUS START DATES) FOR THE DATA IN TABLE 19 (IN £10,000,000)

Year	*Quarter*	*Value*	*Yearly cumulative value*	*Total: Jan.–Dec.*	*Total: Apr.–Mar.*	*Total: Jul.–Jun.*	*Total: Oct.–Sep.*
1974	1	233	233				
	2	254	487				
	3	264	751				
	4	253	1004	1004			
1975	1	261	261		1032		
	2	286	547			1064	
	3	300	847				1100
	4	295	1142	1142			
1976	1	296	296		1177		
	2	312	608			1203	
	3	320	928				1223
	4	325	1253	1253			

Note that the period totals appear against the last quarter in that period. So, for instance, the total, 1100, for quarter 4 of 1974 and quarters 1, 2 and 3 of 1975, appears against the third quarter of 1975. As these periods start and end at different points, there is only *one* total appearing against any quarter. It represents the sum of the figures for that, and the three preceding quarters. These totals can, then, all be combined to give a single set of figures. Because they are all annual totals, and because they 'move along' from quarter to quarter, they are called 'moving annual totals' (MAT). It is evident that there can be no moving annual totals for the first three quarters of a series, as there are not three preceding quarters' figures to sum. The moving annual totals for the data in table 19 are thus:

Year	*Quarter*	*MAT (£10,000,000)*
1974	1	–
	2	–
	3	–
	4	1004
1975	1	1032
	2	1064
	3	1100
	4	1142
1976	1	1177
	2	1203
	3	1223
	4	1253

It is common to display the original figures, the cumulative total and moving annual total figures for a year together on one graph. This is called a 'Z-chart'.

Self-check

Plot the Z-chart for 1975 of the above figures.

This chart appears in figure 43. In practice, Z-charts are more usually drawn with monthly figures. They show several aspects of the figures all at once and are useful for getting a broad picture. The moving annual totals themselves reflect any underlying movements in the figures, because the seasonal and random variation has been smoothed out of them. It is always useful to see the original figures on a graph, as it gives a clearer picture of what is happening. The cumulative total is also of interest because its slope shows how fast business is increasing, or not, as the case may be. The chart's name is derived from the fact that it looks like a Z, because the first monthly (or quarterly) figure coincides with the start of the cumulative total line, which, itself, meets the MAT line at its end.

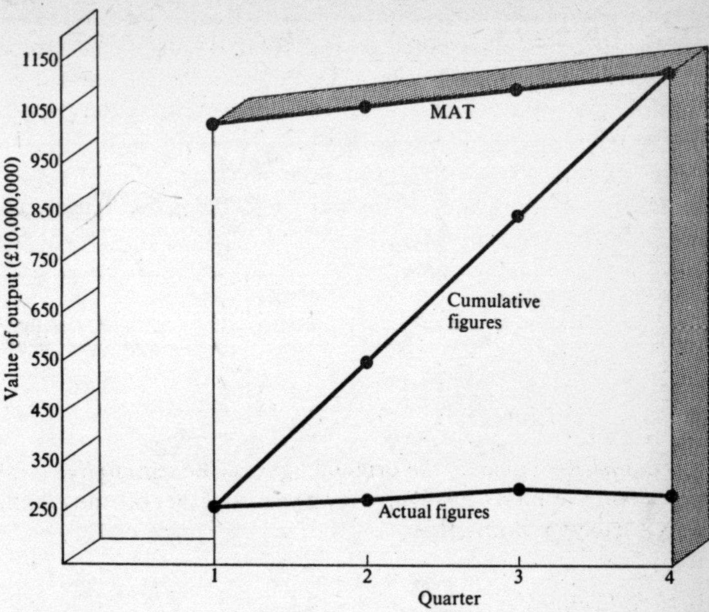

Figure 43. Z-chart of data in table 19 for 1975

Moving the average along

While the moving annual total reflects the trend, the figures it gives are, of course, yearly totals and so cannot be directly compared with the quarterly (or monthly or whatever) figures. In order to do this we may divide each figure by 4 (for quarters, or 12 for months) to give what is then known as a 'moving average'. Unfortunately, this does create some small difficulty where, as with quarterly or monthly figures, there is an even number of figures in the cycle. The reason for this lies in the way the average points are plotted.

You may recall from the discussion on the method of semi-averages that an average for any period must be plotted against the average of the 'time' variable over that period. Now the essence of a time series is that we have figures at regular intervals of time. The time variable has a constant increment from the start of any period to its end, therefore. If there are an even number of time values in the period, their average cannot then be one of these values but must lie between two of them. For example, for time values 1, 2, 3. . .12, representing the twelve months of a year, their average is $\frac{1 + 2 + 3 \ldots 12}{12} = \frac{78}{12} = 6.5$.

For various reasons this makes the analysis difficult, so we generally average again, as follows using the same figures, to *centre* the moving average:

Time	*Quarterly figures*	*MAT*	*4-quarter average*	*Centred average*
1	233			
1.5				
2	254			
2.5			251	
3	264			+/2 = 254.5
3.5			258	
4	253	1004		+/2 = 262
4.5			266	
5	261	1032		+/2 = 270.5
5.5			275	
6	286	1064		+/2 = 280.25
6.5			285.5	
7	300	1100		+/2 = 289.875
7.5			294.25	
8	295	1142		+/2 = 297.5
8.5			300.75	
9	296	1177		+/2 = 303.25
9.5			305.75	
10	312	1203		+/2 = 309.5
10.5			313.25	
11	320	1223		
11.5				
12	325	1253		

If there are an odd number of times in the period, then the first moving average would already be centred on the middle time and so further averaging would not be required. Note there are times (quarters here) at the beginning and the end which have no moving average. It does not matter too much at the beginning, but not having ones for the times at the end is a great drawback, particularly to forecasting. Figure 44 shows the above quarterly figures and quarterly centred averages plotted together. The moving average line represents the trend figures.

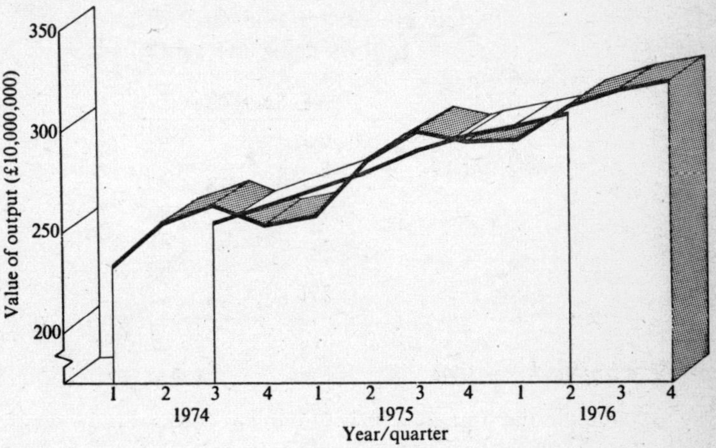

Figure 44. Quarterly figures and quarterly moving averages for data in table 19

While the method of adding up each four-quarterly moving total separately is not too arduous, doing this for twelve-monthly ones can be rather tedious. A short cut for calculating any moving total is to use the previous one, (a) deduct the first figure from it, and (b) add the next one in the series after the end of the previous period to the result. For example:

Monthly figure	*MAT*
63	
67	
68	
66	
62	
63	
65	

68	
69	
72	
65	
64	792
66	792 − 63 + 66 = 795
69	795 − 67 + 69 = 797
65	797 − 68 + 65 = 794
61	794 − 66 + 61 = 789
62	789 − 62 + 62 = 789
65	789 − 63 + 65 = 791
69	791 − 65 + 69 = 795
73	795 − 68 + 73 = 800
75	800 − 69 + 75 = 806
83	806 − 72 + 83 = 817
81	817 − 65 + 81 = 833
78	833 − 64 + 78 = 847

Self-check

Calculate the four-quarterly moving average of the data on Baby Gourmet sales in table 17.

The calculations of the moving average are:

Year	*Quarter*	*Sales*	*MAT*	*Moving average*	*Centred average*
1978	1	100			
	2	100			
				95	
	3	94			93.5
				92	
	4	86			90
				88	
1979	1	88	368		86.125
				84.25	
	2	84	352		82.5
				80.75	
	3	79	337		78.875
				77	
	4	72	323		74.625
				72.25	
1980	1	73	308		70.25
				68.25	
	2	65	289		66.25
				64.25	
	3	63	273		
	4	56	257		

In a previous section, we examined how, with a straight trend line and a knowledge of seasonal variation we could forecast future figures in the time series. Forecasting with a trend found by the moving average method is not so straightforward. A crude method would be to extrapolate the trend from that over the last time period and add the seasonal variation. This can at best operate only over a short time. But, as we have seen, the moving average lags behind the time series figures themselves (by two whole quarters for quarterly figures), so this makes that method very unreliable. For example, if we take the figures for the value of Baby Gourmet sales again, we have earlier calculated the moving average trend. Now the last two moving average trend line figures were 70.25 and 66.25. The trend over the two periods which they represent was thus −4 per quarter. Projecting this to the next quarter (quarter 3 of 1980) gives a trend line forecast of 66.25 − 4 = 62.25. We must now add in the seasonal variation for third quarter. The seasonal variation from a moving average trend can be calculated in a similar way to that for the regression line.

Self-check

Calculate the seasonal variation for the Baby Gourmet sales figures of above.

The calculations are shown below.

Year	*Quarter*	*Sales*	*Centred average*	*Difference*
1978	1	100		
	2	100		
	3	94	93.5	0.5
	4	86	90	−4
1979	1	88	86.125	1.875
	2	84	82.5	1.5
	3	79	78.875	.125
	4	72	74.625	−2.625
1980	1	73	70.25	2.75
	2	65	66.25	−1.25
	3	63		
	4	56		

The average differences for each quarter are then:

Quarter	*Differences*		*Average*
1	1.875	2.75	2.3125
2	1.5	−1.25	0.1250
3	0.5	.125	0.3125
4	−4	−2.625	−3.3125
			Total −0.5625

As they do not add up to zero, these averages have to be adjusted by subtracting −0.5625/4 = −0.140625. This gives the following seasonal variation:

Quarter	*Seasonal variation*
1	2.3125−(−0.140625) = 2.453125
2	0.1250−(−0.140625) = 0.265625
3	0.3125−(−0.140625) = 0.453125
4	−3.3125−(−0.140625) = −3.171875
	Total 0.00000

Going back to projecting the figures then, we adjust the 62.25 trend projection by 0.453125 to get projected sales of 62.7 (£1000) (to one decimal place).

But we know the figure for this period! It is 63. We are already somewhat out in our forecast, then. Projecting further would introduce even more error. However, where the underlying movement of the figures is itself rather irregular, this method is reasonably satisfactory if the irregularities occur over more than five or six time intervals, rather than with greater frequency.

Removing regular fluctuations: seasonally adjusted figures

The techniques of smoothing described up till now remove the random errors as well as the seasonal variation. But we may well want to remove *just* the latter. Suppose we had a set of figures, which showed the number of days lost through illness at a particular factory during some year. Now, we know that more people are ill in the winter than in the summer. We expect there to be some seasonal variation here then, and it would be useful to get rid of it. But we would probably be quite interested to see if any quarter was particularly good, or bad, for any other reason, including random ones such as a very cold winter. Neither the ordinary data given above, nor the trend, would do for this. All we want to eliminate is the seasonal variation itself. We have already discussed how to find this. Having done so, then, all we need to do is to *subtract* it from the figures. The result is what is called deseasonalized or seasonally adjusted data.

Self-check

Calculate the seasonally adjusted Baby Gourmet sales figures from table 17, based on the moving average.

We have already calculated the seasonal variation for these figures. The table below shows this subtracted from the original data, to give the seasonally adjusted figures:

Sales (1000)	*Seasonal variation (from earlier)*	*Seasonally adjusted sales*
100	2.45	97.55
100	0.27	99.73
94	0.45	93.55
86	−3.17	89.17
88	2.45	85.55
84	0.27	83.73
79	0.45	78.55
72	−3.17	75.17
73	2.45	70.55
65	0.27	64.73
63	0.45	62.55
56	−3.17	59.17

Self-check

Calculate the seasonally adjusted values of output from table 19, using the seasonal variation obtained earlier from the regression line.

The calculation is as follows:

Value (£10,000,000)	*Seasonal variation (from earlier)*	*Seasonally adjusted value*
233	−8	241
254	+4.7	249.3
264	+7.3	256.7
253	−4	257
261	−8	269
286	+4.7	281.3
300	+7.3	292.7
295	−4	299
296	−8	304
312	+4.7	307.3
320	+7.3	312.7
325	−4	329

How good is our analysis?

In the previous sections of this chapter we have seen how to extract both linear and non-linear trends from a time series and how to calculate the amount of seasonal variation. We also looked at using a linear trend, and a knowledge of the seasonal variation, to forecast future figures in the time series, and also at using the seasonal variation to deseasonalize the time series figures. What we have not yet looked at in any detail is the random or unexplained variation. If we take the moving average trend figures and add to these the appropriate seasonal variation and subtract the result from the original figures, we obtain the random variation. For this reason it is sometimes called 'residual variation'. For example, take the values for construction out of table 19. We can find the residual variation, using the figures from the self-check on page 178, as follows:

Col. 1 *Quarterly figs*	*Col. 2* *Trend*	*Col. 3* *Seasonal variation*	*Col. 4 (= col. 1 − (col. 2 + col. 3))* *Residual variation*
233	240	−8	+1
254	248	+4.7	+1.3
264	256	+7.3	+0.7
253	263	−4	−6.0
261	271	−8	−2.0
286	279	+4.7	+2.3
300	287	+7.3	+5.7
295	295	−4	+4.0
296	303	−8	+1.0
312	311	+4.7	−3.7
320	319	+7.3	−6.3
325	327	−4	+2.0
			Total 0

If the analysis has been satisfactory these residual errors should not show any bias; that is, they should sum to approximately zero. Nor should they be *consistently* large or show any definite pattern.

Self-check

Do you think the residual variation shown here indicates a reasonable analysis?

The sum of these errors is 0 which is good, nor are they very large on the whole, and there is no consistent pattern. There does not appear to be anything unduly wrong with the analysis, therefore, though there were some large random variations.

Self-check

Calculate the residual variation in the Baby Gourmet figures of table 17, using the results obtained earlier from the moving average method. What can you conclude from them about the analysis undertaken?

The calculations are as follows:

Col. 1 Quarterly figs	*Col. 2 Centred average*	*Col. 3 Seasonal variation*	*Col. 4 (= col. 1 − (col. 2 + col. 3)) Residual variation*
100		+2.45	
100		+0.27	
94	93.5	+0.45	0.05
86	90	−3.17	−0.83
88	86.125	+2.45	−0.573
84	82.5	+0.27	1.25
79	78.875	+0.45	−0.325
72	74.625	−3.17	0.545
73	70.25	+2.45	0.3
65	66.25	+0.27	−1.52
63		+0.45	
56		−3.17	
		Total residual variation	−1.125

There appears to be no evidence of any problem with the analysis, except that the residual variation is of the same order as the seasonal variation which casts doubt on the whole result.

As a final note, it should be pointed out that the data analysed in this chapter was for very short periods. When carried out over a longer time, random variations are cancelled out better, the seasonal variation is more accurate and the trend lines are more representative. Of course, if the figures themselves are unstable, prone to wild fluctuations and large random errors, or otherwise irregular, no amount of analysis will do any good at all.

Review

1 Use the data given in the review on page 180 to calculate:
a the trend by the method of 'semi-averages';
b the moving average trend and plot this;
c the seasonally adjusted figures based on the moving average trend;
d the residual variation and say if the analysis was satisfactory.

2 The *monthly* sales figures for Baby Gourmet for 1978 and 1979 are as below. Draw a Z-chart for the year 1979.

Month	*Monthly sales (£1000) for year* 1978	1979
J	36	32
F	34	29
M	30	27
A	32	28
M	38	28
J	30	28
J	32	27
A	28	26
S	34	26
O	32	25
N	28	24
D	26	23

ANSWERS

1 a The data has to be split into two halves and each averaged. Here, because there are four years, we split into two sets of two years. The average percentage unemployed in each half is $\frac{3.1 + 2.5 + 2.4 + 2.2 + 2.7 + 2.3 + 2.8 + 2.9}{8}$ for 1973 and 1974 and

$$\frac{3.4 + 3.7 + 4.9 + 5.1 + 5.5 + 5.6 + 6.2 + 5.8}{8}$$

for 1975 and 1976.

These are $\frac{20.9}{8} = 2.6125$ and $\frac{40.2}{8} = 5.025$.

The mid-points of each period are then used and the two points are plotted on the graph and joined. This is shown in figure 45, together with the original data. Did you get the correct time values for each point? They are 4.5 (i.e. halfway between the 4th and 5th quarters) and 12.5 (i.e. halfway between the 12th and 13th quarters).

b The moving average trend is shown calculated below. The figures are also plotted on the graph in figure 45.

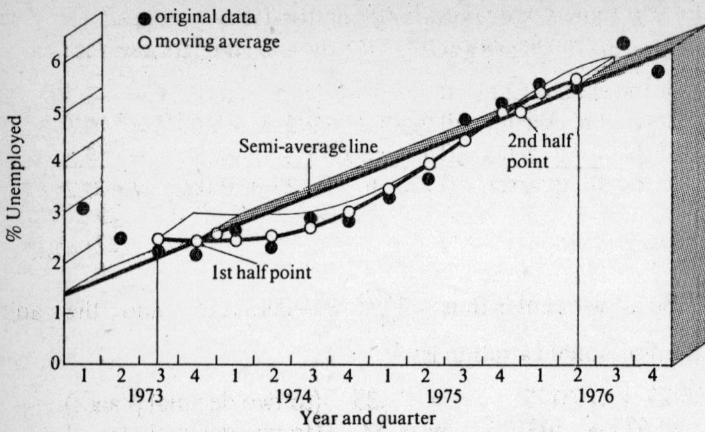

Figure 45. Graph of review 1 (page 200)

Year	*Quarter*	*Data*	*MAT*	*4-quarter average*	*Centred average*	*Data – average (for use in next part of review)*
	1	3.1				
1973	2	2.5				
				2.55		
	3	2.4		2.45	2.50	−0.1
	4	2.2	10.2	2.40	2.425	−0.225
	1	2.7	9.8	2.50	2.45	0.25
1974	2	2.3	9.6	2.675	2.5875	−0.2875
	3	2.8	10.0	2.85	2.7625	0.0375
	4	2.9	10.7	3.20	3.025	−0.125
	1	3.4	11.4	3.725	3.4625	−0.0625
1975	2	3.7	12.8	4.275	4.00	−0.3
	3	4.9	14.9	4.80	4.5375	0.3625
	4	5.1	17.1	5.275	5.0375	0.0625
	1	5.5	19.2	5.60	5.4375	0.0625
1976	2	5.6	21.1	5.775	5.6875	−0.0875
	3	6.2	22.4			
	4	5.8	23.1			

Did you remember to centre the figures?

c The seasonal variation *from the moving average trend* is:

for the 1st quarter: $0.25 + -0.0625 + 0.0625 = 0.25$
for the 2nd quarter: $-0.2875 + -0.3 + -0.0875 = -0.675$
for the 3rd quarter: $-0.1 + 0.0375 + 0.3625 = 0.3$
for the 4th quarter: $-0.225 + -0.125 + 0.0625 = -0.2875$

Total -0.4125

The adjustment is thus $\frac{-.4125}{4} = -0.103125$, and the adjusted seasonal variation is:

$0.25 + .103125 = .35$ (to two decimal places)
$-0.675 + .103125 = -.57$ (to two decimal places)
$0.3 + .103125 = .40$ (" " " ")
$-0.2875 + .103125 = -.18$ (" " " ")
for the four quarters respectively. Note that we *subtract* $-.0975$ and so, in fact, *add* .103125.

To get the seasonally adjusted figures, these variations have to be added to the original figures. The results are:

Year	*1*	2	3	4
1973	3.45	1.93	2.8	2.02
1974	3.05	1.73	3.2	2.72
1975	3.75	3.13	5.3	4.92
1976	5.85	5.03	6.6	5.62

Did you remember to make the adjustments again? And did you subtract them from the initial figures as required? (Note: subtracting a negative number is equivalent to addition.)

d The residual variation is what is left when the trend and seasonal variation are removed from the figures. The calculations for this are:

Raw Data =	*Trend* +	*Seasonal variation* +	*Residual variation*
3.1			
2.5			
2.4	2.50	.40	−.50
2.2	2.42	−.18	−.04
2.7	2.45	.35	−.10
2.3	2.59	−.57	.28
2.8	2.76	.40	−.36
2.9	3.02	−.18	.06
3.4	3.46	.35	−.41
3.7	4.00	−.57	.27
4.9	4.54	.40	−.04
5.1	5.04	−.18	.24
5.5	5.44	.35	−.29
5.6	5.69	−.57	.48
6.2			
5.8			

The analysis does not look all that good. The residual variation is of the same order as the seasonal variation. Furthermore, it is always negative for the third quarter and for the first too and always positive for the second, which isn't random. This seems to indicate that the estimate of the seasonal variation is incorrect, and that it should be greater. (Note that if some figures were added to and subtracted from the estimates of the seasonal variation, it would be all right if they were to balance out.)

2 In order to draw the Z-chart, the cumulative totals for the year are needed together with the moving annual total. The calculations to obtain these are:

Month	Data	1979 Cumulative totals	MAT
J	32	32	376*
F	29	61	371
M	27	88	368
A	28	116	364
M	28	144	354
J	28	172	352
J	27	199	347
A	26	225	345
S	26	251	337
O	25	276	330
N	24	300	326
D	23	323	323

The chart itself appears in figure 46.

*The first figure here is the sum of the monthly sales from February 1978 to January 1979.

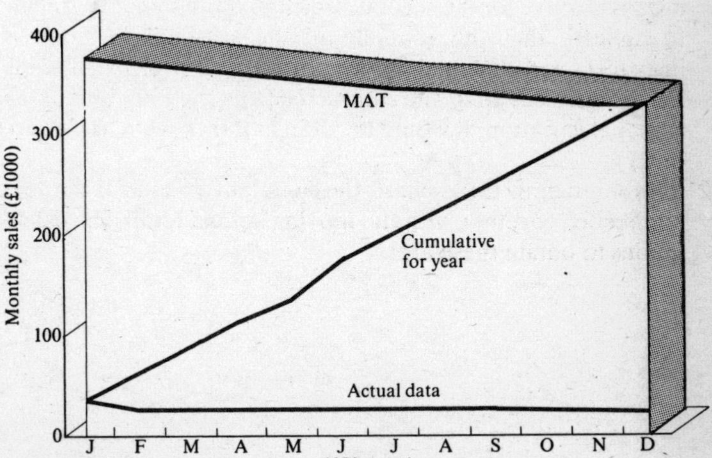

Figure 46. Z-chart for review 2 (page 201)

Part 2
Informing others

Scenario 4
A company magazine

As you read through the following scenario, make a mental note of the uses of the visual presentation of statistics. Look out, too, for ways in which statistics are misused in the scenario.

George Mason, the managing director of Gourmet Foods Ltd, had recently been on a course on industrial relations. One of the ideas put forward there was that a 'house magazine' to keep employees in touch did a lot to improve such relations. He was rather taken with this and asked the personnel director, Mary Fletcher, to start one up.

The annual wage round was due soon and George felt that if the company's rather poor trading record were made clear to the workforce, using the company magazine, it could help to moderate the claim. He asked Mary to pay particular attention to this in the first issue. She enlisted the help of Roger Court, the marketing director, and David Lowe, the finance director.

Roger was asked to write something about current sales and the future prospects. David was asked to write on the current financial position of the company. Both were asked to write specifically with the intention of giving as clear as possible a picture without getting over-complicated and going into too many details.

When Mary received their efforts, she read them through. To her horror they contained so many figures that she felt swamped. Despite her request, neither seemed to have really tried to simplify the situation for the benefit of the employees. They wrote as if for their professional colleagues. Mary felt that if they were left as they were, these articles would do little for the managing director's cause. They may even do it positive harm.

Remembering that a picture was 'worth a thousand words' and that, presumably, this meant that it was worth a good many numbers too, Mary asked both authors to try to put the figures into pictures and diagrams. This they did, to very good effect, and Mary was very pleased with the result.

The house magazine was published and everyone agreed that it was a great success. The employees thought the two articles were very informative.

One sour note was struck, however. There was a good deal of criticism from employees with a knowledge of statistics that some of the statistics given in the magazine were misleading. They were at pains to point out that there was no question of these statistics being wrong, merely that they gave an erroneous impression. The suspicion was that this was done deliberately to influence employees with regard to the coming pay negotiations.

If that was the intention, the laugh was on management. The shop stewards had reacted by saying that, if the company could afford to spend money on things like a magazine, it could afford a good wage rise. The managing director was livid. He swore he'd never take any notice of bright ideas again.

In many instances statistics are intended for someone who is a technical expert and who needs the detailed information gleaned from the raw data by statistical methods. But often, as in the scenario, the statistics are intended for the layman who is not familiar with the technical details and who only requires to 'get the picture'. Statisticians have devised ways of presenting information in such cases. These depend on putting the figures into some visual form, graphical or pictorial, or a combination of both.

The prime consideration is to capture the essence of the figures, but in an 'immediately accessible' manner. It must, however, do this without unduly distorting the 'facts'. From a statistical point of view, these 'facts' should be conveyed as impartially as possible, but with commentary about their *statistical* significance where appropriate.

There was a suspicion that the presentation was deliberately distorted in the house magazine in the scenario. To someone with a knowledge of statistical methods this suspicion would be aroused by telltale omissions, by deliberate vagueness, by unsubstantiated claims and by specific 'tricks' in presentation. The laymen might not be familiar with these devices, but the statistician certainly should be.

Chapter 6 describes the various ways in which statistical data can be presented effectively, while Chapter 7 deals with some of the ways in which it may be deliberately, or perhaps even unknowingly, distorted. Readers should look around for examples of both good and bad practice in the media. And don't forget, always apply a critical eye to any statistical presentation or report that you do come across.

After having studied these chapters you should be able to present statistics in an appropriate way visually and to analyse critically the presentation of statistics by others.

6 Presenting the information visually

Getting the picture

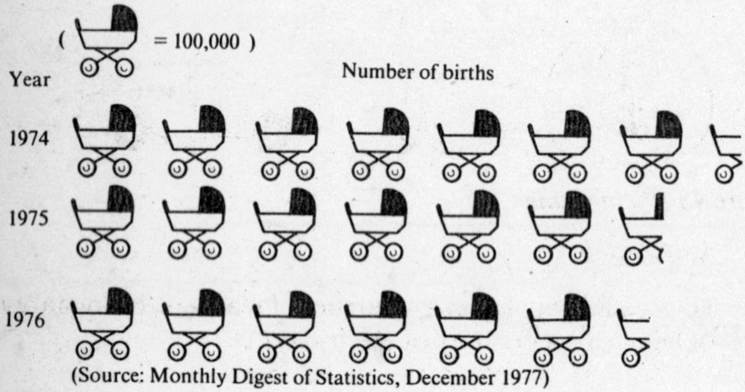

(Source: Monthly Digest of Statistics, December 1977)

Figure 47. Number of babies born in the UK 1974–6

Look at figure 47. It shows how many babies were born in the UK in the years 1974 to 1976. One point to notice immediately is that the source of the figures is quoted. Where there is a source like this it should *always* be given so that the reader may, if he so wishes, check it up, or obtain the exact figures. This is true of *all* the diagrams and graphs of this unit so it should be continually borne in mind. You should not have any difficulty understanding figure 47 even without having read this chapter. Its whole purpose is to be simple and straightforward. It could have been used in the Gourmet Foods house journal to explain why the company couldn't expect an expanding market for its baby food. Displays like this are called 'pictograms'. They are probably the simplest way of presenting statistical information.

In them, some picture symbol, here a pram, is used to represent a certain variable. Other examples are a money bag to depict an amount of money, a stylized figure of a person to depict a number of people, a car to depict a number of cars and so on, as in figure 48. The general idea is that the symbol should correspond in some obvious way to the variable. If, for instance, the people are miners, the stylized figure would be shown wearing a miner's helmet.

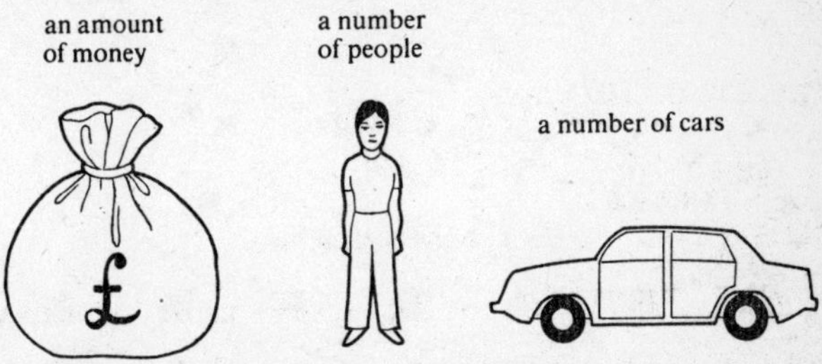

Figure 48. Pictograms

Self-check

How could you depict **a** a number of teachers, **b** a quantity of beer, or **c** a quantity of electricity?

The most obvious way of representing the teachers would be by a stylized figure in a mortar-board and gown. What was used for the beer would depend on what exactly was being portrayed. If we were showing beer consumption a beer mug would be suitable. If, on the other hand, it was beer production, a barrel would be better. Electricity presents somewhat of a problem. It doesn't actually come packaged in anything. Electricity production could be depicted by a stylized picture of a power station, e.g. with the cooling towers prominant. Electricity consumption is not easy. A pylon could be used, but it is not terribly satisfactory.

Having fixed on the symbol, two more questions need to be answered. What is the value of each symbol and how do we depict higher and lower ones? These questions are interrelated. To take the last one first. We can use either a number of symbols to represent more, and *part* of the symbol to represent less, as in figure 47, or we can make the size of the picture proportional to the value. Figure 49 illustrates this in terms of amounts of money. If size is used, the first question reduces to one of scale, otherwise it reduces to one of selecting suitable units to work in.

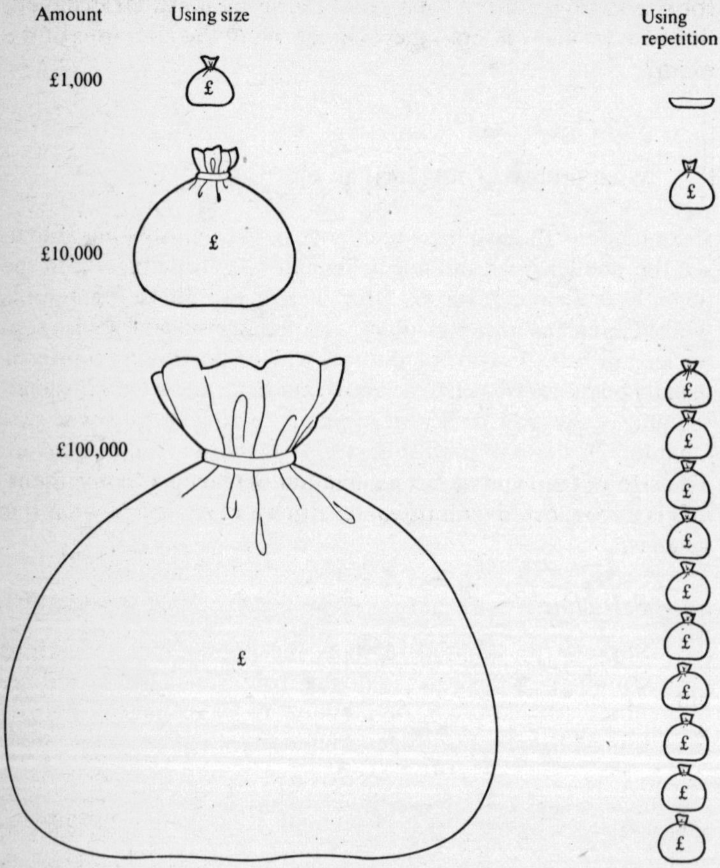

Figure 49. Two ways of depicting £1000, £10,000 and £100,000

If it is a question of scale, then we need to select one which will make the smallest value visible and the largest capable of appearing on at most one page, and preferably a great deal less. It should be noted that height is *not* size, as figure 47 where the *area* of the money bag is proportional to the value of money it represents. This means that a doubling in height *and* width, for example, will *quadruple* the size; that is, will make it represent *four* times as much money. This means that once we have chosen the size for the smallest value, the largest size is also determined. Suppose we want to show the populations of the countries of the earth?

Self-check

What problem could this cause?

It could mean that we have to choose between not being able to see the smaller ones and not being able to get the bigger on the page. New Zealand, for example, has three million inhabitants whilst China has over 800 million. In practice such large discrepancies are rare, however, and this way of portraying figures is usually possible. Because the above method can be very misleading and because of difficulties in constructing it, however (see Chapter 7), the one used in figure 47 is more often employed. The size of the symbol here is fixed at whatever is convenient, and is unconnected with its value. But we must decide what this value is.

Self-check

Suppose we wanted to show the populations of various countries of the earth, ranging from New Zealand's three million to China's 837 million or so. We could use stylized human figures, but what population should each represent.

We have to strike a balance between having too many symbols for the large values and having an unrecognizably small part of the symbol for the small values. No more than about twenty symbols should be used for any value. With the populations this means that each symbol should represent about

$$\frac{837{,}000{,}000 \text{ (the population of China)}}{20} = 41{,}850{,}000.$$

On the other hand no population should be less than about a twentieth of the value of one symbol, giving a maximum value of

3,000,000 (the population of New Zealand) × 20 = 60,000,000. So if each symbol represents 50 million people, this is about right. Figure 50 shows how the UK's, New Zealand's and China's population would be represented in this way. As can be seen, it would be very difficult to display a population smaller than that of New Zealand together with China's.

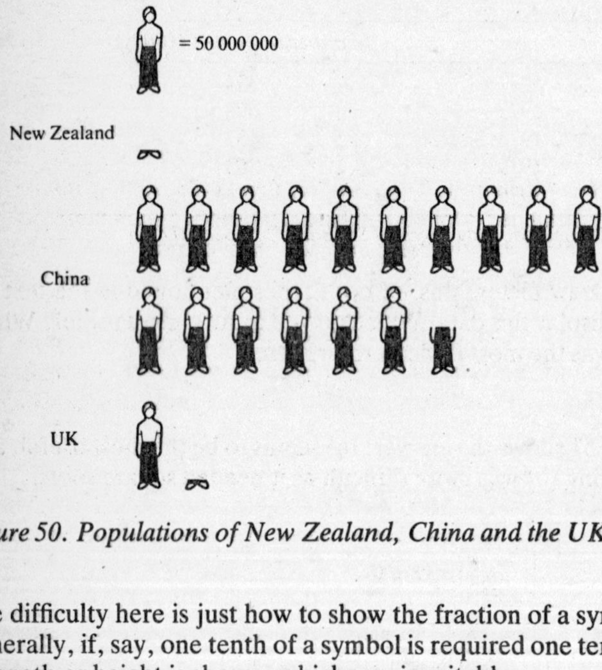

Figure 50. Populations of New Zealand, China and the UK 1976

One difficulty here is just how to show the fraction of a symbol. Generally, if, say, one tenth of a symbol is required one tenth of its length or height is shown, whichever is suitable.

> ### *Self-check*
>
> Why is this unsatisfactory?

We saw before that, properly, it is *area* that is proportional to value. Here we are using a linear system. It would be very awkward, however, to try to show a tenth of the area of the irregular shapes that are often used for symbols. This method of representing figures is thus fairly rough. It does not matter too much, though, as can be seen from figures 47 and 50. Only a general picture is intended to be given anyway.

Self-check

Imports of colour televisions into the UK in 1972 to 1976 were:

Year	*Number imported (1000s)*
1972	334
1973	693
1974	437
1975	263
1976	214

(Source: *Monthly Digest of Statistics*, October 1977)

Draw pictograms, of both types mentioned in the text, to display this data. Which do you think is most useful? Which was the most difficult to prepare?

Figure 51 shows the answer. (a) seems to be the most useful, and preparing (b) was more difficult as it needed square roots.

(a)

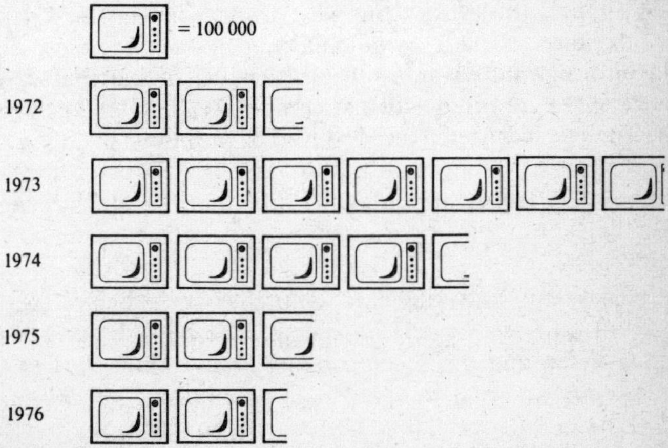

(b)

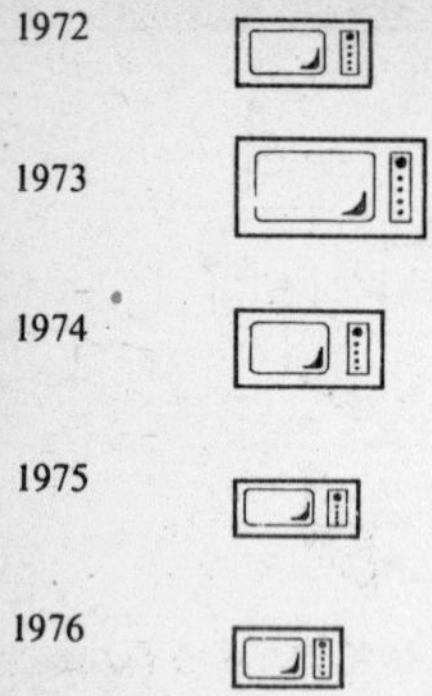

Figure 51. Imports of colour TVs into the UK (Source: Monthly Digest of Statistics *Oct. 1977)*

Just one final point about pictograms. Sometimes the value of the symbol is written on it, particularly if it is of the type where its size is proportional to its value. Alternatively, a value can be written by the side of a symbol, or of the last one in a group of them. Such additions are not necessary unless it is particularly important that an exact figure is conveyed in the diagram.

The long and the short of it

Look at figure 52. It depicts the same data as was shown in figure 47. Though this wasn't the way it appeared in the Gourmet Foods home journal, it would have been one way of presenting the information. Diagrams like this are called 'bar charts'. They must not be confused with histograms (see Chapter 9 in Volume *1*). The two are used for very different purposes: histograms for displaying frequency distributions, and bar charts for displaying sets of data from different sources or times. Unlike histogram rectangles, too, bars do *not* represent data by their area but by their *length*.

This way of displaying data is more accurate than pictograms, but not quite so visually appealing. The bars should all be of equal width and the accompanying scale should start at zero. These points are taken up again in the next chapter. Note that, though the bars are shown horizontally in figure 52, they could equally well have been vertical.

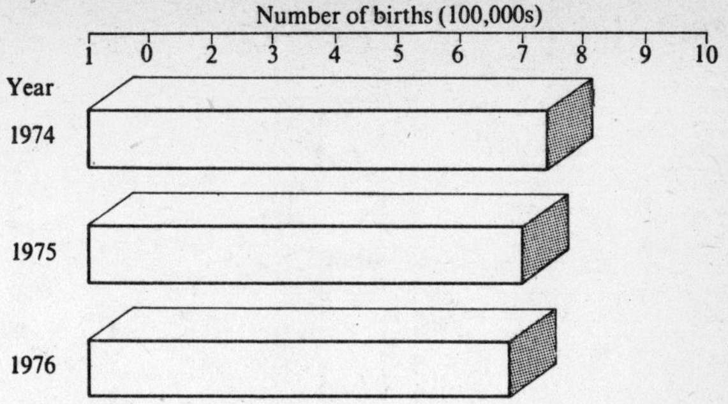

Figure 52. Number of babies born in the UK 1974–6 (source: Monthly Digest of Statistics*)*

Self-check

What would a bar chart of the populations of the UK (56 million), New Zealand and China look like? Draw one to show these three populations so that they can be compared.

Here both 3 million and 837 million would need to be shown as well as the UK's 56 million. It is the largest figure that determines the scale used and the bar for this should almost, but *not* completely, fill the available space. The other figures, including the smallest, will thus have the lengths of their bars determined also. Figure 53 shows the bar charts for these populations. As can be seen, it would be difficult to display meaningfully a population smaller than that of New Zealand together with China's.

Making comparisons

One reason why a bar chart may be preferred to a pictogram is that dual, or even multiple, comparisons can be made. Look at figure 54(a). This is what is called a 'multiple bar chart'. It shows the price indexes for three classes of goods for the years 1974–76. You can see that, as well as allowing us to compare one index with another, it also lets us compare all three over time. This is a

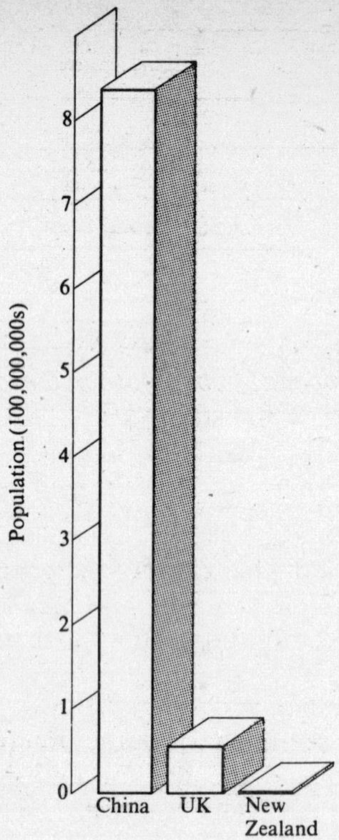

Figure 53. Populations of China, the UK and New Zealand 1976

particularly useful feature of bar charts. Whilst it can be done with pictograms, the results tend to be somewhat confusing.

With a multiple bar chart, of course, there is always more than one way to present it. Figure 54(b) shows the same data as figure 54(a), but with the grouping the opposite way round. Which way is used depends on the exact purpose of the diagram.

Self-check

What difference in effect have figure 54(a) and 54(b)?

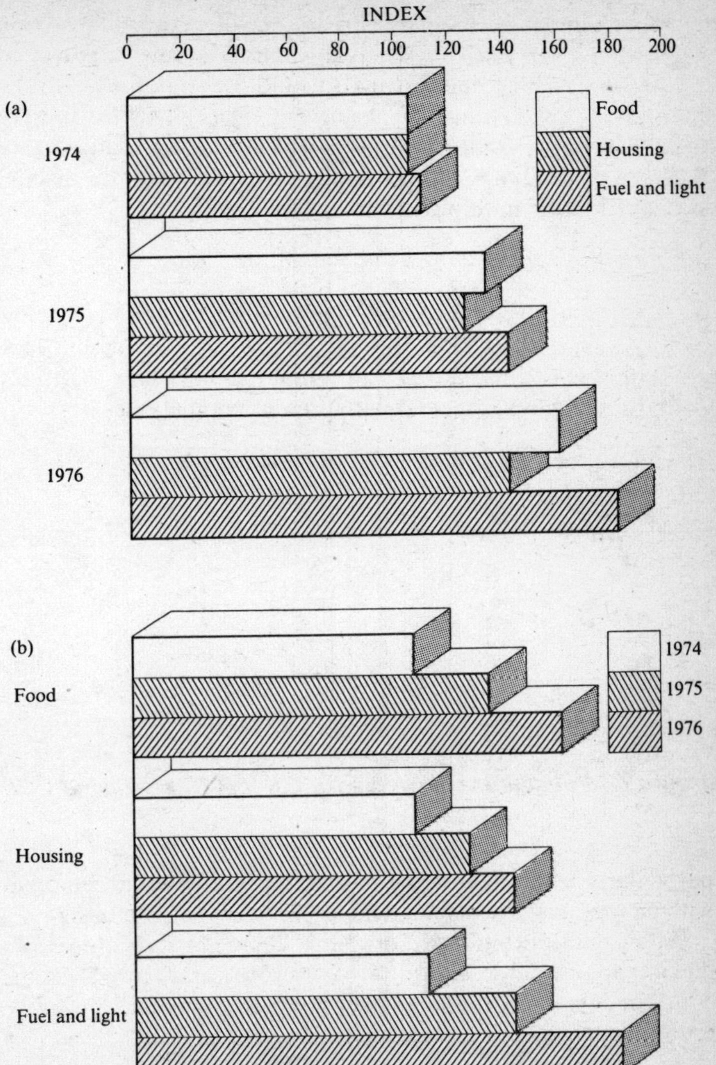

Source: *Monthly Digest of Statistics*

Figure 54. Retail price indexes for food, housing and fuel and light 1974–6 (15 January 1974 = 100)

The first figure makes it easier to compare the three indexes with each other as they are physically together. The reverse is true of the second. Which one was used would depend on which relationship we most wanted to bring out. Figure 54(a) is a more usual way of presenting information of this nature than is figure 54(b). A general rule, if there is no specific reason to choose one, is that the lesser multiple of bars is used.

Self-check

Suppose that the projected populations for the UK, New Zealand and China in the year 2000 are 62, 4.5 and 1196 million respectively. Draw a multiple bar chart to display these figures, together with present populations.

It would appear as in figure 55.

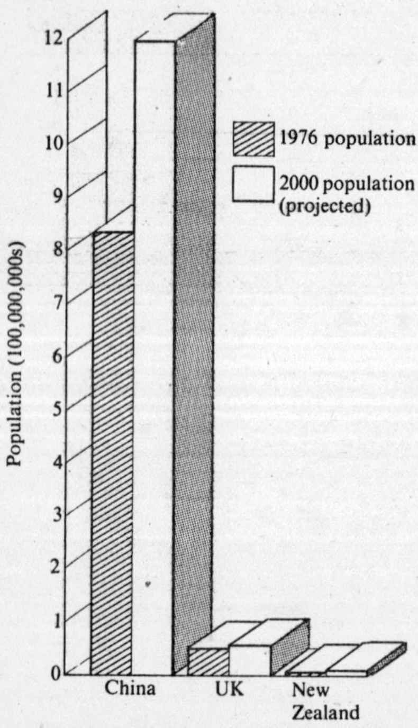

Figure 55. Population of the UK, China and New Zealand

Showing the components

Another reason why bar charts may be used is that they can easily represent composite figures. Look at figure 56. This shows the birth figures of figure 47 as composites of those for England, Wales, Scotland and Northern Ireland. Of course, these could have been displayed in a multiple bar chart. However, this would not show the UK totals at all clearly. It is very difficult, though not totally impossible, to achieve a similar effect with pictograms. Such charts are called 'component bar charts'.

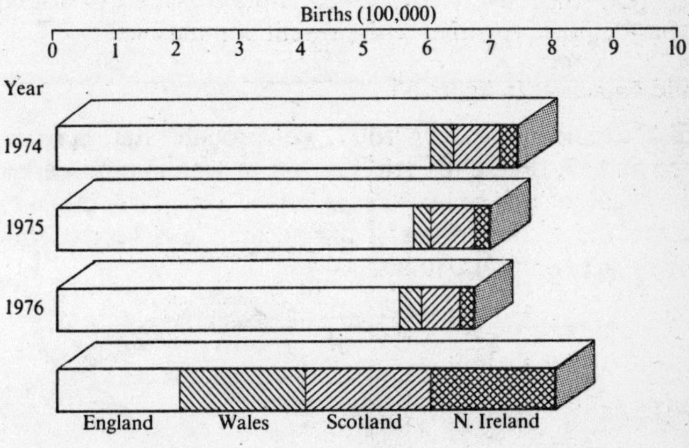

Figure 56. Births in the UK as composite of numbers of births in England, Wales, Scotland and Northern Ireland 1974–6 (source: Monthly Digest of Statistics*)*

Self-check

Draw a component bar chart of the data below:

GOURMET FOODS LTD SALES 1979–80

Brand of product	*Average value of sales/month (£1000s)* 1979	1980
Baby Gourmet	20	16
Gourmet Soups	93	87
Gourmet Preserves	21	19
Gourmet Potted Pastes	6	7
Quick Gourmet	112	121
Totals	252	250

Your chart should look like figure 57. You probably notice, from figures 56 and 57, that, although it is easy to see the differences in totals, because each component is moved along, it is difficult to compare these. Nevertheless, this technique is very useful where there are composite totals.

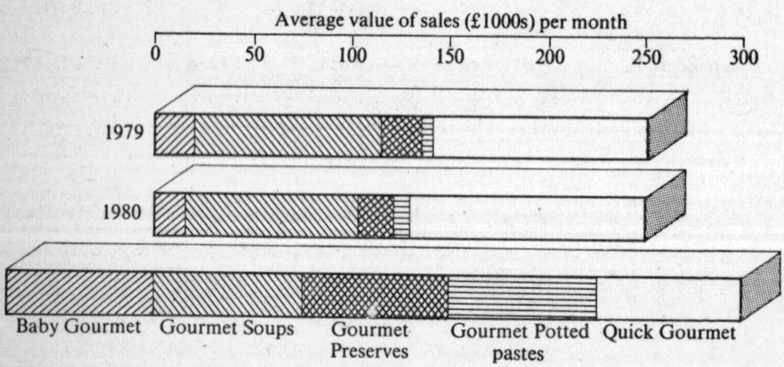

Figure 57. Gourmet Foods Ltd sales 1979–80

There is no reason why we should not have multiple component bar charts. The only problem is they tend to give a rather confused picture unless they are well done. The golden rule of all statistical diagrams is to be as simple as possible consistent with their aims, so such diagrams should only be used if there is an overriding reason for doing so.

Self-check

You are given the following figures (which repeat, in part, those in the self-check on page 217) (source: *Monthly Digest of Statistics*, December 1977):

Year	*Colour TVs*		*B/w TVs*	
	Imports	*Exports*	*Imports*	*Exports*
		(1000s)		
1972	334	29	352	47
1973	693	40	463	70
1974	437	104	241	79
1975	263	227	433	48
1976	214	237	546	116

Construct a multiple bar chart to show how imports and exports of coloured TVs varied from year to year, and a component bar chart to show how imports of both coloured and black and white TVs changed from year to year. Construct, too, a diagram which shows all the above data.

The multiple bar chart and component bar chart are shown in figures 58 and 59. To show all the data it would not be unreasonable, in this case where there are only two components, to use a multiple component bar chart, as shown in figure 60.

Just three further points about bar charts. Sometimes they are shown with descriptions and/or the actual values or percentages written on or near the bars themselves. Even if this is done, it is preferable to still have a scale by the bars. Also, negative values, e.g. loss as opposed to profit, can be shown by drawing the bars the opposite way and marking the scale that way appropriately (see figure 60(a)).

Finally, the bars may be touching each other, or apart, as desired. In the case of multiple bar charts there may, as in figure 54 and so on, be a combination of both methods.

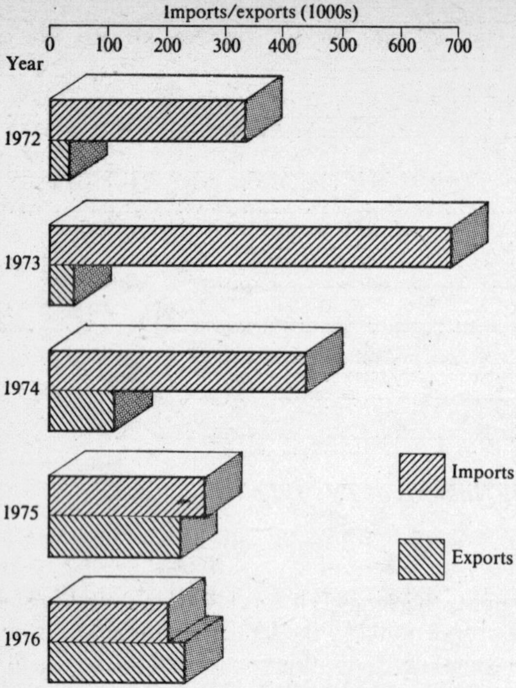

Source: *Monthly Digest of Statistics* December 1977

Figure 58. Imports and exports of colour TVs 1972–6

A piece of the cake

Look at figure 61. This shows the figures for Gourmet Foods sales for 1980, that were given earlier. This time they are displayed in the form of what is known as a 'pie chart'. These are used when there is one figure which can be broken up into several different components and no comparison is to be made with another. So we can show only one year's sales in this way. Other years would need separate pie charts. This type of diagram shows how the 'cake' (or, according to its name, the 'pie') is divided.

In pie diagrams, the angle at the centre in each piece (or, what

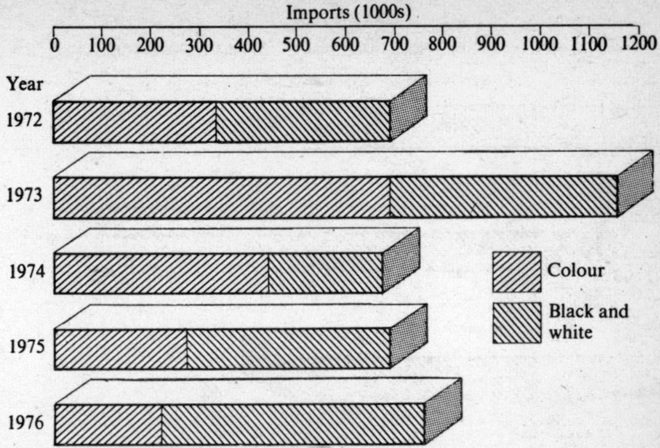

Source: *Monthly Digest of Statistics* December 1977

Figure 59. Imports of TVs 1972–6

is equivalent, the length of the arc of the circle cut off by the piece) is proportional to the value represented. Since there are 360° in a complete circle, this means that the angles in the pieces add up to 360°, which must thus represent the total of all the values. For example, in the case of the Gourmet Foods Ltd's 1980 sales, 360° represents 250 thousand. So the 16 thousand of Baby Gourmet sales is represented by a piece with an angle of $360° \times \frac{16}{250} = 360° \times .064 = 23.04°$.

Self-check

What are the angles for the other sales?

For the Gourmet Soups the angle is $360° \times \frac{87}{250} = 360° \times .348 = 125.28°$.

For the preserves it is $360° \times \frac{19}{250} = 360° \times .076 = 27.36°$.

For the potted pastes it is $360° \times \frac{7}{250} = 360° \times .028 = 10.08°$.

Finally, for Quick Gourmet it is $360° \times \frac{121}{250} = 360° \times .484 = 174.24°$.

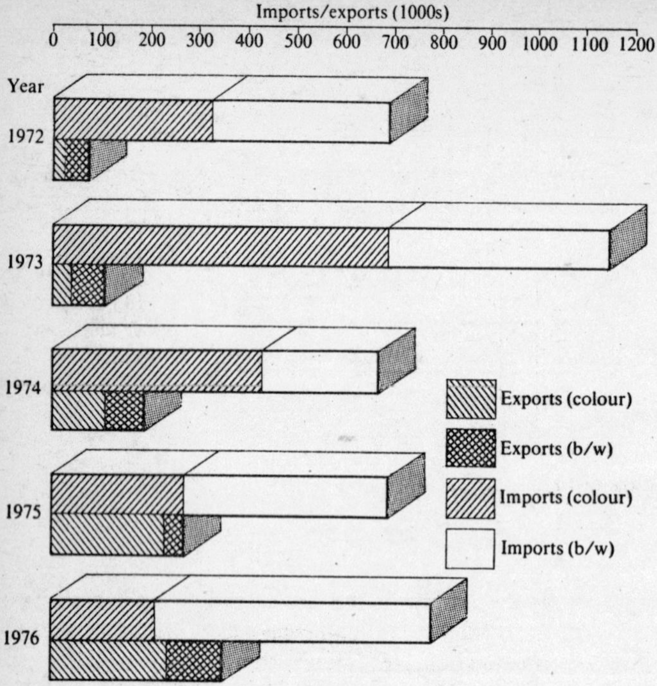

Source: *Monthly Digest of Stratestics* December 1977

Figure 60. Imports and exports of TVs 1972–6

To summarize, then, we get angles of:

Baby Gourmet	23.04°
Gourmet Soups	125.28°
Gourmet Preserves	27.36°
Gourmet Potted Pastes	10.08°
Quick Gourmet	174.24°
Total	360.00°

These, then, are the angles shown in the pie diagram of figure 61.

Figure 60(a).

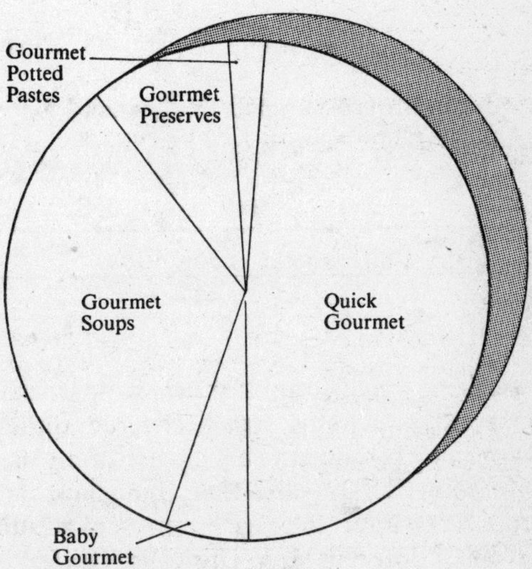

Figure 61. Gourmet Foods Ltd sales 1980

Self-check

A company's assets are as follows:

Vehicles	15	£ thousand
Plant & equipment	60	,,
Land	50	,,
Stock and work in progress	18	,,
Debtors	2	,,
Cash	5	,,
Total	150	,,

Draw a pie diagram for this data.

First, we need to find the angles. They are:

Vehicles	$360° \times \frac{15}{150} = 360° \times .1 = 36°$
Plant & equipment	$360° \times \frac{60}{150} = 360° \times .4 = 144°$
Land	$360° \times \frac{50}{150} = 360° \times .3333 = 120°$
Stock and work in progress	$360° \times \frac{18}{150} = 360° \times 0.12 = 43.2°$
Debtors	$360° \times \frac{2}{150} = 360° \times .0133 = 4.8°$
Cash	$360° \times \frac{5}{150} = 360° \times .0333 = 12°$
Total	360°

The corresponding pie diagram is shown in figure 62.

As with the other diagrams already covered, the actual figures or percentages may be added to each piece of the diagram if it is felt they are required. Note also that, though pie diagrams *may* be compared, if the totals they each represent are different, the circles must be of different size. This causes difficulties and it is not recommended that pie diagrams are used to make comparisons in this way, unless percentages are used when, of course,

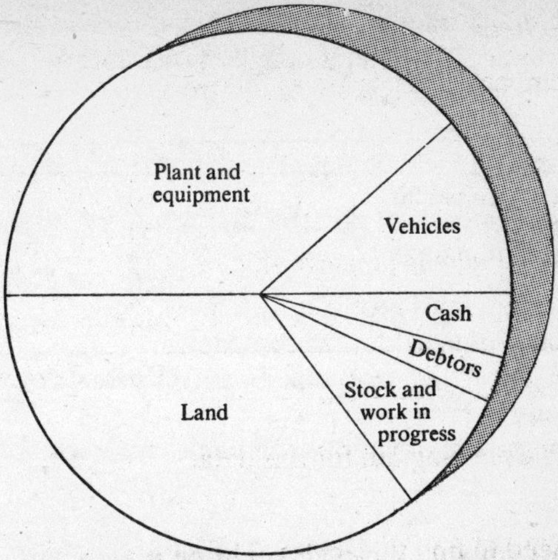

Figure 62. A company's assets

the totals in each case are 100%. Even then, it is often difficult to keep both charts in proper view to compare them.

Which type of diagram do we use?

There are many different ways in which statistics can be presented, some of them very imaginative. What have been included here up till now are the standard diagrammatic ones. Tables and graphs are going to be dealt with in the second half of the chapter. Perhaps, though, one other type of diagram deserves attention and that is the 'cartogram'. This is used extensively in atlases. It is that method of colouring or shading regions of maps to show population density, height above sea level and so on. In business it might, for example, show the sales in each sales region.

Which diagram is used in any specific case depends on a number of factors. If detail is of very little concern, a pictogram is usually the best method. The eye can judge the lengths of the bars in bar charts fairly well, so where a greater accuracy is required they should be used. Pie charts, while they look attractive, are not as easy to judge, in terms of size, as bars, though the parallel with cutting up a cake (pie) is a very useful aid to understanding. The general rule is clarity without distortion of the data.

Self-check

Which methods of presentation would be suitable for each of the following?

1 A company's profits by divisions.
2 The profits of various companies.
3 The profits of various companies broken down into those made at home and abroad.
4 The profits of various companies for each of two years.

ANSWERS

1 The most suitable method would be a pie chart. There is a definite 'sum' which is to be 'divided' among the different divisions. If you said a bar chart, then this is not quite so good as it doesn't emphasize that an amount is being shared out. You could have said a pictogram but, again, it doesn't clearly show this division aspect.
2 It is wrong to use a pie chart here: there is no 'cake' being shared that can be identified as such. Pictograms would be acceptable, but a bar chart would bring out the comparison best. It would be a simple bar chart, since it is straight profits we are comparing.
3 Here we have two different factors in operation: the company and the source of the profits. To show the company a bar chart could be used as in **2**. But to show the source of profits, it would have to be a component bar chart. Although it could be shown as a multiple bar chart, the fact that the profits are broken down really indicates it should be a component one. It would be difficult to draw a good enough pictogram to show all this information. It would definitely be wrong to use a single pie chart, as there is more than one firm to be shown with the source of profits. A pie chart would be suitable if we just wanted to show the source of profits of one firm.
4 Here, again, there are two factors: the firm and the year. But we can't use a component bar chart here, since we can't say

the profits have been broken down into sub-units (except if we take 'profits over two years' to be a sensible number to operate with). The multiple bar chart is suitable here. It would not be easy to draw an adequate and clear pictogram. A pie chart would be incorrect as there is no 'sharing of a cake'.

Review

1. Use the data in table 22 to draw a pictogram depicting the sales of the various flavours of Baby Gourmet food in 1980.
2. Use the same table and show, in the form of a bar chart, the sales of the various flavours in 1979.
3. Using the same data, draw a multiple bar chart to show sales of the flavours in 1979 and 1980.
4. With this data again, draw a component bar chart showing the sales of Baby Gourmet foods in 1979 and 1980, and by each flavour.
5. Again, with the same data, draw a pie chart to show the proportions of total sales for the various flavours in 1979.

TABLE 22. SALES OF BABY GOURMET FOOD BY FLAVOUR 1979–80 (£000s) PER MONTH (AVERAGE)

Flavour	*Year* 1979	1980
Venison Broth	5	5
Creamed Asparagus Tips	4	3
Caviarette	3	2
Partridge Stew	3	3
Bilberry Desert	3	2
Passion Fruit Desert	2	1

ANSWERS

1–6 See figures 63 to 67, which follow.

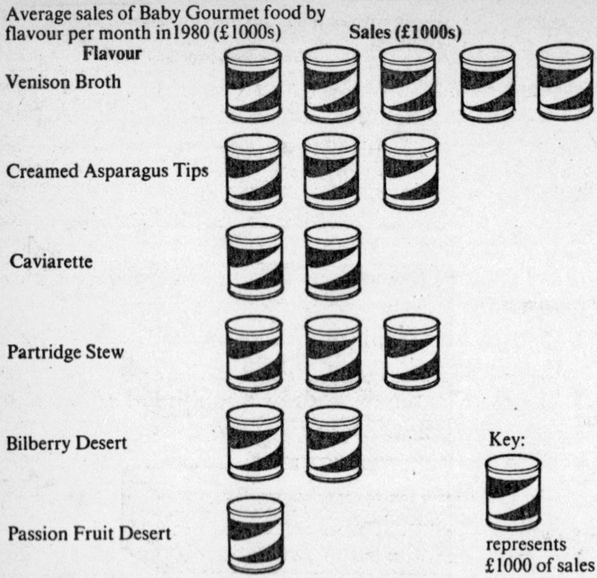

Figure 63. Pictogram for review 1 (page 233)

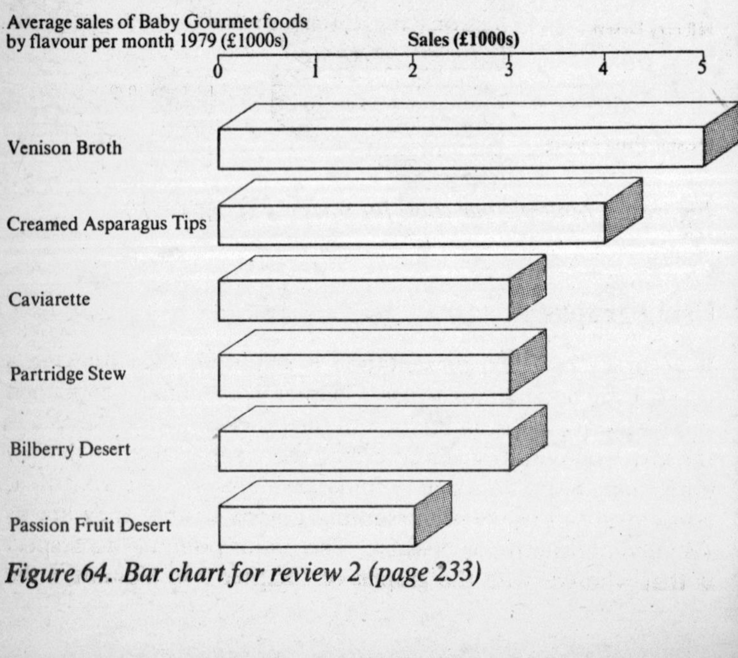

Figure 64. Bar chart for review 2 (page 233)

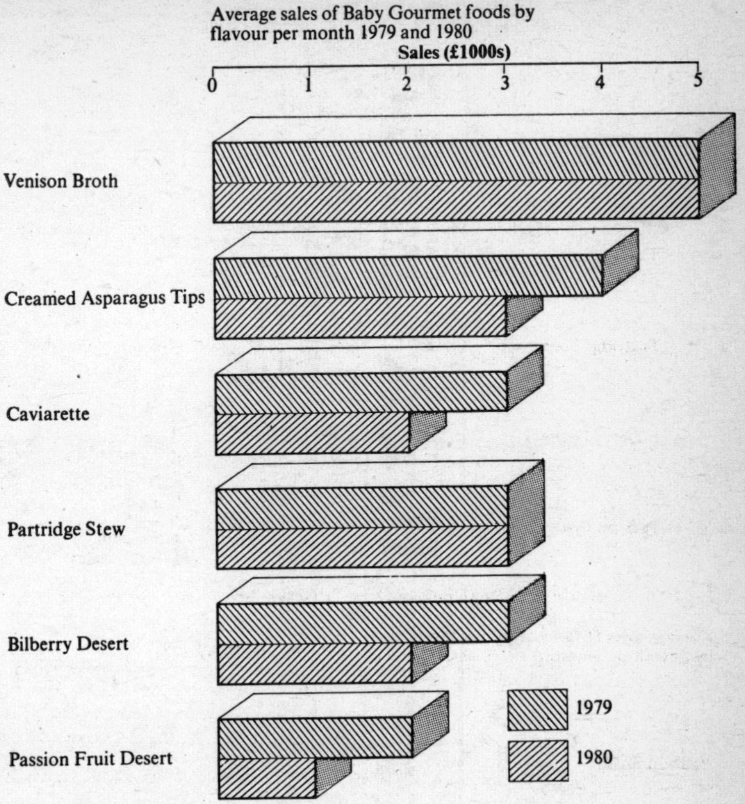

Figure 65. Multiple bar chart for review 3 (page 233)

Using graphs

If accuracy in visual presentation is required, then drawing a graph is the best method to use. Chapter 9 in Volume *1* explained the basics of graphs, in relation to the processing of data. While the histograms and ogives described there can be used to display data, their prime function is statistical. This section will, then, concentrate on ways of presenting graphs so that they are as visually informative as possible. The major point in this respect is that whereas with the graphs of Chapter 9 in Volume *1* the

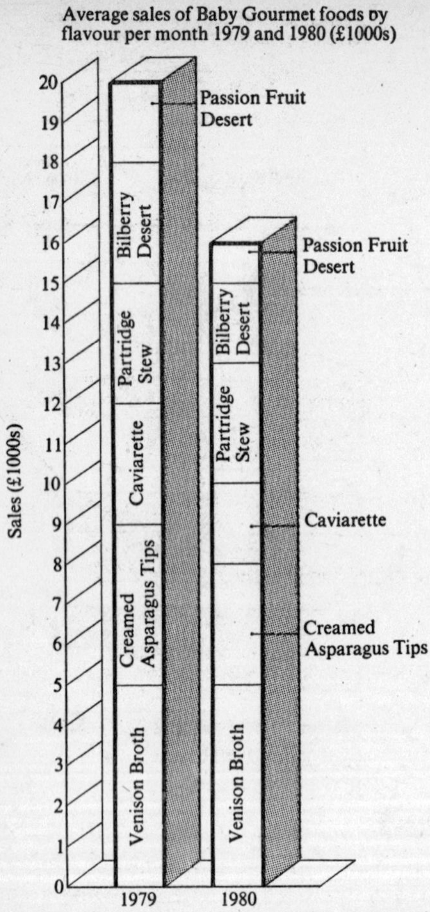

Figure 66. Component bar chart for review 4 (page 233)

lines should be drawn as thin as possible so as to generate accuracy, for display purposes they should be somewhat thicker. This is because we want to make them visually clear. Figure 68 illustrates this. It is a graph that might have been in Gourmet Foods' house magazine to show the decline in sales of Baby Gourmet foods in 1979.

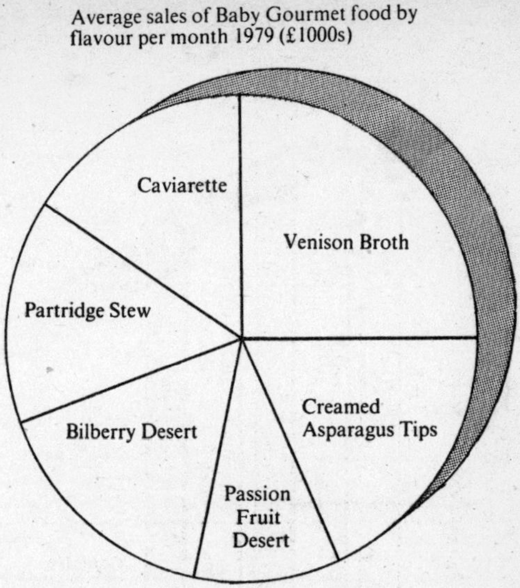

Figure 67. Pie chart for review 5 (page 233)

Self-check

Make a list of points that you notice about figure 68 that represent 'good practice' when drawing a graph.

The following are generally regarded as good practice:

- the title should be displayed clearly without interfering with the graph itself;
- each axis should be labelled with the name of the variable it represents;
- each axis should show a scale for the values of the variables it represents, with negative values clearly marked as such;
- vertical scales should normally begin at zero;

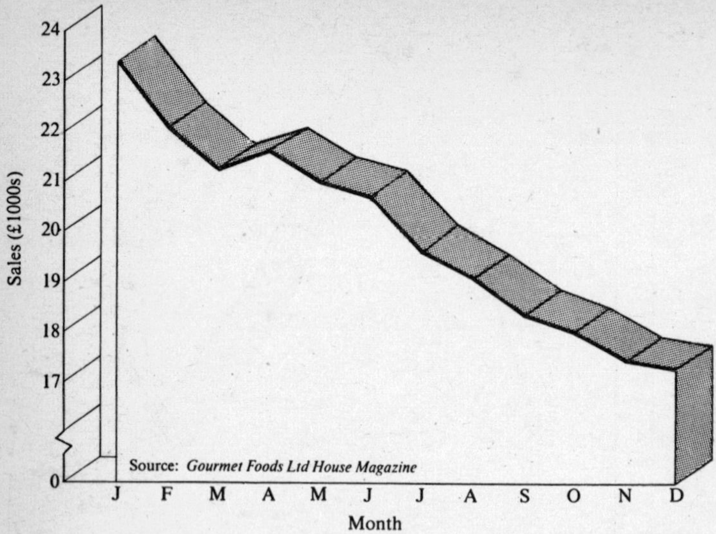

Figure 68. Sales of Baby Gourmet foods (£1000) 1979

- in cases where the above rule is not practicable, the axis may be 'broken' (as shown in figure 68) to indicate that some of it has been omitted;
- graphs should not appear cramped and choice of scales is of vital importance in this respect;
- the source of the figures should be quoted whenever applicable.

Two for the price of one

It is sometimes useful to display more than one line on a single graph. Look at figure 69, for instance, which shows the figures on imports and exports of coloured televisions from the self-check on page 225. Note that here each line is labelled for easy identification. Doing this enables two or more sets of figures to be compared directly with each other as with the import and export figures. Sometimes we only wish to compare the 'ups' and

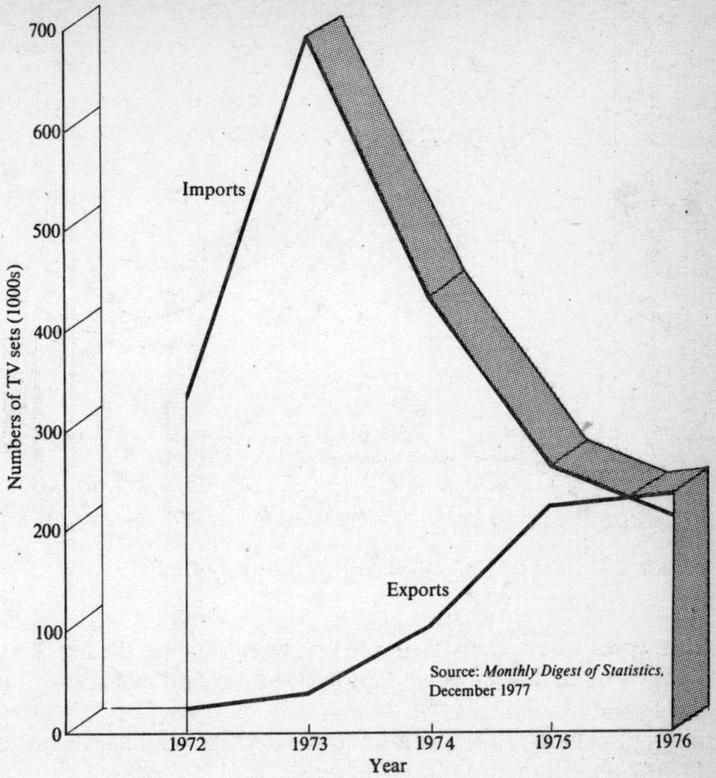

Figure 69. Import/export of colour TVs 1972–6

'downs'. In such cases, the different sets of figures may not even be in the same units. We can do this by plotting the two corresponding curves on one graph and using *two sets of vertical axes* as shown in figure 70. This represents the import volume index and the imports of TVs. You can see that there is one vertical axis on the left, showing the index number, and another on the right, showing the imports of TVs. Note that this time different types of lines have been used, dotted for the imports and unbroken for the index, instead of labels as in figure 69. They could still be labelled if required, though.

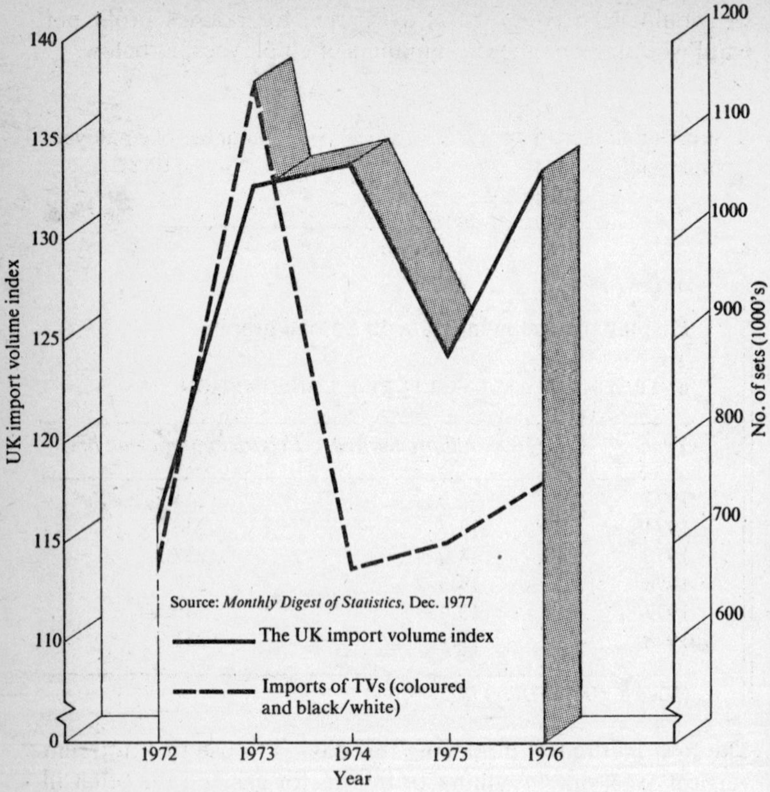

Figure 70. Imports of TVs into the UK and the import index 1972–6

Let's take another example. Suppose we wanted to produce a graph showing, together, the gross profit per employee in a firm and the number of employees, over some time period.

Self-check

How could we do it?

We could draw lines on the graph representing both sets of figures. Because they are expressed in different units, once again we would need two vertical axes, one for pounds profit per employee and the other for numbers of employees, as below.

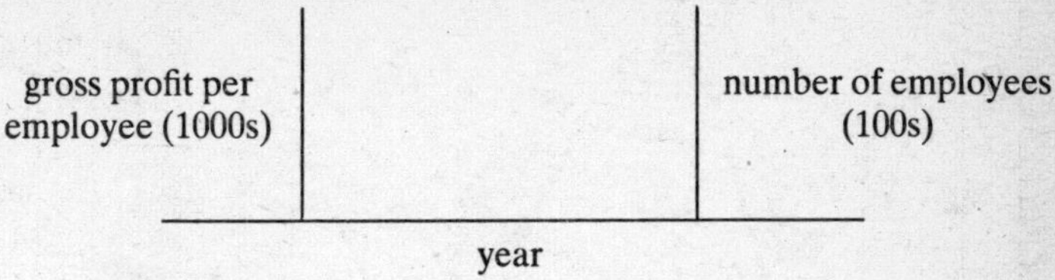

Self-check

Display the following data all on one graph:

ENERGY AVAILABLE FOR PUBLIC CONSUMPTION

Year	*Gas (1000 million therms)*	*Electricity (tera watt hrs)*
1973	12.0	244.7
1974	13.7	236.7
1975	14.0	237.3
1976	14.5	239.5
1977	15.4	246.3
1978	15.9	251.9

(Source: *UK in Figures 1975–79*)

The best method of displaying this data is to use two different vertical axes, one in billions of therms for gas and the other in tera watt hours for electricity. Such a graph is shown in figure 71. Note that it does *not* mean that where the two lines are near roughly equal amounts of energy were obtainable from gas and electricity: the two scales are, as they stand, independent. Only the pattern of ups and downs has any meaning in the relationship between one line and the other.

One particular type of graph used when there are more than one set of figures is the 'multi-layer graph'. Figure 72 shows one for the export of colour and black-and-white TV sets. It is the graphical equivalent of the component bar chart and is employed when one figure is the sum of several others. The diagram is built up 'layer by layer' by adding in successive component figures. There is no statistical reason why layers should be in any particu-

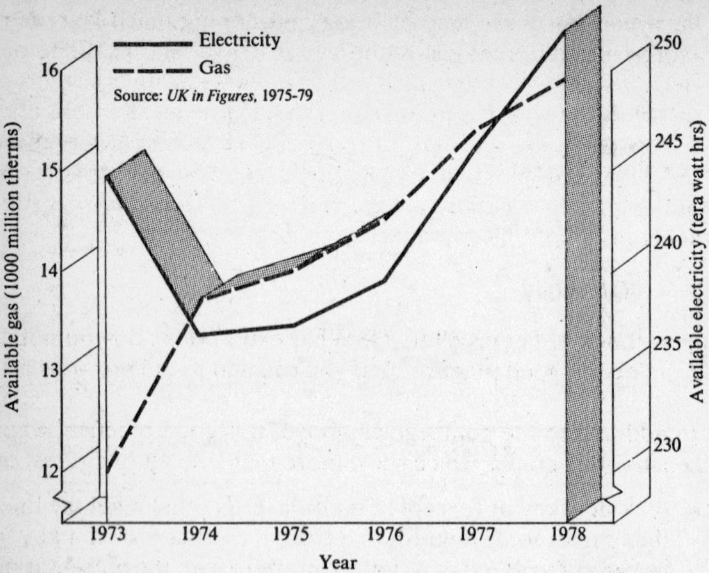

Figure 71. Available energy from gas and electricity in the UK 1973–8

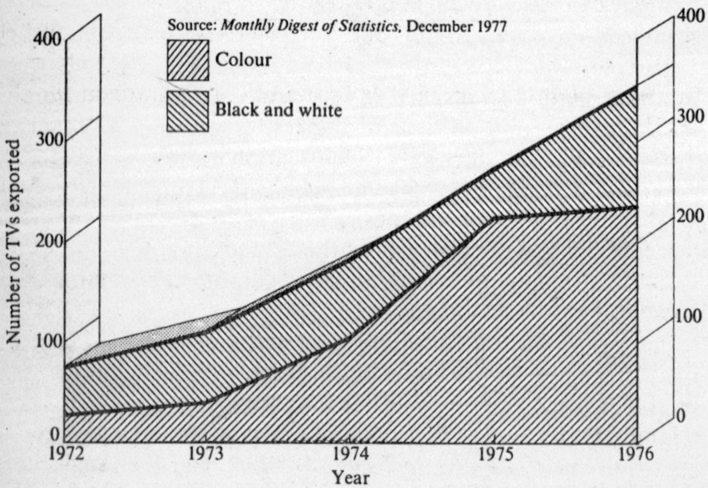

Figure 72. Exports of colour and black-and-white TVs 1972–6

lar order, but there may be a logical one; e.g. each layer may represent a different age group and it would be sensible to put these in order. All the figures will be in the same units so there is no need for two separate vertical axes. However, it is helpful to the clarity of the diagram if the vertical scale is shown both on the left and on the right as in figure 72. Because the proportions of the graph are important, the vertical axis should *always* start at zero for multi-layer graphs.

Self-check

Look at figures 69 to 72. What extra points do you notice about 'good practice' that you can add to the previous list?

In addition to the points given above, it is good practice, when constructing graphs which show more than one set of figures, to

- provide a key or (except in multi-layer graphs) label the lines themselves to distinguish one from the other – such a key to be carefully placed so as not to interfere with the presentation of the graph;
- provide only the minimum number of different lines; too many can easily result in confusion;
- choose the scales so that one line can easily be distinguished from another;
- always start the vertical axis on a multi-layer graph at zero.

Self-check

Draw a multi-layer graph to show the following data.

WORKING POPULATION IN UK (MILLIONS)

Year	*Men*	*Women*	*Total*
1973	16.2	9.4	25.6
1974	15.7	9.4	25.1
1975	16.1	9.7	25.8
1976	16.2	9.8	26.0
1977	16.3	10.1	26.3*
1978	16.2	10.2	26.4

(Source: *UK in Figures 1975–79*)

*Rounding errors mean that the sum of the men's plus the women's figures does not equal total figure here.

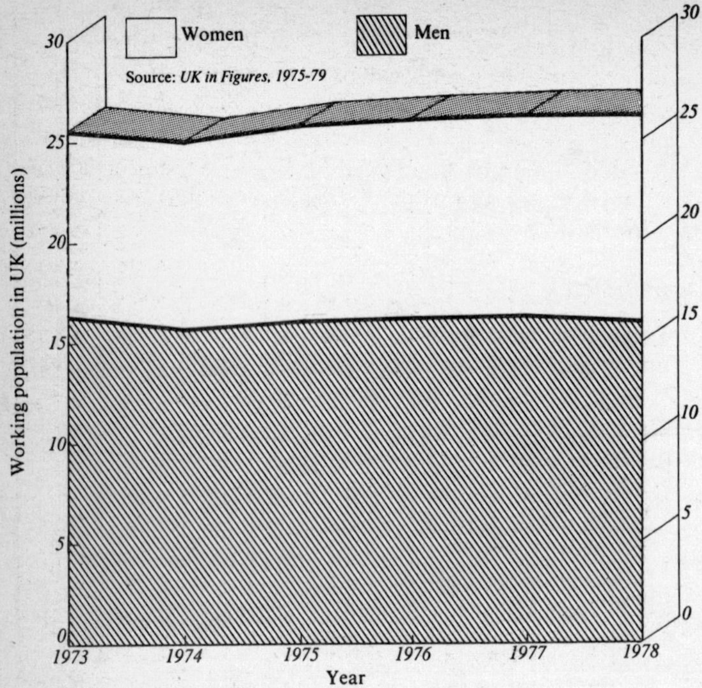

Figure 73. UK working population 1973–8

The graph is shown in figure 73. Note that when there is little variation in the figures, the points are, as here, often difficult to plot because the vertical axis has to start at zero.

Tables of figures

In some cases there are either too many variables to conveniently get on a graph, or it is thought important that the full figures are clearly stated. Then a table is the best way of displaying the data. Now it is not quite as easy to draw up a *good* table as might be at first imagined. Look at table 23 for example. (This was one left out of Gourmet Foods' house magazine!)

				Years of service					*Years of service*					*Totals*		
				0 to 2	*2 to 5*	*5 to 10*	*10 to 20*	*20 ↓*	*0 to 2*	*2 to 5*	*5 to 10*	*10 to 20*	*20 ↓*			
Category of work	*Unskilled*	*Age*	*16-18*	3	0	0	0	0	8	0	0	0	0	3	8	11
			18-25	2	2	1	0	0	7	16	3	0	0	5	26	31
			25-40	1	3	3	1	1	6	13	7	3	1	9	30	39
			40 →	0	1	1	0	0	10	12	15	9	3	2	49	51
	Skilled	*Age*	16-18	0	0	0	0	0	0	0	0	0	0	0	0	0
			18-25	1	2	2	0	0	0	0	1	0	0	5	1	6
			25-40	1	2	5	1	0	0	1	2	0	0	9	3	12
			40 →	0	2	4	2	1	0	0	2	1	0	9	3	12
	Clerical	*Age*	16-18	0	0	0	0	0	4	0	0	0	0	0	4	4
			18-25	0	2	1	0	0	3	5	2	0	0	3	10	13
			25-40	0	1	0	1	0	1	2	1	0	0	2	4	6
			40 →	0	0	1	1	0	0	0	1	0	0	2	1	3
	Managerial	*Age*	16-18	0	0	0	0	0	0	0	0	0	0	0	0	0
			18-25	0	0	0	0	0	0	0	0	0	0	0	0	0
			25-40	0	0	2	15	0	0	0	2	1	0	17	3	20
			40 →	0	0	2	8	3	0	0	1	1	1	13	3	16
				Male					*Female*							
				Sex												
		Totals		6	6	5	1	1	31	41	25	12	4	19	113	132
				2	6	11	3	1	0	1	5	1	0	23	7	30
				0	3	2	2	0	8	7	4	0	0	7	19	26
				0	0	4	23	3	0	0	3	2	1	30	6	36
				8	15	22	29	5	39	49	37	15	5	79	145	224

TABLE 23 BAD EXAMPLE OF A TABLE: EMPLOYEES OF GOURMET FOODS LTD 1980 BROKEN DOWN BY AGE, SEX, CATEGORY OF WORK PERFORMED AND YEARS WITH COMPANY

Self-check

List the things you think are wrong with it.

Firstly it tries to do too much. There are too many variables for the table to be clear enough, especially the way it is arranged. Next, the 'sex' headings are stuck awkwardly in the middle. They should have been at the top. One very poor aspect is the totals. There are no labels to indicate clearly to what they correspond. While it is not impossible to work it out, it should not be necessary to have to do so. The sub-totals are also too far away from the figures that constitute them. They should appear as totals with each section. For example, the male totals should appear in the 'male' column. A clue that the table is a poor one is that so many of the entries in it are zero; this is always a bad sign.

While these are the major drawbacks, there are also other poor aspects of style. We saw, in Chapter 8 in Volume *1*, how we should always be clear about the class boundaries. In this table it is not clear where they start and end in the case of age and years of service. 16–18, 18–25 and so on should, for example, be 16 and under 18, 18 and under 25 and so on. The column and row headings, too, are over complicated. We don't need 'age' and 'sex' as separate and independent headings. In addition it is not good form to have the writing vertical, as 'category of work' is, for instance. It should either be horizontal or on its side. Finally the various sections of the table are not clearly partitioned.

In general:

- all tables should be labelled clearly, concisely and informatively;
- all columns and rows should be clearly and concisely labelled;
- it should be made clear what units are being used – (£1000s), (kg), etc.;
- any table should be sectioned neatly and clearly by lines, and preferably framed by lines also;
- where the table is complex, lines of differing thickness, or single and double-ruled lines, etc., should be used to mark off sections, particularly sub-totals;
- totals and sub-totals should be included, where appropriate, and should be placed immediately to the right of, or below, the figures of which they are the totals;

- tables should not contain too many figures;
- class boundaries should be very clearly specified;
- notes should be included where appropriate, e.g. where some figure is different in some way to what might be expected.

Though there are many different kinds of table and many ways of constructing them, the above rules should always be adhered to.

Self-check

How should the data in table 23 have been presented?

If the table is to be broken up, which it almost certainly should be, the age of the employee and his or her years of service would be the best candidates for appearing in separate tables, as the two are very much connected. This is one reason why there are so many zeros. No one between 16 and 18, for example, can possibly have been longer than two years with the company. Also, these variables give rise to a lot of rows or columns. We could have two tables, then, one showing age, sex and category of work and the other length of service, sex and category of work. The one with the ages in is shown in table 24.

Category of work	Male					Female					Total male and female
	16 and under 18 yrs	18 and under 25 yrs	25 and under 40 yrs	40 and over	Total male	16 and under 18 yrs	18 and under 25 yrs	25 and under 40 yrs	40 and over	Total female	
Unskilled	3	5	9	2	19	8	26	30	49	113	132
Skilled	0	5	9	9	23	0	1	3	3	7	30
Clerical	0	3	2	2	7	4	10	4	1	19	26
Managerial	0	0	17	13	30	0	0	3	3	6	36
Totals	3	13	37	26	79	12	37	40	56	145	224

TABLE 24 EMPLOYEES OF GOURMET FOODS LTD 1980 BROKEN DOWN BY AGE, CATEGORY OF WORK AND SEX

Self-check

Draw the other table to the one in table 24. This time have sub-totals for each length of service, by males, females and both, and for each category.

This table is shown in table 25. A slightly different style of presentation has been used to show how it may vary.

Of course, some detail is inevitably lost in the above process. It is, for example, no longer possible to see the different categories of work broken down by age of employee. If this was important, either the break-up should be performed in a different way or a further table constructed.

Review

1 Draw a suitable graph for the following figures:

Year	*Export of goods (£1000 million)*	*Import of goods (£1000 million)*
1974	15.6	20.8
1975	18.8	22.8
1976	25.4	29.0
1977	32.2	33.9
1978	35.4	36.6

(Source: *UK in Figures 1975–79*)

2 Draw a suitable graph for the following figures:

Year	*Local authority rates income (£1000 million)*	*Government tax income (£1000 million)*
1974	3	9
1975	4	14
1976	5	17
1977	5	17
1978	6	19

(Source: *UK in Figures 1975–79*)

	Years of service															
	Under 2			2 and under 5			5 and under 10			10 and under 20			20 and over			
Category of work	M	F	T	M	F	T	M	F	T	M	F	T	M	F	T	Total male and female
Unskilled	6	31	37	6	41	47	5	25	30	1	12	13	1	4	5	132
Skilled	2	0	2	6	1	7	11	5	16	3	1	4	1	0	1	30
Clerical	0	8	8	3	7	10	2	4	6	2	0	2	0	0	0	26
Managerial	0	0	0	0	0	0	4	3	7	23	2	25	3	1	4	36
Totals	8	39	47	15	49	64	22	37	59	29	15	44	5	5	10	224

M= male F = female T =total

TABLE 25 EMPLOYEES OF GOURMET FOODS LTD 1980 BROKEN DOWN BY LENGTH OF SERVICE, SEX AND CATEGORY OF WORK

3 Draw a suitable graph for the following figures:

Year	*Days lost through disputes (millions)*	*Numbers unemployed (mid-year estimates) (millions)*
1973	7.2	0.6
1974	14.8	0.5
1975	6.0	0.9
1976	3.3	1.3
1977	10.1	1.5
1978	9.4	1.4

(Source: *UK in Figures 1975–79*)

4 Draw a suitable graph for the following figures:

IMPORT OF GOODS (£1000 MILLION) FROM

Year	*EEC*	*Rest of Europe*	*N. America*	*Oil-exporting countries*	*Elsewhere*
1975	8.3	3.1	2.8	3.0	4.8
1976	11.1	4.0	3.9	3.9	6.1
1977	13.6	4.6	4.5	3.4	7.8
1978	15.7	5.0	4.9	3.1	5.9

(Source: *UK in Figures 1975–79*)

5 Construct a table which shows the data of review 4, together with the information below, in one table:

EXPORT OF GOODS (£1000 MILLION) TO

Year	*EEC*	*Rest of Europe*	*N. America*	*Oil-exporting countries*	*Elsewhere*
1975	6.0	3.1	2.1	2.3	5.4
1976	9.0	4.0	3.1	3.2	6.1
1977	11.9	4.9	3.8	4.3	7.3
1978	13.7	4.5	4.2	4.6	8.4

(Source: *UK in Figures 1975–79*)

ANSWERS

1 The graph is shown in figure 74. It is a dual graph. A layer one will not do since the two variables cannot sensibly be added together. Since the values are very similar, it is better to use the same axis for both sets.

2 The graph is shown in figure 75. Here it is also a dual graph, for the same reason as in review **1**. However, there need to be two different scales as the two sets of figures are rather different in size. Furthermore, it is basically the comparison with the movements of the figures that is of interest and not so much their actual values. You would not be too wrong, however, if you used a layer graph, since it can be argued that the two sets of figures represent two forms of 'tax' and so can be added together.

3 Here a dual graph can be used to good effect again. Since the two sets of figures are in different units there *must* be two different scales. If you just used one, look to see that one variable is measured in days and the other in persons. Figure 76 shows the result.

4 For these figures a layer graph is best. The picture is one where a quantity, here the amount of goods imported into the UK, is split into several different components. Figure 77 shows such a graph.

5 Table 26 shows the answer. This is not the only table that could be drawn to show these figures. You may well have divided each of the columns into two, one for imports and one for exports. This would, however, make the totals shown in the answer given difficult to present. The table could easily be presented with the columns and rows the other way round; that is, with the year along the top and so on, and this would be quite correct.

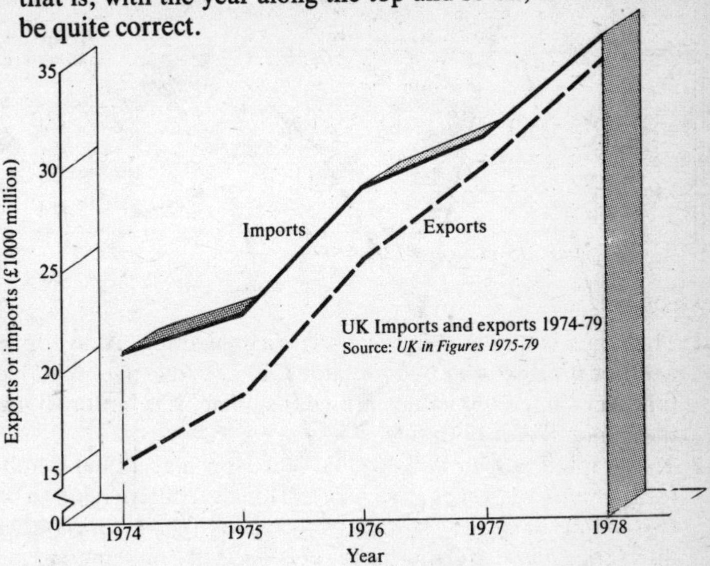

Figure 74. Graph for review 1 (page 248)

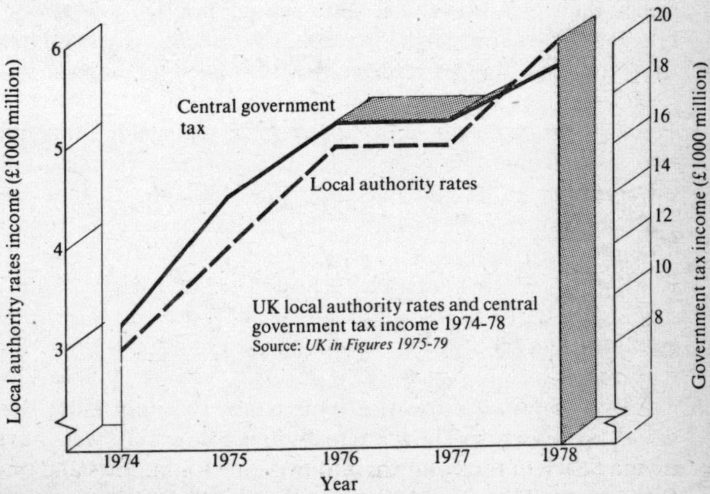

Figure 75. Graph for review 2 (page 248)

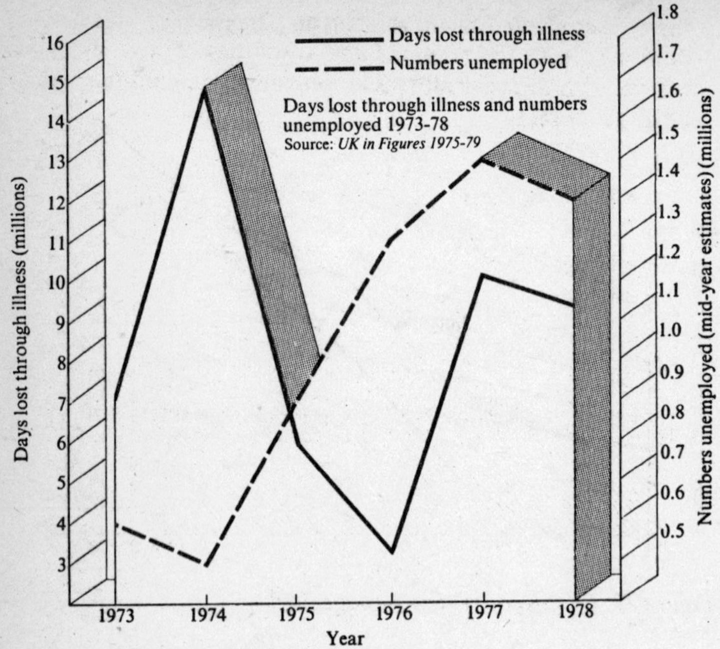

Figure 76. Graph for review 3 (page 249)

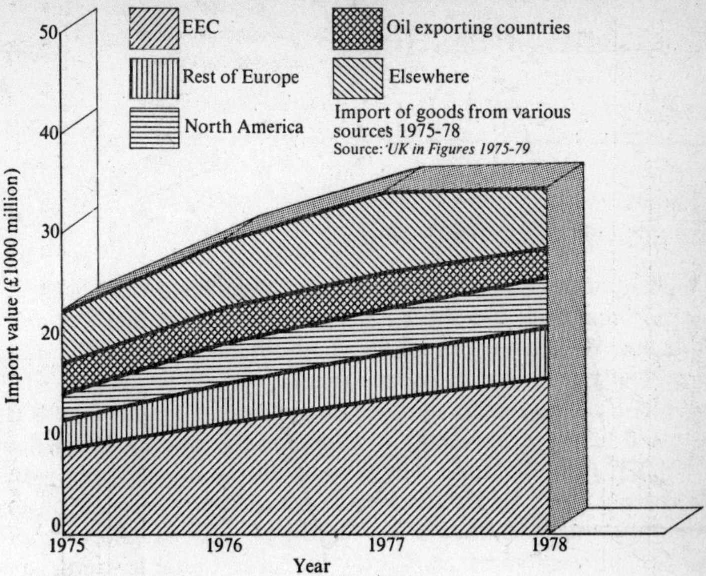

Figure 77. Graph for review 4 (page 249)

TABLE 26. Import and export of goods to/from UK 1975-78 (£1000)

		Place					
Year	Imports or exports	EEC	Rest of Europe	North America	Oil exporting countries	Elsewhere	Total
1975	Imports	8.3	3.1	2.8	3.0	4.8	22.0
	Exports	6.0	3.1	2.1	2.3	5.4	18.9
1976	Imports	11.1	4.0	3.9	3.9	6.1	29.0
	Exports	9.0	4.0	3.1	3.2	6.1	25.4
1977	Imports	13.6	4.6	4.5	3.4	7.8	33.9
	Exports	11.9	4.9	3.8	4.3	7.3	32.2
1978	Imports	15.7	5.0	4.9	3.1	5.9	34.6
	Exports	13.7	4.5	4.2	4.6	8.4	35.4

Source: *UK in Figures 1975-79*

7 Lies, damned lies and statistics

Where can distortion occur?

The title of this chapter comes from a quotation from Disraeli. He said that there are three kinds of lies: lies, damned lies and statistics. While statistics can be an invaluable aid to business, it is perfectly true that they can be used merely to 'bamboozle' people. It is thus necessary to be on your guard against this. But it would be a grave mistake to condemn the whole of statistics for this reason. To do so would be to 'throw the baby out with the bath water'. Bad statistics are not always the result of an attempt to mislead; they are often the product of ignorance of the discipline of statistics. Certainly, here, a little learning can be a dangerous thing. The aim of this chapter is to point out some of the most common ways in which statistics may be distorted.

The two volumes of this book have so far shown you how:

- data is collected, either by taking a census or by sampling;
- data is processed, if necessary, by taking averages, constructing indexes, making grouped frequency tables, etc.;
- decisions are made according to the results of statistical tests made on the data, or on information derived from it;
- data, and decisions, are communicated to others.

At any stage in this process the statistics can become distorted, either deliberately or accidentally.

For example, the managing director in the scenario wanted to influence the wage negotiations by showing that Gourmet Foods Ltd could not afford a large wage rise. The intention may well have been to 'let the facts speak for themselves', on the assumption that they were bad enough. But there is always a temptation to present statistics in a way which emphasizes what it is we want to show. One glaring instance of this is, of course, in advertising, where manufacturers make all kinds of claims about their products.

This chapter looks at each of the stages mentioned above and investigates where, exactly, distortion may creep in. Naturally, in practice, not all the opportunities for distortion listed in the chapter will necessarily occur in one statistical exercise. But at no time will there ever be such an exercise in which there is no opportunity at all.

When examining statistical results, then, be on your guard against being taken in by any of the tricks or mistakes described in this chapter. Do not think that they are rare; the literature abounds in stories about them, and examples crop up every week. You must also take care not to draw any unwarranted conclusions yourself, even from good statistics. Consider, for example, a remark made by a cabinet minister responsible for education. This contains a far from obvious fallacy. What he said, basically, was that statistics showed that not all those qualified to teach mathematics in schools were doing so. He inferred that if a large proportion of these teachers could be persuaded to actually teach mathematics, the chronic shortage of teachers in this area would be cured.

Self-check

Can you guess where the fallacy lies? What kinds of teachers would be qualified to teach mathematics that aren't doing so?

Of course, the statement as it stands is true. But what we should really ask is, Why aren't such teachers teaching mathematics? The answer is that a lot of them have mathematics only as their second subject and that they teach their first subject all the time. 'So what?' you may ask. Well, in the majority of cases this first subject is physics or another scientific or technical subject in which there is also a shortage of teachers. So the solution is no real solution at all. We solve the shortage of mathematics teachers by creating a shortage in other areas.

It is often necessary, then, for us to look behind the statistics, perhaps even to ask for *further* statistics to clarify the picture. When using statistics, in addition to looking for distortions in them, always think very carefully before drawing any conclusions from them, therefore.

Who says?

No analysis of data collected is worth anything at all if that data is not both reliable and representative. One of the most common faults in data collection is to use a biased sample. This type of error was discussed in Chapter 6 of Volume *1*. While it is often very difficult indeed to obtain a totally unbiased one, many statements are made, in the media and elsewhere, which are based on results from samples which are far from unbiased.

In business, one type of biased sample that is continually encountered is the one that is self-chosen.

Self-check

Any firm which sells goods or services is bound to get some complaints. What do they tell the firm about the quality of the goods or services?

Certainly if the goods or service offered changes in quality the number of complaints received should also alter. But suppose complaints are running at a fairly steady level, what information can be extracted from their level? While it is true that complaints received by a company about one of its products or services might well be warranted in most cases, in many instances they are not. Furthermore, there are probably a number of slightly faulty products about which complaints are not received because the purchasers are too lazy or perhaps shy to make one. Their action may be to buy from a different source next time. There is thus a danger that a company will underestimate the dissatisfaction felt with its products and will only find out from falling sales that this is so.

'Phone-ins' to radio stations are another way in which a sample selects itself. Any findings based on these should be treated with suspicion. Capital Radio, the London commercial station, has a 'hit line' on which listeners can vote for their current favourite singles. The top ten records are played each weekday.

> *Self-check*
>
> What can record companies gather from the results? Can they, for instance, conclude that these are the most popular records?

It is clear that the sample certainly cannot be guaranteed to be representative. For one thing, it is unlikely that anyone without a phone would take the trouble to go to a call box. For another, those who do bother to phone are almost certain to be somewhat different, on average, from those who don't. They would, for example, tend to be more interested in music. They may be strong 'fans'.

Indeed, presumably, if someone was fanatical enough, they could phone in hundreds of times for some record. It must be said, incidentally, that Capital Radio itself makes no claim about the representativeness of this sample. The record companies should, and no doubt do, look at such results with a certain degree of scepticism. There is, anyway, a reasonably reliable survey of actual record sales which they can use.

In other cases, just how the sample is collected is never made clear. In TV commercials there is a favourite phrase, 'Tests show. . .' or, to try to sound even more convincing, 'Laboratory tests show . . .'. This is generally followed by a statement the truth of which the viewer is in absolutely no position to judge.

> *Self-check*
>
> What kind of things would we need to know in order to be able to judge any such claim properly?

Well, we would want to know what the test was, how those tested were chosen, and how many there were of them. We would also need the significance level of the result. In fact we would need a great deal more information than could be realistically put on TV.

Then there are those 'housewives' who vow that they will never change their brand of washing powder only to be convinced by a demonstration wash that there is a better one. How were they selected? Giving their names adds spurious credence to the whole thing. But what it all boils down to is that we are to take the information given in TV commercials 'on trust'.

There are many other examples of biased samples, questionnaire surveys where the response rate is down in the ten-per-cent range, interviews with women supermarket shoppers which purport to yield results applicable to women or, even worse, people as a whole, and so on. But there is also a way of distorting the results with what is actually a true random sample.

Self-check

Suppose a company tests its product on a number, say twenty, of random samples of people. It finds that *one* of them yields a result which favours its product at the 5% level of significance. It then publishes the data *on this sample alone*. What will people think from the published results, and what is actually the case?

Even someone versed in statistics would think that this was the only sample taken and that such a result would happen only 5% of the time (i.e. in only one in twenty samples) by chance if the null hypothesis was true. So the probability of this result *not* really reflecting the worth of the product would, on this basis, be taken to be one in twenty. But, *in fact*, there were twenty samples, *each of which*, with a 5% level of significance, had a probability of 1/20 of happening to be significant by sheer chance. So we can calculate the probability of at least one of the samples giving a significant result.

Self-check

What kind of distribution do we have here?

We have a binomial distribution with twenty trials and probability of 'success', i.e. a significant result, equal to 1 in 20 or .05, and so of 'failure', i.e. not a significant result, of 19 in 20 or .95.

Self-check

So what is the probability of getting one sample, at least, significant?

Well, the probability of getting *no* significant results in twenty samples, if the null hypothesis is true, is $\frac{19}{20} \times \frac{19}{20} \times \ldots$ (20 times) $(\frac{19}{20})^{20}$ which is about .36 (to two decimal places). The probability of getting at least one is $1 - .36 = .64$. That is, if the null hypothesis is true, and the product is nothing special, a 5% significant result in one sample or another of the twenty, has an almost two-in-three chance of occurring. This is far higher than the one-in-twenty chance of a significant result occurring if only one sample were taken.

Juggling the figures

Having collected the figures, something can then be made out of them. It is at this stage that some judicious juggling can get from them the picture that is wanted. One way that has already been mentioned (in Chapter 10 of Volume *1*) is to choose, from the various averages available, the one that is nearest to what is required. With a skewed distribution, the median, mode and mean will all give different values. This point has been covered fairly thoroughly previously and so won't be covered again here.

TABLE 27. SALES INDEXES 1977–81

Year	*Sales index 1977 = 100*	*Sales index 1979 = 100*
1977	100	80
1978	120	96
1979	125	100
1980	120	96
1981	105	84

Index numbers offer a great deal of scope for juggling, too. Look at table 27. This shows two indexes for the sales of some company, one with 1977 as base year and the other with 1979.

Self-check

How many *points* rise is there from 1977 to 1979: **a** in the first index (with 1977 = 100); **b** in the second index (with 1979 = 100)? Comment on the result.

The two answers are 25 and 20. By choosing a base year in which sales were low (1977), we emphasize the rises. By choosing one in which they were high (1979) we de-emphasize rises. We can't of course, have one of two such indexes going up while the other goes down, but we can disguise the extent of the movement. To see why this is so, look at a simple problem.

Self-check

A company's sales drop by 10% one year, but then they rise again by 10% the next. Does this mean that they are back to their original level?

Well, let's make up some figures. Suppose sales start off at 100 million. They then drop 10% to 90 million. The next year they go up by 10%, i.e. by 9 million, to 99 million. The answer to the above question is 'no', therefore. We are *not* taking a percentage of the *same figure* in each case. Similarly, with the index numbers, the results are different, even though the years (1977 to 1979) are the same in both cases, because they are percentages of different amounts.

How we actually describe rises and falls in the figure or index can make a difference too.

Self-check

What is the actual percentage fall (*not points* fall in the index) between 1980 and 1981?

It is, using the first index, $\frac{100 \times (120 - 105)}{120} = \frac{1500}{120} = 12.5\%$. This is, of course, the same for both indexes. That is, it is also $\frac{11 \times (96 - 84)}{96} = \frac{1200}{96} = 12.5\%$.

Self-check

And what is the fall in *points* over the same time: **a** in the first index; **b** in the second index?

The points falls are 15 and 12, respectively. So *all three* measures of change are different and the one that best suits the presenter can be used. This is not strictly juggling, but it can make a difference as to how the figures are viewed, especially by those unfamiliar with index numbers.

A dramatic effect can be obtained by changing from a Laspeyres index to a Paasche or vice versa. Take the following simple situation. The price of commodity A in a given year is £5 a kilogramme and of B is £10 a kilogramme. The purchased quantities of A and B are 40 kg and 30 kg respectively. In a later year the price of A is £10 a kilogramme and of B is £5 a kilogramme, with purchased quantities being 20 kg for A and 40 kg for B.

Self-check

Calculate the Laspeyres and the Paasche price indexes for the later year with the earlier as base year.

The Laspeyres index is

$$100 \times \frac{(40 \times 10 + 30 \times 5)}{40 \times 5 + 30 \times 10} = 100 \times \frac{(400 + 150)}{(200 + 300)} = 100 \times \frac{550}{500} = 110.$$

The Paasche index is

$$100 \times \frac{(20 \times 10 + 40 \times 5)}{(20 \times 5 + 40 \times 10)} = 100 \times \frac{(200 + 200)}{100 + 400} = 100 \times \frac{400}{500} = 80.$$

So, with these particular figures, if we use the Laspeyres index we find that 'prices' rise and, if the Paasche, then they fall. This shows that extreme care is required when dealing with index numbers. You must be very clear as to exactly what is being measured and how.

The reader is reminded of the index of retail prices, as introduced in Chapter 12 in Volume *1*, for example. That excludes family 'expenditure' on 'income tax, national insurance, life insurance premiums and payments to pension funds, premiums for household contents insurance, subscriptions to trade unions, friendly societies, hospital funds, church collections, etc., cash gifts, pools and other betting payments, doctors', dentists', etc. fees, and *capital* sums or mortgage payments for house purchase or structural alterations' (from the Supplement to the *Monthly Digest*). It should also be recalled that the weights used to calculate this index change from year to year.

As mentioned in Chapter 12 in Volume *1*, then, the retail prices index cannot be said to be totally representative of expenditure. Furthermore it is a *price* and not a cost or expenditure index. Great care should then be taken when using it for wage bargaining, and so on. The same is true of all the other indexes that are produced. The whole basis of their construction needs to be gone into before making use of them.

Review

1 'Statistics seldom offers certainties, so you are quite justified in slanting the presentation according to what you regard as the most probable interpretation.' Comment on this statement.

2 'Seven out of ten top tiddley-winks players recommend Flippo finger guards. Why don't you get some today?' What more information would you want before you followed this advice?

3 A newspaper has a form in it one day which asks people to post it to the proprietors saying how they intend to vote at the next election. Can the newspaper sensibly predict the result of that election from the replies?

4 'Tests show that 69.3% of dogs prefer Bonzo to any other available dog food.' What questions would you like to ask the manufacturers of Bonzo?

5 The trading position of Ebeneezer Scrooge Ltd, makers of Christmas novelties, is so bad, and unemployment so high, that employees take a 5% cut in wages to try to keep their jobs. Scrooge promises them that as soon as he can he will give them a 5% rise again to get them back to their old level. What (deliberate?) mistake has Scrooge made?

6 Write two very short reports on the figures below, one trying to put them in as good a light as possible, the other in as poor a one. You can perform any legitimate change on the figures that you wish. For example, you can change the base month.

Quarter	*Index of productivity per employee Garish Gadgets Ltd 1980 (Jan. 1970 = 100)*
1st	200
2nd	180
3rd	160
4th	150

7 In a particular factory in 1978, labour costs were £400,000 and raw materials costs £200,000. In 1980, labour costs were £600,000 and raw materials £840,000. The average hourly wage costs per worker (i.e. the 'price' of labour) rose 60% over the period but the price of raw materials dropped by 60%. Calculate two labour and materials 'price' indexes; one which shows these figures in the best light and one which shows them in the poorest, using weighted price relatives.

ANSWERS

1 Your answer should point out that individual bias is probably unavoidable in cases where there is no clear-cut answer, as is often the case in statistics, but that

(a) it should be reduced to an absolute minimum;

(b) any assumptions, etc., that are made should be clearly stated;

(c) sufficient detail is given for the reader of the statistics to be able to check out the various considerations for himself, e.g. sources;

(d) where there are known statistical techniques for dealing with bias or for resolving conflicting evidence, these should always be used.

As far as the statement goes, then, 'the most probable

interpretation' is certainly what should be given, but it is not correct that it should be 'what you regard' as that, but what the statistical techniques yield as that wherever possible.

2 Here, you should indicate that some questions should be asked such as:

(a) Are they really what would generally be called 'top' players?

(b) Are they getting paid for saying it, or being given free Flippo guards?

(c) Do they actually use Flippo guards in important tournaments?

(d) If they are suitable for these top players, does this necessarily mean that they are suitable for me?

3 You should say that it cannot. The replies will form a very biased sample. For a start, those who read that newspaper will probably have something in common in their political views. Think of the readers of some of the papers you know and think if you can't predict what political views most of them will have. In addition, those that send in the form will be a biased sample of the paper's readership. They are more likely to be politically active, for example. Certainly, they will have something in their personality that causes them to send back such forms.

4 The kinds of question you should ask are:

(a) What tests?

(b) Did you really give the dogs a choice from *every available* dog food?

(c) Under what conditions were the dogs offered each of the different foods?

(d) How large a sample of dogs was it, and was there anything special about it?

(e) Is the result significant at, say, the 1% level?

5 You should say that the 5% rise is not going to give them back their original wages since the 5% is of their new, lower wage, whereas the cut was 5% of their old, higher wage.

6 The way to present these figures in as bad a light as possible is to use them as they stand and to give the decreases in percentage points. For example, the decrease in productivity from the first to the second quarter was 20 *percentage points*. To the uninitiated this looks as if it were a drop of 20% in productivity. To present them in a good light, the figures can be expressed as percentages of the first quarter's figures. So, for example, looking at it this way the decrease in productivity from the first to the second quarter is now 10% (the true figure indeed for the actual drop).

7 If the current (1980) weights are used, the index is

$$\frac{£600{,}000 \times 160\% + £840{,}000 \times 40\%}{£600{,}000 + £840{,}000} = \frac{96{,}000{,}000 + 33{,}6000{,}000}{1{,}440{,}000}$$

$$= \frac{129{,}600{,}000}{1{,}440{,}000} = 90.$$

If the base year (1978) weights are used, the index is

$$\frac{£400{,}000 \times 160\% + £200{,}000 \times 40\%}{64{,}000{,}000 + 8{,}000{,}000} = \frac{64{,}000{,}000 + 8{,}000{,}000}{600{,}000}$$

$$= \frac{72{,}000{,}000}{600{,}000} = 120.$$

Depending on which is used, then, there is either a 10% fall or a 20% rise! Note that the relatives used are 160% and 40%. The former is a 60% rise and the latter a 60% drop, as stated in the question.

On the face of it

Having collected the data and summarized it where necessary, we then look to see what it can tell us. We may have to perform tests, or analyse the data further, but we may be able to get something out of it before doing that. In any case a very useful step before going on is to ask ourselves just what it is that has been collected. If it is someone else's data we can ask the same question about that. Very often, when a careful examination is made, what they say they obtained and what they actually got are two different things.

Take, for instance, official figures on suicides. When these are examined, Catholic countries have significantly lower suicide rates than others. It is then tempting to assume that Catholics are less prone to suicide than others. But is this a justifiable conclusion?

Self-check

Can you think of any other possible reason, involving the data actually collected, why such a difference should be found?

If we look carefully at what data we have, we see that we have *not* got figures for suicides, but only for deaths *officially attributed* to suicide. It is quite feasible that, in a Catholic country, in which suicide is regarded as immoral, officials would be reluctant to put the cause of death as suicide if any other conceivable (though perhaps slightly less probable) cause could be found.

The whole question of the correspondence between what actually happens and what is recorded is very important. For example, any claim that some figure is increasing, or decreasing, should be looked at very carefully if the evidence is based on recorded data. Take the crime rate: a recent article in one of the national papers put forward the idea that increased spending on the police actually increases the crime rate; the reasoning being that the efficiency with which crimes are recorded is increased. This would result in an increased crime *rate* even if there were no actual increase in *crime*.

Another way of getting a sudden increase, or decrease, in some figure is to alter the definitions on which it is based. This is a favourite trick of governments when in a tight corner. For example, say some safety limit is set for workers in a particular industry, like the allowable exposure to radiation when working with nuclear fuels. Figures can then be quoted for workers exposed to dangerous levels. If these figures start to get too high, a simple way to bring them down is to revise *upwards* the definition of what is a dangerous level. And don't think this sort of thing doesn't happen; it does. When a milk board for a particular region in the United States was faced with a huge batch of milk with strontium 90 levels exceeding the official safety limit, this limit was upped. Economic pressures are the cause of such actions.

Often increasing knowledge can affect how events are classified officially. For instance, the cause of death of many babies in the last century was put down to 'teething'. It is highly improbable that any such entries appear today. One effect on business is the increased knowledge we have of illnesses caused by exposure to dangerous chemicals and other work hazards. Under these circumstances we certainly cannot assume that changes in the death rates from such causes necessarily indicate any *real* change in the number of deaths from them. We should have to have other evidence to support any conclusion like this.

One cautionary tale taken from marketing research concerns the Ford Edsel car in the USA. It was designed based on the results of an exhaustive marketing survey to find out what kind of a car people wanted to drive. They were asked such questions as, 'How many doors should the model have?', 'How large a boot is wanted?' and so on. The answers received were combined and averaged to give the outline specification for the model. The detailed specification was based on this and engineering considerations. Sales of the model when it was produced were, to say the least, disappointing.

Self-check

Can you guess why?

The company thought that the summarized data showed what type of a car 'Mr Average' wanted, presumably. But, of course, it did no such thing. To take an absolutely extreme illustration, suppose we ask a group of people what colour car they want and half say yellow and half red. Would it be a sensible step to produce an orange one? The Edsel was, then, a 'mish-mash' which pleased hardly anyone.

Great care should be taken, then, in working out exactly what data has been collected, even if the methods of collection themselves are above reproach. Indeed this area is the one that generates most mistakes and misunderstandings, as opposed to deliberate deceptions. There is a strong movement nowadays towards what can be called the 'search for meaning' approach. One aspect of this is the increasing emphasis on in-depth interviews in market research. This seeks to look behind the figures themselves and not to just accept them uncritically. On the face of it the data may appear to be one thing, in reality it may be something quite different.

Jumping to conclusions

There are basically two ways in which erroneous conclusions may be drawn. One is to make ones which are not at all warranted by the data. The other is to draw valid ones but then to go on to say that something else is proved, actually without any real foundation for it. This latter is the 'trick' used most often to deliberately deceive. Darrell Huff in his book *How to Lie with Statistics* gives a very good example of the latter. A writer of a letter to an American magazine was defending a company which was making earnings of 1.1 per cent of sales. You can't call it profiteering to make only just over $10 on every $1000 invested during a year, he wrote. But, as a later writer to the same magazine pointed out, the jump from profit on sales to profit on investment is totally unwarranted. Suppose you were to go out every day and buy an article for £1.00 and sell it for £1.01 the same day.

> *Self-check*
>
> What would be the percentage profit on sales over a year?

Well, it would be 1%. In fact it would be 1% whatever period you chose.

> *Self-check*
>
> What would be the total investment, and what percentage profit would be received on this over a year?

The initial investment would be £1. But this is also equal to the total investment since every time you made a sale *you would recoup the £1, and get your profit*. The percentage profit on the investment over the whole year is thus 365%, if you literally sell an article every day. Even if you only work weekdays it's around 250%! This is really a straight exercise in arithmetic. A different example, based on a different misconception, is given in the same book.

Statistics will show up any differences between two sets of figures and it will tell us whether or not these are *statistically* significant.

What it won't tell us is what they indicate. For example, the death rate for the Navy in the Spanish–American war was nine per thousand. For civilians in New York at the same time it was sixteen per thousand.

> *Self-check*
>
> Was it, therefore, safer to be in the Navy at war than at home in New York?

Well, common sense tells us that it could not have been. The error here is that like isn't being compared with like. New York contained the normal range of ages presumably, whereas the Navy consisted of people in an age range where the death rate should in any case have been minimal.

One common trick is to pick on some set of figures that can be seen to improve from before some given event, such as the election of a new government, to after it, then give that event as the *reason* for the improvement. Figures that don't improve aren't, however, blamed on the new government. Indeed, an attempt is generally made to put the onus on the previous one. In business the event in question may, for example, be a new management. In order to show that these improvements are actually caused by the new government, new management, or whatever, it must be shown that they *would not* have happened otherwise. Similarly, to show that deteriorations are *not* caused by the change, it must be shown that they *would*.

The whole business of causation is difficult. We saw in Chapter 4 how two sets of figures which are statistically correlated do not necessarily imply a cause and effect relationship, as was demonstrated with the smoking and cancer controversy. Let's look at another example.

> *Self-check*
>
> There is a reasonably strong correlation between the index of retail prices and the average working wage. Does this mean that high wage rises cause inflation?

By itself, it certainly doesn't. The correlation no more proves this statement than it does the converse, that high inflation leads to higher wages. We would have to go elsewhere to find proof to support either claim. Of course, neither of those statements may be true. In fact, there could be some 'hidden correlate', i.e. some common cause, or there could be a complex interplay between wage rises and inflation so that, to some extent, each causes the other.

In this discussion of unwarranted conclusions, we should mention the 'extrapolation' of the trend in a time series into the far future. The assumption that 'it has been growing at 5% per annum over the last few years, so it will continue to do so', and ones like it, are dangerous in the extreme. At one time there were some rather simplistic ideas about continuous economic growth. The oil price rises of the 1970s put a rather abrupt stop to those. Any projection into the future must be treated with great restraint. It can only represent our 'best guess' given what data we have, and as such could easily turn out to be wrong. This is taken up further in the next section.

Lastly, it is worth saying something about probability.

Self-check

Do you have a better chance of winning a premium bond prize if you buy all your certificates in a block, i.e. with consecutive numbers, or scattered about?

Some people (erroneously) believe that it is better to buy them in a block, on the basis presumably that this gives ERNIE a 'bigger target to aim at'. Others (equally erroneously) think that a good scatter is better as, in that way, the 'net is spread wider'. In fact, because the chance of any *one* bond winning is *independent* of that of any other one, it makes not the slightest difference what its number is, or what the numbers are of any bonds its owner possesses. Of course, the more bonds owned the better the chance of winning, but it is immaterial what their numbers are.

Self-check

Assuming that the chances of any given premium bond winning the top prize in a draw are 1 in 1,000,000,000, and it has just won it, what are the chances of it winning it again in the next draw?

Some people seem quite surprised at the answer, which is 1 in 1,000,000,000 still. That is, the fact that it won the last draw is of no relevance to the probability of it winning the next. If someone asked you what the chances are of a tossed coin coming down heads would you need to ask first how many times it had come down heads before? Not if you could assume it was unbiased, you wouldn't.

Both of the above results are dependent on the fact that the events described, i.e. getting a head and winning the premium bond draw, are *independent*. That is, one toss or draw has no effect on the next. This is as distinct from cases where successive events are dependent, for example the probability of someone being absent from work on any day is dependent to some extent on whether or not they were absent the day before.

Do you get the picture?

One of the most fruitful areas for finding distortions of the facts is the presentation of statistics. It is, of course, the layman that these are aimed at. At their crudest, these distortions involve leaving out all the information that a statistician would want to assess the statistics presented. These are such things as sampling methods, sample size, definitions, classification systems, processing methods and so on. This is typical of advertisements which tend to simply make bold claims, like 'Tests show that seven out of ten women can't tell margarine from butter.' We have discussed this kind of thing previously. There is a great deal of scope for biasing the presentation in the use of diagrams and graphs.

Self-check

Look at figures 78 and 79. These both show the sales of

Baby Gourmet food from 1978 to 1980 (at 1978 prices). Figure 79 is a graph that appeared in the Gourmet Foods house magazine, mentioned in the scenario. Comment on any faults you can see in the presentation of this in comparison with figure 78.

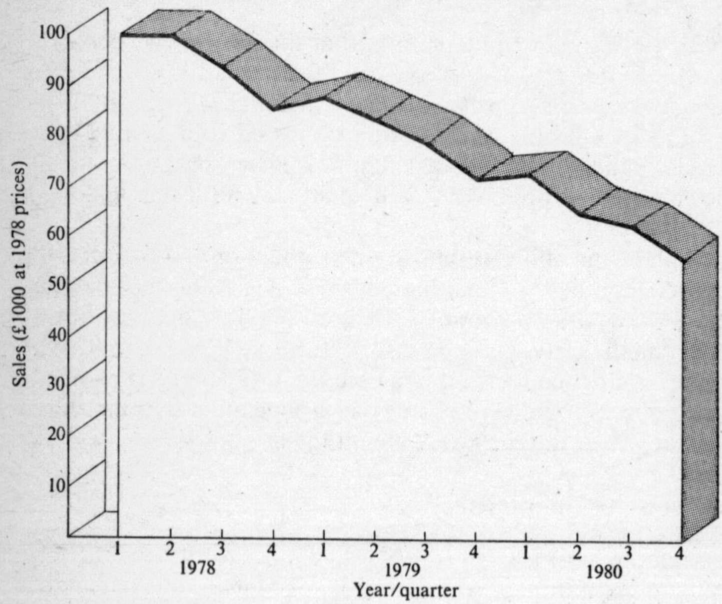

Figure 78. Quarterly sales of Baby Gourmet foods 1978–80 (£1000 at 1978 prices)

In both cases it is clear that sales are dropping badly. However, by starting the vertical axis at 50 in figure 78, the impression of a fall is much greater. Also the vertical scale in figure 78 is different so as to emphasize the fall even more. Of course, the same thing can be done with rises. Let's look at an example of this, but using a bar chart, instead of a graph.

Self-check

Look at figures 80 and 81. These show the increase in

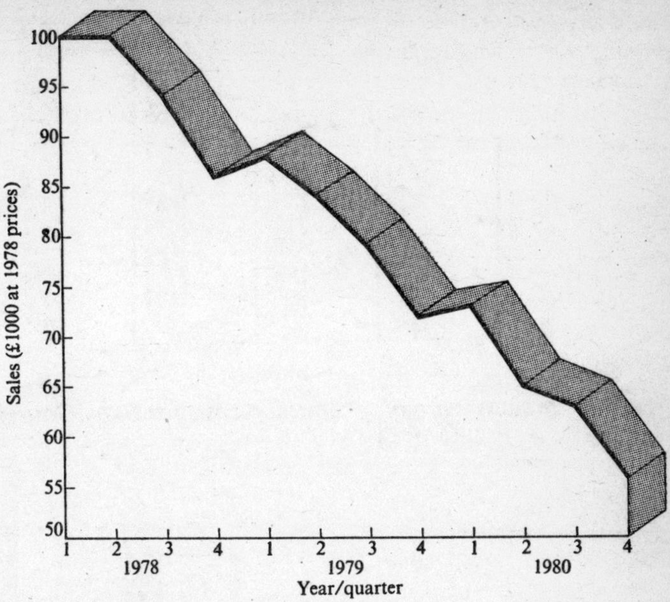

Figure 79. Quarterly sales of Baby Gourmet foods 1978–80 (£1000 at 1978 prices)

> variable production costs for Baby Gourmet from 1977 to 1980. Figure 81 is the one that appeared in the Gourmet Food house magazine. Comment on its inadequacies in relation to the other diagram.

It has the same faults as did the graph in figure 79. The vertical scale doesn't start at zero and is stretched to make the differences look bigger. Additionally, in this case, the bars are shown next to each other to emphasize the differences.

Some quite dramatic effects can be obtained in graphs where there are two vertical scales.

> *Self-check*
>
> Look at figure 82. This is another example from the Gourmet Foods house magazine. What comments do you have about this?

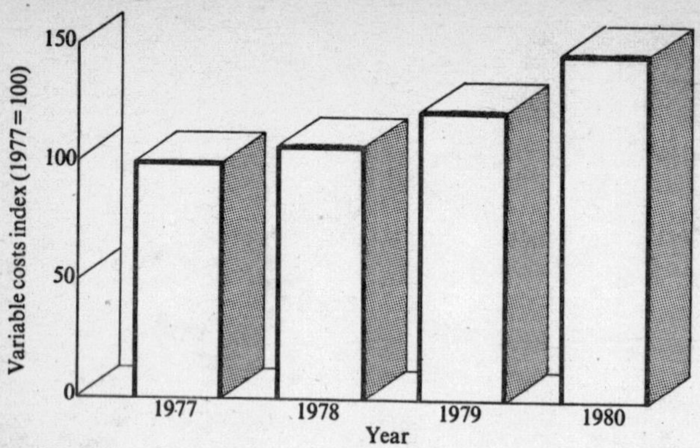

Figure 80. Index of variable production costs for Baby Gourmet food 1977–80 (1977 = 100)

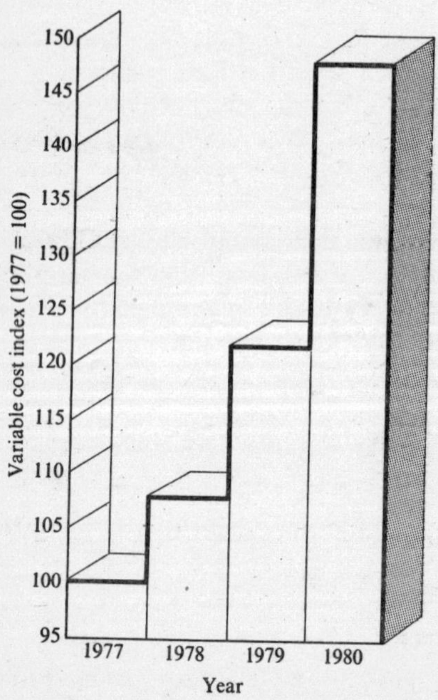

Figure 81. Index of variable costs for Baby Gourmet food 1977–80 (1977 = 100)

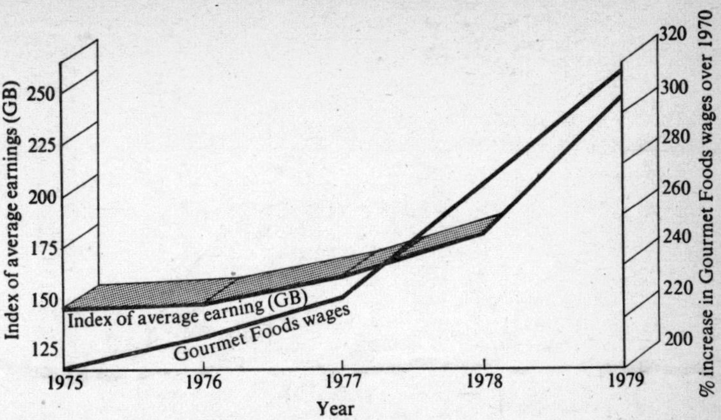

Figure 82. Gourmet Foods Ltd and national earnings 1975–9

This graph is totally and completely misleading. For a start, the two indexes are not really strictly comparable, if 'wages' means what it says. Secondly, the index of average earnings is not given a base year. In fact, it is 1974. That for Gourmet Foods is, of course, 1970. This, in itself, makes the Gourmet Foods figures actually greater than those for Great Britain for a start. But the really crafty trick is that, by not making the connection between the two sets of figures, the two vertical scales can be made different. This allows the wages scale to be stretched out so that it looks as though Gourmet Foods wages overtake those for Great Britain as a whole. In fact, whereas over the period the national average earnings went up by around 73% $(100 \times \frac{248 - 143}{143})$, Gourmet Foods wages went up by only 60% $(100 \times \frac{320 - 200}{200})$.

Pictograms also offer another chance to distort the picture.

Self-check

Look at figure 83. This is another gem from the Gourmet Foods house magazine. This purports to show how much more Gourmet Foods has to pay out in wages in 1980 than it did in 1970. Can you see what the trick is?

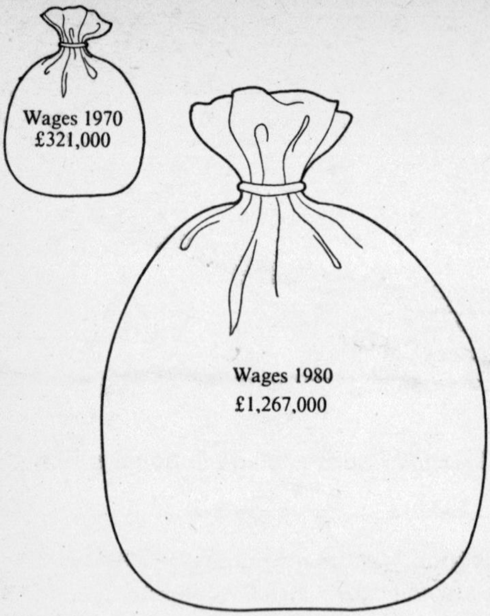

Figure 83. Gourmet Foods Ltd total wages bill 1970 and 1980

It is simply that the bag of money for 1980 is twice as *high* and so is four times as big as the one for 1970. This gives an impression of a much greater difference than there really is.

Lastly, a look at projections from time series.

Self-check

Figure 84 shows a trend line and projections into the future for unemployment. What are your comments on it?

What has been done is to take the increase from the second quarter of 1980 to the third and project this into the future. The figures are seasonally adjusted so they do show the trend plus the random variations. While there might be some point in projecting like this for a month, to do so for two years is entirely unwarranted. As it happens, it looks as though this projection is, in the short term, an underestimate. Have a look at the latest figures and see what did happen!

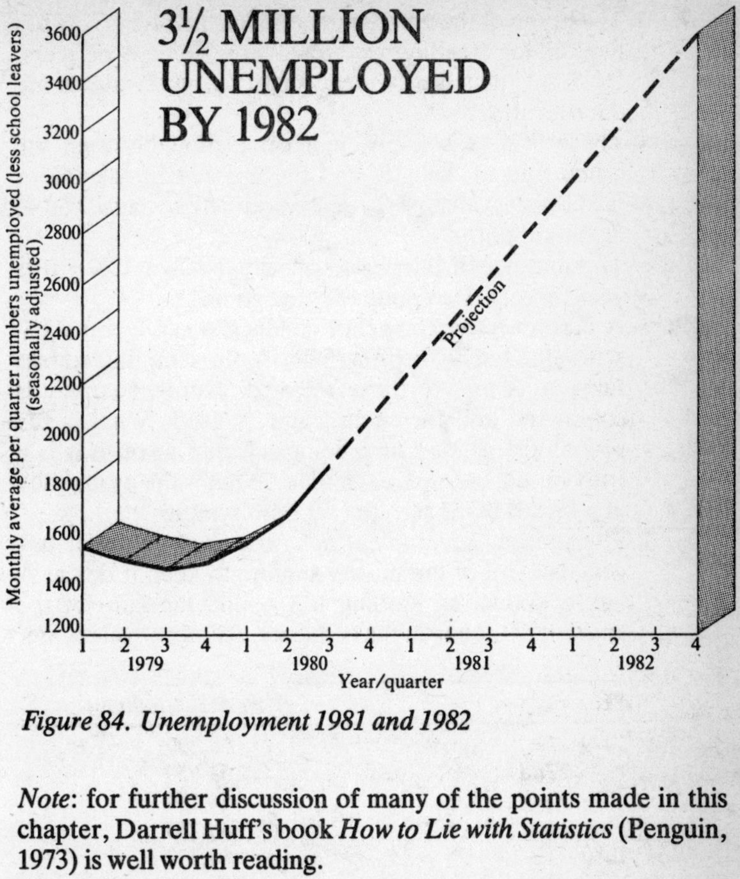

Figure 84. Unemployment 1981 and 1982

Note: for further discussion of many of the points made in this chapter, Darrell Huff's book *How to Lie with Statistics* (Penguin, 1973) is well worth reading.

Review

1 At present the government are planning to force schools to publish their examination results. If school A has higher passes and grades at 'A' level than school B, does this mean A is a better school than B?

2 Because of the poor economic situation, a firm shortens the period of credit it allows to its customers. What effect do you think this could have on statistics on debtors?

3 The graph of the number of accidents involving cars has been going steadily upwards over a number of years. Does this necessarily mean that driving standards are deteriorating?

4 There is a reasonably high correlation between the crime rate in the UK and the number of televisions sold. Does watching the television tend to cause you to turn to crime?

5 The number of telephones installed in the UK grows year by year. How long can that go on?

6 A market research agency conducts a survey on a 1% random sample of firms from some sampling frame. Firm A is one of those selected. Another survey is conducted and the same frame is used. What is the probability of that firm being selected again if it is a truly random sample each time? What is the probability of a firm B being selected for both samples?

7 The present government has, as one of its major targets, control of the money supply, to keep it down. A figure known as Sterling M3 is one measure of the amount of money in the economy. Its recent values are:

Year/quarter			*Sterling M3 (£ million)*
1979	1st	quarter	50,390
	2nd	,,	52,650
	3rd	,,	54,180
	4th	,,	55,750
1980	1st	,,	56,770
	2nd	,,	58,720

Draw a graph to show these figures in **a** the most favourable light, and **b** the least favourable light, from the government's point of view.

8 Comment on the effect of figure 85.

9 Figure 86 shows the index for industrial production together with the one for average earnings. Comment on the presentation.

10 A firm increases its profits from £100,000 to £120,000

over a year. Draw a pictogram to exaggerate this increase as much as possible.

11 The mean temperatures (°C) in England and Wales in January for 1975 to 1977 were 7.2, 6.2 and 3.5. Project this into the future. Is Britain due for a new ice age?

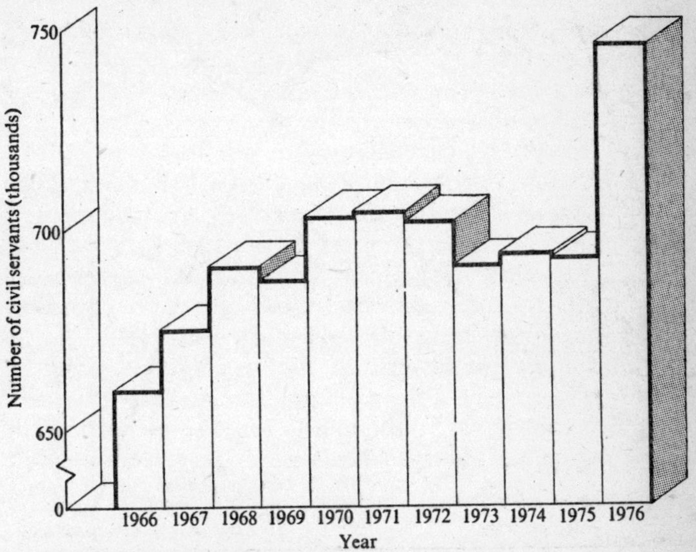

Figure 85. The massive increase in the Civil Service

ANSWERS

1 Your answer should be 'no'. For a start, you would need to know what type of pupil attended each school. Selective schools ought to have better results at 'A' level than other mixed types of school. Also, it presupposes that results at 'A' level are an indication of the goodness of the school, which might not be true for some other considerations.

2 If the firm did not make any adjustments, it would probably result in an apparent sudden increase in the number of debtors. Those on the books already, but over the new limit, would, for example, now be included in the total. Of course,

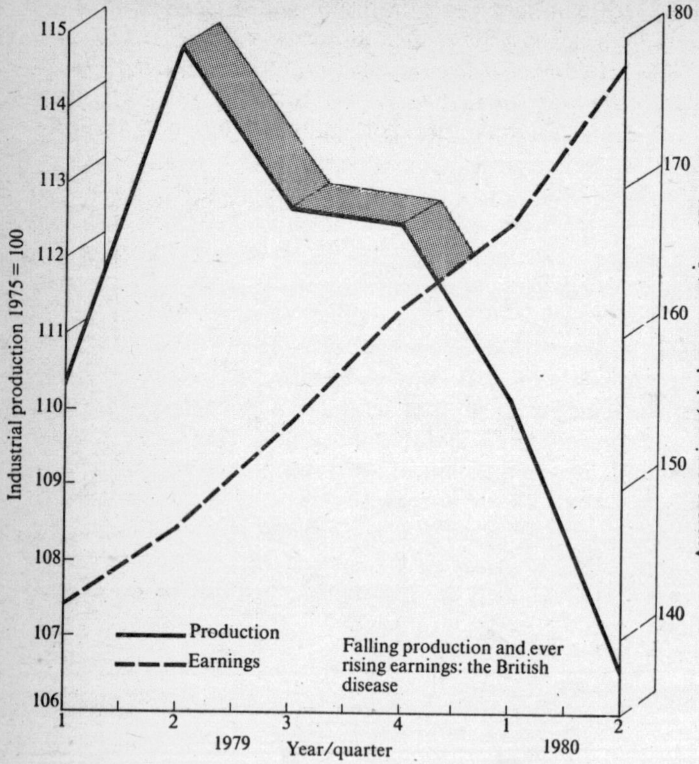

Figure 86. Production and earnings indexes 1979–80

there is also a likelihood of customers not being able to meet the new time as easily anyway, so increasing the figures.

3 No it doesn't. One of the major reasons is that there are just more cars. Of course, this does not mean that driving standards are not deteriorating, but it does not constitute proof that they are. On the figures alone, it could be, for example, that the road conditions are getting worse, causing more accidents, or even that the modern cars are more shoddy and so cause more. Other evidence, of course, leads us to reject these two, but the point is that they are reasonable explanations of the figures.

4 Some people might like to think so and, indeed, it may be partially true. However, the figures do not prove that; they merely show that the two sets of figures have grown together. You might equally wrongly wish to argue that criminals watch more television (though here again it is possible that this is so!). The correlation is probably due to the effect of the march of 'progress' on society.

5 Fairly obviously, when every home and every workplace has a telephone the total number will not increase very much from then on. Population increases may add to the total, but not significantly. Projections which show an indefinite increase are therefore ridiculous.

6 The probability is .01, i.e. 1 in 100. If you got any different answer remember that the fact that it was chosen in the first sample *has no effect* on the chances of it being in the second one. On the other hand, if we look at a firm and ask *in advance* what will be its chances of being included in both samples then the probability is .01 × .01 = .0001 or 1 in 10,000. If you do not follow this, read the chapter on probability again and then the relevant part of this chapter once more.

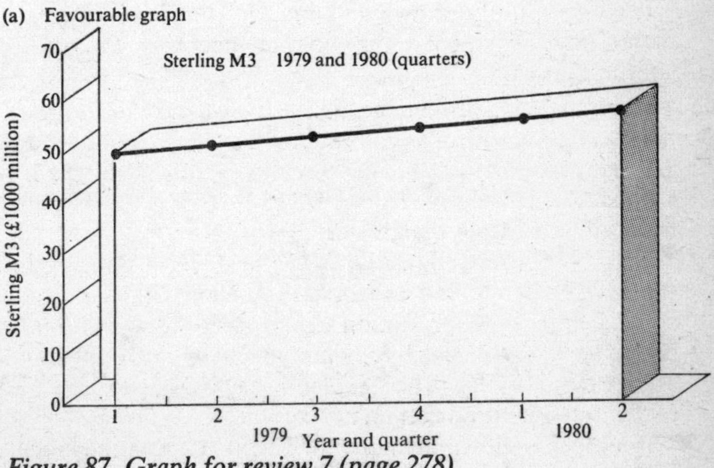

Figure 87. Graph for review 7 (page 278)
(a). Favourable graph

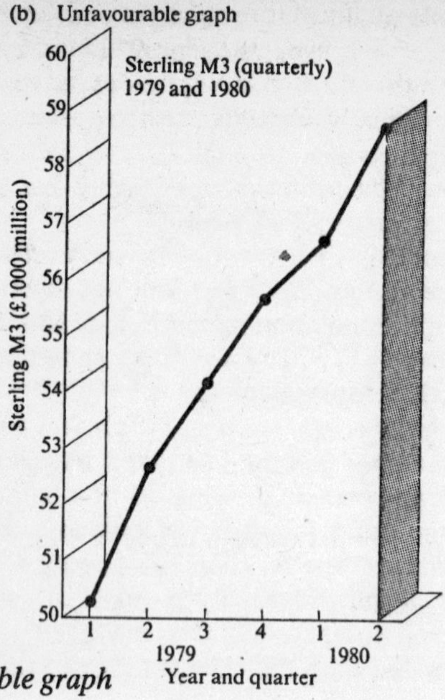

(b). Unfavourable graph

7 The two graphs are shown in figure 87. The idea is to either flatten out or steepen the line by choosing the scales appropriately.

8 Though there is a broken line on the right-hand axis, the bars themselves are shown as continuous. The lengths of the bars are thus very misleading. That is not to say that there was not a considerable increase from 1975 to 1976, but the diagram makes it look bigger than it was.

9 The graph is arranged so as to give the steepest slope in the space given. Note the use of the non-zero starting point again. There is an implication visually that the two lines are on the same scale, which they are not. In any case the units are totally different. The heading is also meant to lead the reader into making a certain conclusion.

10 The answer is shown in figure 88. The idea is that the height of the money bag is increased by 20% making an increase of much more in the area of the bag.

11 Not on the basis of just three observations, it isn't. This could be a result of random changes. Of course, if there was a continuing decline, then it would bear investigation. Even then, it would be dangerous to extrapolate too far into the future.

Figure 88. Pictogram for review 11 (page 279)

Scenario 5
A new bonus scheme

This scenario, and the chapter which follows, helps you to see how all the elements which make up 'business statistics' can be brought together to solve a particular business problem. Simply read through the scenario and then move straight on to Chapter 8 which, with its series of brief self-checks, acts as a sort of commentary on the scenario.

Some years ago, when the sales of Baby Gourmet foods were expanding, primarily because of a baby 'boom', the Gourmet Foods management were faced with the problem of raising production somehow. One way of doing it would have been to introduce regular overtime, which wasn't being worked then. But the managing director felt that the productivity at the Baby Gourmet plant was poor and it had been declining over recent years. He said that it needed increasing first. So he asked the board if they had any ideas about how to do that.

The personnel director, Mary Fletcher, thought that possibly motivation was lacking as workers there were paid at a flat rate. She suggested putting them on a bonus scheme. The plant manager, Martin Gray, was approached for his views. He thought that some bonus scheme was quite a good idea. He did have some points to make about it, however.

He pointed out that it was a team effort at the plant and that individual bonuses were not feasible. He did believe that a collective bonus scheme was possible, though, and it was this course that he recommended. The personnel director and the managing director both agreed. They decided between them that a standard weekly production would be decided upon. If this was exceeded, then the production staff, chargehands and foremen would get a bonus. There would be no deductions if it wasn't. Office and other such staff would not participate in the scheme.

Naturally, the company didn't want to find itself paying out a fortune in bonuses for no increase in output, so the standard couldn't be set too low. On the other hand, the workers wouldn't be very pleased if they worked hard, increased output and didn't get any bonus. Mary Fletcher suggested simply taking the average weekly production over the last year. Martin Gray didn't think that would be wise. He felt that productivity per worker was fairly low at the time and that bonuses should only be begun to be paid at a somewhat higher production than the recent average. Anyway, it was only an average and it covered holiday weeks when production was low or zero.

The sense of Martin's point was acknowledged by the others and, after some discussion, it was decided to ask for the assistance of the works study section. They would go into the plant and assess the situation. In particular they would estimate how much time-wasting, etc., went on. Martin was given the job of negotiating with the shop stewards. He would first have to persuade them to cooperate with the works study team.

When he met them, he emphasized that it was to everyone's advantage to have a scheme that would work, from the management's point of view as well as from theirs. He also promised that no one would lose from any scheme that was implemented and that nothing would be deducted from the wages if the standard production was not achieved. It was, nevertheless, with some reluctance that they agreed to cooperate with the study.

The works study team went into the plant and observed the workers there for some weeks. They recorded the time taken to set up the machines, to repair them and so on. All this data was recorded and average times for all the various operations calculated. In addition, the team estimated the percentage of production lost through avoidable time-wasting and so on. This data, taken into conjunction with production figures over the last year, was used to set the standard.

The average production in jars per week over the last year had been 50,712 (to nearest 1). The works study team reckoned that in a normal week, i.e. one in which nothing interrupted production, 54,000 jars could easily be produced. They also estimated the time required for setting up and repairs to be ninety minutes a day. A proposal was put to the shop stewards' committee based on these figures. The suggested bonus payments for the machine operators were:

Production per week	*Bonus per worker per hour*
less than 54,000	nil
54,000–54,999	0.5p
55,000–55,999	1.0p
56,000–56,999	1.5p
57,000–57,999	2.0p, etc.

Similar figures were suggested for other groups of workers. The bonus was to be paid on all hours worked. The shop stewards did some calculations. The basic wage was £14.70 a week or 35p an hour. Over the previous year, production had averaged 50,712 jars a week. If this figure was raised by 1000 jars, it was just under a 2% increase. Now 2% of 35p is 0.7p. The stewards would have liked to have seen this increase and told Martin this was what they wanted. Furthermore, they said bonuses should start at 50,000–50,999 jars.

Martin Gray then explained to the stewards that the full increase couldn't be paid for all hours worked as $1\frac{1}{2}$ hours a day were used for setting up and repairs. Also he didn't agree that the last year's average should be used as standard. Works study had shown that 54,000 was quite a reasonable target. Thus each 1000 extra jars was only an 1.85% increase. As a 5-day, 42-hour week was worked, the productive hours (i.e. less the $1\frac{1}{2}$ hours a day above) were only 34.5 a week. Only *these* hours should be paid for at the increase of 1.85% on 35p i.e. of .6475p. *Overall* then, the increase per hour worked should be only the weighted average of 0p and .6475p; that is,

$$\frac{.6475 \times 34.5 + (0 \times 7.5)}{34.5 + 7.5} = \frac{22.33875}{42} = 0.531875\text{p}.$$

Since it would be difficult to calculate the bonus with this kind of figure, .5p had been chosen.

The shop stewards could not agree with this reasoning. They felt that setting up and repair time should be paid for at some bonus rate, even if it wasn't the full one earned. They were also adamant that a standard of 50,000 was a fair standard. He explained that the figure of 50,712 jars was only an average, and that some weeks it had been much less, e.g. during the holidays.

In order to help the shop stewards appreciate this, Martin showed them a graph of weekly production for the previous year. He also showed them a graph of weekly productivity over several years, together with a trend line illustrating that it had decreased somewhat overall. This, together with increased orders, was why rather more overtime had been worked recently, he explained. The mention of overtime reminded the shop stewards that there wouldn't be so much of that if the new bonus scheme worked. They decided to do some more calculations.

Overtime in the evening, which was when virtually all of it was worked, was paid at time-and-a-half. If they were to take the management's figures of 54,000 jars produced in 34.5 hours, or about 1565 jars per hour, it would require approximately $\frac{2}{3}$ hours of overtime to produce 1000 extra jars; i.e. every machine operative would get 35p × $\frac{2}{3}$ hours × $1\frac{1}{2}$ overtime rate, equals about 35p extra. On the management's bonus scheme, as it stood, they would receive 42 hrs × 0.5p equals 21p extra. This convinced them they shouldn't agree to those terms. So they proposed that, instead of .5p, it should be .65p and that bonuses should start at 5200 jars.

Martin considered the shop stewards' suggestion. He believed that with a good bonus scheme, production could go up to around 56,000 jars in a good week. With his proposal this would cost the company 2 × 42 × .5p = 42p per operative. Reducing the standard from 54,000 to 52,000, but keeping the .5p, would cost an extra 2 × 42 × .5p = 42p per operative. Leaving the standard at 54,000 and putting up the rate to .65p would cost a total of 2 × 42 × .65p = 54.6p. Obviously it was better to give in on the .65p rather than on the standard, so he put this to the shop stewards; a standard of 54,000 but a bonus rate of .65p.

The stewards still rejected it, but they did say they would put it to a vote of the workforce. Martin said he would like to test out opinion first. He didn't want to put forward a plan that would be rejected. The stewards said that they didn't mind him doing this, but they would only accept a vote in favour from all. So the meeting broke up and, later that day, Martin saw ten of the machine operators selected at random. The shop stewards had already put their point of view to them; now Martin put his. He then asked them how they thought they would vote. Seven said they would accept the scheme as put forward, one didn't know, and two said they would reject it.

When they had left, Martin worked out that the chances of getting seven out of ten or more saying they would accept his proposal if there was really a fifty–fifty split were only about one in twenty. He thought he was willing to take that chance. So he called in the shop stewards and told them to hold their vote. This they did a few days later. Though they recommended rejection, there was a majority in favour of acceptance. Martin now had to put this to the board for ratification. This all went smoothly and an agreement was signed between unions and management lasting a year.

The bonus scheme was a great disappointment to the workers. In the following year the average weekly production rose from 50,712 to 54,123 jars, an increase of 6.7%. The average weekly earnings of the machine operatives, on the other hand, rose by only 4.6% from £14.70 a week to £15.38. They were also annoyed by the fact that the national average wage had gone up by 5.3% and retail prices by 6.4% over the same period, as measured by their indexes. When the agreement expired the shop stewards negotiated a better deal. This time they were backed by the workforce.

All this was many years ago, of course. In fact the bonus scheme didn't last for very long. The baby boom passed and sales began to fall.

Gourmet Foods were no longer interested in paying for high production so their heart wasn't in the bonus scheme. The workforce became more and more annoyed with breakdowns of the machinery which brought down the production figures. A flat rate wage was reintroduced.

Basically the whole of the following chapter is a commentary on this scenario. All that will be said here, therefore, is that, whereas all the other chapters, in Volumes *1* and *2*, have been devoted to one topic, the next one looks at the whole picture. Remember that a statistical investigation consists of collecting and processing data, drawing conclusions and presenting the results. All of these stages were involved explicitly or implicitly in the scenario.

8 Gathering the data and making a case

Introduction

This chapter looks at the statistical processes described in previous chapters, but taken together. The scenario includes all these different aspects used in devising and evaluating a bonus scheme. Obviously it cannot include examples of all different ways of collecting data, of processing it, of testing it, of making decisions based on it and of presenting it. What it does do, it is hoped, is to show how each of the different aspects of statistics is involved in solving (or, in the case of the scenario, not really solving) a business problem. The following sections will, then, look at the part played by these different aspects in the scenario.

Collecting the data

Self-check

Identify the examples of data collection, either explicit or implicit, in the scenario. Note which were samples.

The works study engineers collected data on work rates by observation. It was this data that was used as the basis for the bonus rates. Data was also abstracted from the company's documents on past production figures. The question was raised as to whether the standard production figure should actually be the average of the weekly production figures over the previous year. Later, Martin shows the shop stewards a graph of productivity over time. The data from which this was compiled needed to have been collected.

Self-check

What data would this have been?

As well as production figures, man-hours worked to get that production would be needed. Productivity would then be the ratio of production to this figure. At the same time, Martin also mentions sales, and hours of overtime worked. All this data would need to have been abstracted from the firm's records.

Martin collected some data himself, using an interview. Here it was also a sample, of the workforce's opinions in fact. This is the only case where sampling is explicitly used in the scenario. However, there is an implicit reference to samples. The retail price index and the index of average earnings, mentioned later, also involve samples. By inference, too, the last two paragraphs of the scenario involve abstraction of data on production, wages and sales. There, too, data on machine breakdowns would be collected.

The collection of data plays a very important part in statistics. Any amount of statistical processing cannot make up for poor data, though, as we have seen, it can make up for a lack of the complete data, provided we have a reasonably sized random sample. In business statistics, much of the data is taken from the records of the business concern itself. It is thus of vital importance that these are comprehensive and reliable. A great many statistics of use to business are collected by governments. We are fortunate in Britain to have an excellent statistical information service to business. Many companies carp about filling in government questionnaries asking for various details. What they must remember is that they use the results of such surveys themselves – or, at least, if they don't, they should do. One important way of gathering information not included in the scenario is by a sample survey carried out by a market research agency.

Processing the data

Before any conclusions can be drawn from data it must be collated and processed. This may be just a matter of arranging it in tabular form, or finding an average, or it may involve working out a sampling distribution and calculating levels of significance and so on.

Self-check

What examples of processing can you find in the scenario, again either explicit or implicit?

One important figure calculated in the scenario is the average weekly production. It doesn't specifically state which type of average was used.

Self-check

Which one do you think it was?

Almost certainly it was the arithmetic mean. In fact, it was this that caused many of the problems. Had the mode been chosen, or at the least some modal class, then the interpretation that was put on this figure by the shop stewards would have been more correct. Remember, the mean is more affected by extremes, like the Christmas holiday production figures, and so on, than the mode or the median. It was also the arithmetic mean that was used by the shop stewards to find the average production per hour so as to make an estimate of overtime required. The works study team would probably have used the arithmetic mean too, when calculating average times for the various operations. They would also have worked out standard deviations.

A weighted mean was involved in calculating the overall bonus per hour from that paid for non-productive and productive hours. Weighted means were also involved in calculating the earnings and retail price indexes, mentioned at the end of the scenario.

Martin himself did a small calculation to find the probability for the sample result when questioning the workers.

Self-check

What distribution would he have used?

The sampling distribution in the case in question was the binomial, with probability half and ten trials.

Of course, many of the other statistics quoted would have come from tables which someone would have had to compile. Figures for production, for example, wouldn't just all be listed randomly. Again, in business it is important to put data in as clear a form as possible, for one thing to cut down the possibility of misinterpretation and also to ease finding the right data.

Drawing conclusions

There was one case in the scenario of a statistical test, and this was Martin's little opinion sample. Here he came to the conclusion that the workforce would probably accept his proposal, as, indeed, they did. He made the decision to let the vote go ahead. Business is, of course, made up of continual decisions. Statistics helps by indicating some probable consequences of taking various actions. Generally, the major factor in business is cost. If we know the probabilities and the costs associated with the various possible outcomes of an action, we can decide whether or not to take that action. We saw this in connection with the quality testing in Chapter 2.

The scenario does, however, include other examples of conclusions being drawn from the data, though without a formal statistical test being involved. In the first paragraph, the managing director draws a conclusion from the data on productivity, namely that it was declining. This crops up again, later, when Martin shows the shop stewards a graph of productivity over several years. There was a conclusion reached by the works study team, too, based on the data they collected. This was that a production level of 54,000 jars a week was a reasonable standard. The shop stewards made an estimate of the overtime required to produce 1000 extra jars, based on the year's hourly average production. This too was a conclusion based on available data.

There is also an interesting case here of a possible wrong conclusion being drawn. It concerns the average production, the standard production and the bonus. In the last but one paragraph of the scenario, it is stated that production in the following year rose by 6.7% to 54,123 jars. But this is only within a 1000 of the standard of 54,000 jars. Thus (goes the *false* argument) the average bonus must have been .65p per hour. This is a percentage increase of $\frac{.65}{35} \times 100\% = 1.9\%$ (to one decimal place). But the percentage given in the scenario is 4.6%.

Self-check

Where is the fallacy?

The false argument wrongly assumes that *under*-achievement also affects the bonus. Some figures will illustrate this. Rather than give fifty-two weeks' worth of them, only eight will be used. Suppose the production during these is 48,913, 48,787, 56,819, 57,732, 58,749, 47,300, 57,314 and 57,370.

Self-check

What is their arithmetic mean?

It is $\frac{432,984}{8} = 54,123$, as in the scenario.

Self-check

What bonuses would be paid in each week?

In the first two weeks there would be no bonus. In the next three the bonus would be $3 \times .65 = 1.95$p, $4 \times .65 = 2.6$p and $5 \times .65 = 3.25$p per hour respectively. The next week would yield no bonus again. The last two weeks would both give bonuses of $4 \times .65 = 2.6$p per hour.

Self-check

What is the total and average bonus for the eight weeks?

The total bonus is $1.95 + 2.6 + 3.25 + 2.6 + 2.6 = 13$p per hour. Over eight weeks this averages to $\frac{13}{8} = 1.625$p per hour.

Self-check

What percentage of the 35p per hour basic rate is this?

It is $\frac{1.625}{35} \times 100 = 4.6\%$ (to one decimal place) of the basic rate, the same as in the scenario. Actually, it would have been quite possible for the average production to have been *less* than the standard and still to have had bonuses earned.

Presenting the data

Self-check

What examples of the presentation of data are there in the scenario?

The only direct reference to the presentation of data in the scenario is where Martin shows the shop stewards the production and the productivity graphs.

Self-check

Why do you think Martin showed them a graph rather than the figures?

It was because of the visual impact of the graph. Like most time series, these figures would fluctuate. It is generally only when displayed in the form of a graph that the trend can be seen. It is for this kind of reason that presentation is important. It is also, as we saw in the last chapter, why it is easy to mislead people by presenting the statistics in a certain way.

There are, of course, many indirect references to presentation in the scenario. The production, wage breakdown and other figures mentioned would all have appeared in tables of some kind. So too, of course, would the retail price index and the average earnings index. Presentation is important in such cases so that required figures may be easily extracted from the whole.

Conclusion

You have now worked through both volumes of this book. I

hope you have obtained an idea of the stages and processes involved in a statistical investigation and of the various techniques involved. The book was not intended to turn you into a professional statistician. Rather its aim has been to give you a knowledge that will enable you to understand the importance of statistics to business practice, to use statistical information in your work with understanding so as to derive the greatest benefit from it, and to follow critically statistical data and arguments presented by others. The book has tried to present the fundamentals of statistics in a clear and consistent way. It is hoped that you will use it as a springboard to study statistics in greater depth.

Review

1 A rival car manufacturer has produced some statistics which claim to show that his model is better than yours. You wish to gather some other statistics to counter this claim. You decide to have a number of drivers of each model interviewed to obtain gradings out of twenty for a number of points on each car such as reliability, comfort and so on. How would you go about getting suitable data? (Include in your answer sampling methods, interview schedule design and so on.)

2 Suppose 72 drivers are interviewed, 36 of each model, and the average grades over all questions they each allocate to their cars are as follows:

Your model				*Rival model*			
15	13	14	15	16	13	12	12
13	15	13	15	14	15	15	11
14	14	15	14	15	13	15	13
12	15	12	15	15	11	12	12
15	12	14	14	14	15	13	16
11	13	12	15	12	15	11	14
14	15	13	14	13	14	14	15
13	16	13	16	11	13	12	14
15	15	14	16	15	13	14	14

Construct a frequency table for each set of figures. Calculate the means and standard deviations of each also.

3 Is the difference between the two sets of grades significant at the **a** 5% level; **b** 1% level?

4 What exactly does the above result tell us? Is it really what is needed?

5 How would you present the collected data diagramatically, fairly and without distortion, giving as good an overall picture as possible? (You can assume the answers to the individual questions are available.)

ANSWERS

1 Your answer should include the following points. While the manufacturer *may* have an adequate sampling frame on owners of his own model – though this is unlikely for a mass-produced car, he is not going to have one for the model produced by his rival. The sample must, then, be one selected ultimately on a quota basis, or possibly a cluster sample.

To get some sort of fair representation, however, the sample must be a multi-stage one, with stratification at one or more stages. The area of the country, the socio-economic type and other similar variables should be used for stratifying.

The sample size should be sufficient to give reliable results. More precisely, it should be large enough to give a satisfactorily small sampling error.

The questions on the interview schedule should be selected carefully so as to be relevant to the question in hand, i.e. the 'goodness' of the cars. The best procedure to find what are suitable criteria is to get, from a sample of the population (and *not* just drivers), a list of what features they feel to be important in a car. The ones mentioned most frequently could then be used in the interview schedule of above. This sample, too, should be a multi-stage one with stratification by socio-economic group, etc.

The conduct of the interviews should be as described in Chapter 3 of Volume *1*, with all the usual controls in operation.

2 The frequency table can be constructed by working through the list of numbers and tallying. The result is as below:

Grade	*Manufacturer's model tally*	*Rival's model tally*	*Manufacturer's model frequency*	*Rival's model frequency*
11	/	////	1	4
12	////	~~////~~ /	4	6
13	~~////~~ //	~~////~~ //	7	7
14	~~////~~ ////	~~////~~ ///	9	8
15	~~////~~ ~~////~~ //	~~////~~ ////	12	9
16	///	//	3	2
Total			36	36

The mean and standard deviations can be calculated as follows:

MANUFACTURER'S MODEL

Grade	*Frequency*	*Grade × frequency*	*Grade × (grade × frequency)*
11	1	11	121
12	4	48	576
13	7	91	1183
14	9	126	1764
15	12	180	2700
16	3	48	768
Totals	36	504	7112

RIVAL'S MODEL

Grade	*Frequency*	*Grade × frequency*	*Grade × (grade × frequency)*
11	4	44	484
12	6	72	864
13	7	91	1183
14	8	112	1568
15	9	135	2025
16	2	32	512
Totals	36	486	6636

The mean of the manufacturer's own model is $\frac{504}{36} = 14$, while the standard deviation is

$$\sqrt{\left(\frac{7112}{36} - \frac{504^2}{36^2}\right)} = \sqrt{(197.55 - 14^2)}$$

$= \sqrt{(197.55 - 196)} = \sqrt{1.55} = 1.24$ (to two decimal places).

The mean difference of the rival's model is $\frac{486}{36} = 13.5$, while its standard deviation is

$$\sqrt{\left(\frac{6636}{36} - \frac{486^2}{36^2}\right)}$$
$$= \sqrt{(184.33 - 13.5^2)}$$
$= \sqrt{(184.33 - 182.25)} = \sqrt{2.08} = 1.44$ (to two decimal places).

3 The difference between the means of the two sets of data is 14.0 − 13.5 = 0.5. To find out if this is significant, an estimate of the standard error of the difference between means is needed. From Chapter 4, this figure is:

$$\sqrt{\frac{1.44^2}{36} + \frac{124^2}{36}}$$
$$\sqrt{\frac{2.08}{36} + \frac{1.55}{36}}$$
$$\sqrt{\frac{3.63}{36}} = \sqrt{.10} = .32$$

(to two decimal places).

The null hypothesis is that the difference between the means of the marks awarded by all owners of the two types of car (i.e. the populations) is really zero (and the actual difference found in the samples is due to sampling error) while the alternative hypothesis is that it isn't. So we have a two-tailed situation. The standard error of the difference between the means is as calculated above; that is, .32. So we need to look at $\frac{.5}{.32} = 1.56$. The difference is thus not significant at both the 5% and the 1% level.

4 The result tells us that the average score *over all questions* was not significantly higher for the manufacturer's model than for the rival one. What it does not tell us is on how *many* of the questions it scored higher. So, for example, a reasonable

difference in marks on just one or two questions in favour of the manufacturer's model, and a slight difference in favour of that of the rival on all other questions, could lead to no *average* difference in favour of the former. Whether or not this is what we want is then debatable. It would probably depend on just how important we regarded those points on which there was a great difference. If they were only minor, then the large number of small differences would probably outweigh these.

5 The data could probably best be displayed by using multiple bar charts. The average scores of each model could be shown for each of the questions asked, the length of the bars being proportional to the mark allocated. You may have given some other answer, but this method is one of the best that could be used as it brings out the data clearly.

Appendix: Standard normal tables

These tables show the probability of the standard normal value, here called z, being exceeded.

Z	.00	.01	.02	.03	.04	.05	.06	.07	.08	.09
0.0	.5000	.4960	.4920	.4880	.4840	.4801	.4761	.4721	.4681	.4641
0.1	.4602	.4562	.4522	.4483	.4443	.4404	.4364	.4325	.4286	.4247
0.2	.4207	.4186	.4129	.4090	.4502	.4013	.3974	.3936	.3897	.3859
0.3	.3821	.3783	.3745	.3707	.3669	.3632	.3594	.3557	.3520	.3483
0.4	.3446	.3409	.3372	.3336	.3300	.3264	.3228	.3192	.3156	.3121
0.5	.3085	.3050	.3015	.2981	.2946	.2912	.2877	.2843	.2810	.2776
0.6	.2743	.2709	.2676	.2643	.2611	.2578	.2546	.2514	.2483	.2451
0.7	.2420	.2389	.2358	.2327	.2296	.2266	.2236	.2206	.2177	.2148
0.8	.2119	.2090	.2061	.2033	.2005	.1977	.1949	.1922	.1894	.1867
0.9	.1841	.1814	.1788	.1762	.1736	.1711	.1685	.1660	.1635	.1611
1.0	.1587	.1562	.1539	.1515	.1492	.1469	.1446	.1423	.1401	.1379
1.1	.1357	.1335	.1314	.1292	.1271	.1251	.1230	.1210	.1190	.1170
1.2	.1151	.1131	.1112	.1093	.1075	.1056	.1038	.1020	.1003	.0985
1.3	.0968	.0951	.0934	.0918	.0901	.0885	.0869	.0853	.0838	.0823
1.4	.0808	.0793	.0778	.0764	.0749	.0735	.0721	.0708	.0694	.0681
1.5	.0668	.0655	.0643	.0630	.0618	.0606	.0594	.0582	.0571	.0559
1.6	.0548	.0537	.0526	.0516	.0505	.0495	.0485	.0475	.0465	.0455
1.7	.0446	.0436	.0427	.0418	.0409	.0401	.0392	.0384	.0375	.0367
1.8	.0359	.0351	.0344	.0336	.0329	.0322	.0314	.0307	.0301	.0294
1.9	.0287	.0281	.0274	.0268	.0262	.0256	.0250	.0244	.0239	.0233
2.0	.0228	.0222	.0217	.0212	.0207	.0202	.0197	.0192	.0188	.0183
2.1	.0179	.0174	.0170	.0166	.0162	.0158	.0154	.0150	.0146	.0143
2.2	.0139	.0136	.0132	.0129	.0125	.0122	.0119	.0116	.0113	.0110
2.3	.0107	.0104	.0102	.0099	.0096	.0094	.0091	.0089	.0087	.0084
2.4	.0082	.0080	.0078	.0075	.0073	.0071	.0069	.0068	.0066	.0064
2.5	.0062	.0060	.0059	.0057	.0055	.0054	.0052	.0051	.0049	.0048
2.6	.0047	.0045	.0044	.0043	.0041	.0040	.0039	.0038	.0037	.0036
2.7	.0035	.0034	.0033	.0032	.0031	.0030	.0029	.0028	.0027	.0026
2.8	.0026	.0025	.0024	.0023	.0023	.0022	.0021	.0021	.0020	.0019
2.9	.0019	.0018	.0018	.0017	.0016	.0016	.0015	.0015	.0014	.0014
3.0	.0013	.0013	.0013	.0012	.0012	.0011	.0011	.0011	.0010	.0010
3.1	.0010	.0009	.0009	.0009	.0008	.0008	.0008	.0008	.0007	.0007
3.2	.0007	.0007	.0006	.0006	.0006	.0006	.0006	.0005	.0005	.0005
3.3	.0005	.0005	.0005	.0004	.0004	.0004	.0004	.0004	.0004	.0003
3.4	.0003	.0003	.0003	.0003	.0003	.0003	.0003	.0003	.0003	.0002
3.5	.0002	.0002	.0002	.0002	.0002	.0002	.0002	.0002	.0002	.0002
3.6	.0002	.0002	.0001	.0001	.0001	.0001	.0001	.0001	.0001	.0001
3.7	.0001	.0001	.0001	.0001	.0001	.0001	.0001	.0001	.0001	.0001
3.8	.0001	.0001	.0001	.0001	.0001	.0001	.0001	.0001	.0001	.0001
3.9										
4.0					0+					

0+ indicates a probability of less than .0001.

Index